高等院校航空运输类专业教材精品系列

民航商务英语
CIVIL AVIATION BUSINESS ENGLISH

陆 东 ◎ 主 编
李 季 ◎ 主 审

人民交通出版社股份有限公司
北京

内 容 提 要

本教材为民航商务专业英语教材,全书共分为7章,涵盖了民航商务的各个领域,内容包括航空业概述、市场营销、旅客服务、空运货物、机场、安全及新趋势。为帮助学生理解掌握教材内容,每节均设置了案例导入、重难点术语解释、长难句解析、重点词汇等模块。同时,本教材还提供了重难点词汇音频,扫描书中二维码即可收听学习。

本书可作为高等院校民航商务、民航运输以及相关专业教材,也可供行业相关岗位从业人员参考使用。

图书在版编目(CIP)数据

民航商务英语 / 陆东主编. —北京：人民交通出版社股份有限公司, 2021.12
ISBN 978-7-114-17729-3

Ⅰ.①民… Ⅱ.①陆… Ⅲ.①民用航空—商业服务—英语—教材 Ⅳ.①F56

中国版本图书馆 CIP 数据核字(2021)第 251434 号

Minhang Shangwu Yingyu

书　　名：	民航商务英语
著 作 者：	陆　东
责任编辑：	吴燕伶
责任校对：	孙国靖　魏佳宁
责任印制：	刘高彤
出版发行：	人民交通出版社股份有限公司
地　　址：	(100011)北京市朝阳区安定门外外馆斜街3号
网　　址：	http://www.ccpcl.com.cn
销售电话：	(010)59757973
总 经 销：	人民交通出版社股份有限公司发行部
经　　销：	各地新华书店
印　　刷：	北京印匠彩色印刷有限公司
开　　本：	787×1092　1/16
印　　张：	14.25
字　　数：	331 千
版　　次：	2021年12月　第1版
印　　次：	2021年12月　第1次印刷
书　　号：	ISBN 978-7-114-17729-3
定　　价：	42.00 元

(有印刷、装订质量问题的图书由本公司负责调换)

前言

自莱特兄弟于1903年发明了第一架动力驱动的航空器后,经过一个多世纪的快速发展,航空运输已成为现代化的主要交通方式之一。航空运输与生俱来的国际性特点以及全球贸易一体化,对航空运输岗位从业人员的英语能力提出了更高的现实要求:一线服务岗位从业人员除了要掌握基本的英语听、说能力外,还要求有读、写能力。这是因为岗位中的操作规则绝大部分来源于国际上的通用规则,从业人员只有具备足够的英语资料阅读能力,才能更好地掌握规则、理解规则、应用规则,使服务工作上升到一个更高的台阶,这也完全符合中国民用航空局提出的"人民航空为人民"的服务宗旨。

为企业输送需要的人才一直以来是行业院校的办校方针,在开设民航运输和民航商务专业核心课程的教学过程中,笔者发现学生因缺乏专业英文阅读能力,对行业规则的理解存在较大困难,也影响了对课程的掌握。彼得·贝罗巴巴(Peter P. Belobaba)与辛西娅·巴恩哈特(Cynthina Barnhart)两位教授合著的《全球航空业》(The Global Airline Industry),对整个民航业做了全面而系统的介绍,堪称行业著作的典范,但该著作的适用对象应具备相当的专业能力和英语基础,所以对专业院校的学生而言,直接选用该著作来作为专业英语教材,学生掌握起来较为困难,会影响教材的使用效果;而民航商务专业的其他英语教材主要以口语类教材居多。因此,适合民航商务专业学生用来提升英语资料阅读能力的专业英语教材极少,这也正是本教材编写的初衷和落脚点。

本教材的编写思路是以民航商务为主线,共分为7章内容,具体包括:航空业概述、市场营销、旅客服务、空运货物、机场、安全、新趋势。教材涵盖了民航商务的各个领域,包括了行业最新变化内容,如品牌运价、航空公司多品牌战略、"四型"机场的建设、国际航空运输协会取消"YY"票价、新型冠状病毒肺炎疫情期间"客"改"货"、2021年实施的《公共航空运输旅客服务管理规定》、国际航空运输协会新分销能力(NDC)与全单计划(ONE ORDER)等,力争做到内容全、知识新、全方位、多覆盖。

通过本教材的学习,学生可以提升英语综合能力,特别是读、写技能,还能掌握最新的行业相关专业知识;既为学生掌握后续专业核心课程夯实基础,也能为有一定英语能力的人员全面而系统地了解掌握民航商务业务提供帮助。为了能使学生更容易掌握每节内容,每节首先通过案例导入激发学生学习兴趣;其次,对文章中难理解的术语单独进行详细解释,并在正文中每一个大段落后增加了长句、难句及语法的注解,以便于学生理解掌握;再次,每节重难点词汇均配套了音频,扫描书中二维码即可收听学习;最后,在文章末设置了延展阅读,拓展相关知识点的背景知识。

上海民航职业技术学院陆东老师完成了本教材第2、6、7章的编写及全书的统稿工作;秦缜铮老师完成了第1章和第3章第1~4节的编写;朱晓梅老师完成第3章第4节及第4章的编写;张晴老师完成了第3章第5节及第5章的编写。教材编写过程中还得到了中国东方航空公司陆萍、袁锦华及上海外航服务公司于立瑾等行业专家的大力支持,中国东方航空公司驻日本小松营业部的李季经理完成了本教材的审稿工作,在此深表感谢!

由于编者水平有限,加之时间仓促,教材中如有疏漏、不妥或错误,敬请读者指正。

编　者

2021年8月

目录
Contents

Chapter 1　AIRLINE INDUSTRY OVERVIEW ·················· 1
　Section 1　Industy Evolution ·················· 1
　Section 2　Factors Influencing Mode Selections of Low-cost Carriers and
　　　　　　a Full-service Airline ·················· 8
　Section 3　Introduction of ICAO and IATA ·················· 15

Chapter 2　MARKETING ·················· 24
　Section 1　Passenger Air Fare ·················· 24
　Section 2　Global Distribution System ·················· 35
　Section 3　Electronic Ticket ·················· 42
　Section 4　Code-Sharing and Airline Alliances ·················· 50

Chapter 3　PASSENGER SERVICE ·················· 59
　Section 1　Self-service Check-in Kiosk—CUSS ·················· 59
　Section 2　Travel Information Manual ·················· 66
　Section 3　Baggage ·················· 74
　Section 4　Overbooking ·················· 82
　Section 5　Flight Delay ·················· 89

Chapter 4　AIR CARGO ·················· 97
　Section 1　Air Cargo Market Characteristics ·················· 97
　Section 2　Air Cargo Facilities ·················· 104
　Section 3　Air Cargo Rates and Charges ·················· 112
　Section 4　The Air Waybill ·················· 119

Chapter 5 AIRPORT 127
Section 1 Hub Airport 127
Section 2 Regional Airport 136
Section 3 Beijing Daxing International Airport 144

Chapter 6 SAFETY 153
Section 1 Dangerous Goods Transportation 153
Section 2 Weight and Balance of Aircarft 161
Section 3 Positive Passenger Bag Match 170

Chapter 7 NEW TRENDS 177
Section 1 IATA New Distribution Capacity 177
Section 2 ONE Order Plan 185
Section 3 Build Global "123" Fast Cargo Flow Circle 191

Appendix 1 Extract from airline two character code and ticket settlement code 200
Appendix 2 Airport code of major cities in China 201
Appendix 3 Code of major international cities 202
Appendix 4 Extract from international special fare restrictions 203
Appendix 5 Extract from Singapore TIM 204
Appendix 6 Regulations on passenger service management of public air transport 210

References 220

Chapter 1
AIRLINE INDUSTRY OVERVIEW

Section 1
Industry Evolution

Lead in

Airlines Flying to the Most Countries

Turkish Airlines is the largest airline in Europe and occupies an important position in the world. It now has more than 300 aircrafts, surpassing British Airways, Lufthansa and the United Arab Emirates, second only to the "Top Four" of the United States and the "Top Three" of China, ranking the eighth in the world. Because there are too many international routes, one third of the Turkish air fleets are wide-body aircrafts(Figure 1-1).

Figure 1-1　Turkish Airline

With the geographical advantage of "intersection between East and West", Turkish Airlines has firmly linked the world. Chinese flights rarely go to South America and American flights rarely go to Africa. If there is any enterprise on the earth that has the most extensive and close contact with the world every day, it is undoubtedly Turkish Airlines.

Special Terms

1. RPK: revenue passenger kilometers, measured passenger transport volume [= passenger transport volume of segment (person) × leg distance (km)].
客运里程收入,衡量旅客运输量[= 航段旅客运输量(人) × 航段距离(公里)]。
2. ASK: available seat kilometers(= number of seats available for sale × leg distance).
可用座位公里(= 可供销售的座位数 × 航段距离)。

Text

Globally, the airline industry faced serious financial challenges for much of the first decade of the twenty-first century. Airlines were in serious trouble even before the events of "9 · 11", as the start of an economic *downturn* had already affected negatively the volume of *business travel* and *average fares*. At the same time, airline labor costs and *fuel prices* had been increasing faster than the general rate of inflation for several years. To make matters worse, airlines faced *deteriorating* labor—management relations, aviation *infrastructure constraints* that led to increasing *congestion* and *flight delays*, and dissatisfied customers due to perceptions of poor service.

The Largest Global Passenger Airlines Ranked by RPK

Figure 1-2 shows the largest global passenger airlines, ranked by revenue passenger kilometers (RPK) for 2013. Although the biggest US carriers (Delta airlines, American and United airlines) remained the largest in the world by this measure, the fourth largest passenger airline was Emirates, based in Dubai. With a 14% RPK growth in 2013 compared to 1% ~ 2% growth for the three US carriers, Emirates is poised to leap ahead of the US group in the coming years to become the world's largest airline. The gray bars on this figure identify the other airlines that belong to this new *category* of emerging global airlines, all of which have recently entered the ranks of the largest world airlines due to *sustained* high growth rates. China Southern, China Eastern, and Air China, based in the People's Republic of China, ranked 9, 10, and 12, respectively, and grew by 9% ~ 10% in 2013.

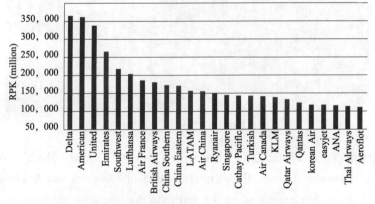

Figure 1-2　Largest 25 airlines ranked by revenue passenger kilometers, 2013

Chapter 1　AIRLINE INDUSTRY OVERVIEW

Notes 1

❶ Airlines were in serious trouble even before the events of "9·11", as the start of an economic downturn had already affected negatively the volume of business travel and average fares.

解释：在"9·11"事件之前，航空公司就已陷入了严重的困境，因为经济衰退的开始已经对商务旅行量和平均票价产生了负面影响。

❷ To make matters worse, airlines faced deteriorating labor-management relations, aviation infrastructure constraints that led to increasing congestion and flight delays, and dissatisfied customers due to perceptions of poor service.

解释：更糟糕的是，航空公司面临着日益恶化的劳资关系，因航空基础设施限制导致的航班日益拥堵和航班延误，以及因服务质量差而导致的旅客不满。

语法：that 引导定语从句，先行词为 constraints。

❸ With a 14% RPK growth in 2013 compared to 1%~2% growth for the three US carriers, Emirates is poised to leap ahead of the US group in the coming years to become the world's largest airline.

解释：阿联酋航空公司2013年的RPK增长率为14%，而美国三家航空公司的客运里程收入增长率为1%~2%，因此阿联酋航空公司有望在未来几年超越美国航空集团，成为全球最大的航空公司。

The Reason for the High Growth Rate of Emerging Airlines

The *emerging global carriers* based in China and South America have been growing at very high rates primarily due to the rapid economic growth and *resultant* increase in demand for air travel in both countries. On the other hand, the emerging carriers of the Middle East have grown at even higher rates, but with a significantly different strategy for growth. As shown in Figure 1-3, these four airlines—Emirates, Qatar, Etihad, and Turkish.

Item	Emirates	Etihad	Qatar	Turkish	Average
Passengers	12.65%	16.26%	15.83%	13.62%	14.59%
ASKs	14.19%	18.66%	20.41%	18.30%	17.89%
RPKs	14.37%	21.84%	19.28%	18.20%	18.42%
Fleet Size	11.68%	11.50%	16.42%	15.30%	13.73%

Figure 1-3　Annual growth rates of emerging Middle East carriers 2007—2012

Each of these emerging Middle East carriers has grown as a result of very similar network strategies designed to carry passengers via their *respective* hub, a major reason why we include Turkish in this group. A large majority of the passengers carried by these carriers on flights to their hubs in Dubai (Emirates), Doha (Qatar), Abu Dhabi (Etihad), and Istanbul (Turkish) are *connecting passengers* with neither origins nor destinations in the *hub city*.

Their hub strategies allow them to operate mostly *large wide-body aircraft*, and the location of their hubs gives them a geographical advantage over traditional connecting hubs in Europe. Looking ahead, the combined fleet orders for these four airlines totaled more than 1,000 aircraft at the end of 2013. If all of these aircraft are ultimately delivered and put into service by 2020, the number of passengers carried by this group will more than double.

Notes 2

❶ The emerging global carriers based in China and South America have been growing at very high rates primarily due to the rapid economic growth and resultant increase in demand for air travel in both countries.

解释：中国和南美的新兴全球航空公司一直在以非常高的速度增长，主要原因是这两个国家的经济快速增长以及由此导致的航空旅行需求的增加。

语法：based 为非谓语结构，表示被动含义。

❷ Each of these emerging Middle East carriers has grown as a result of very similar network strategies designed to carry passengers via their respective hub, a major reason why we include Turkish in this group.

解释：每一家新兴的中东航空公司都能发展壮大，因为他们设计了非常相似的网络策略，即通过各自的枢纽运送乘客，这也是我们将土耳其航空公司纳入这一群体的主要原因。

语法：designed 为非谓语结构，表示被动含义。

Impact of Emerging Airlines Across the Industry

Just as Low-cost Carriers (LCCs) changed the competitive *dynamics* of airline markets in many world regions by offering low fares and introducing innovative operating models emphasizing *productivity* and cost-efficiency, the *emerging global carriers* are *poised* to make a potentially even greater impact. While LCCs focused on *short-haul routes* within regions, the emerging carriers have grown almost *exclusively* by capturing *long-haul inter-regional traffic* between virtually all regions of the globe. Some of their traffic is indeed new air travel generated by economic growth in emerging countries and made possible by the new connections offered by these carriers. At the same time, there is much evidence that a substantial portion of the traffic carried by emerging carriers is being shifted from network *legacy* airlines, in the United States, Asia, and especially Europe. The potential impacts of emerging carriers on global traffic flows and market shares could easily exceed the competitive challenges posed by LCCs to *legacy* airlines.

Notes 3

❶ Just as Low-cost Carriers (LCCs) changed the competitive dynamics of airline markets in many world regions by offering low fares and introducing innovative operating models emphasizing productivity and cost-efficiency, the emerging global carriers are poised to make a potentially even greater impact.

> 解释：正如低成本航空公司通过提供低票价和引入低成本、高效率的创新运营模式，改变了世界许多地区航空市场的竞争一样，新兴的全球航空公司正准备发挥更大的潜在影响。
>
> ② Some of their traffic is indeed new air travel generated by economic growth in emerging countries and made possible by the new connections offered by these carriers.
>
> 解释：他们的一些客流实际上是新兴国家的经济增长产生的新兴航空旅行，这些航空公司提供的新换乘，使其成为可能。
>
> 语法：generated 为非谓语结构，表示被动含义。
>
> ③ The potential impacts of emerging carriers on global traffic flows and market shares could easily exceed the competitive challenges posed by LCCs to legacy airlines.
>
> 解释：新兴航空公司对全球航空流量和市场份额的潜在影响，很容易超过低成本航空公司对传统航空公司的竞争挑战。

Further Reading

The Challenges of Global Airline Industry

More than three decades after the initial deregulation of US airline markets and the subsequent liberalization of many other markets around the world, the global airline industry remains fragile. Airlines around the world are facing competitive pressures from restructured *legacy* carriers, new entrant low-cost airlines, and/or *emerging global carriers*, as already described. The rapid growth of the global airline industry and the continued threat of terrorist attacks make safety and security issues critical to every airline and every airline passenger.

And, the need for expanded aviation *infrastructure*, both airports and air traffic control, is of particular importance to emerging economies of the world such as India, China, Africa, and the Middle East, where much greater rates of demand growth are forecast for both passenger and cargo air transportation. These important challenges- sustaining airline profitability, ensuring safety and security, and developing adequate air transportation infrastructure.

New Words

downturn	[ˈdaʊntɜːn]	n. 经济低迷、衰退
deteriorate	[dɪˈtɪərɪəreɪt]	v. 变坏；恶化
congestion	[kənˈdʒestʃən]	n. (交通)拥塞；充血
constraint	[kənˈstreɪnt]	n. 限制；限定
infrastructure	[ˈɪnfrəstrʌktʃə]	n. (国家或机构的)基础设施
poise	[pɔɪz]	n. 沉着自信；稳重
emerge	[ɪˈmɜːdʒ]	v. 浮现；显现

resultant	[rɪˈzʌltənt]	*n.* 结果;合力;后果
respective	[rɪˈspektɪv]	*adj.* 分别的;各自的
dynamics	[daɪˈnæmɪks]	*n.* 相互作用的方式;动态;力学
legacy	[ˈlegəsɪ]	*n.* 遗产
sustain	[səˈsteɪn]	*v.* 维持(生命、生存);遭受
category	[ˈkætəgərɪ]	*n.* 类别
exclusively	[ɪkˈskluːsɪvlɪ]	*adv.* 唯一地
productivity	[ˌprɒdʌkˈtɪvətɪ]	*n.* 生产率;生产效率

Phrases & Expressions

business travel	商务旅行
average fare	平均票价
fuel price	燃油价格
flight delay	航班延误
emerging global carrier	新兴全球航空公司
connecting passenger	联程旅客
hub city	枢纽城市
large wide-body aircraft	大型宽体飞机
short-haul route	短途路线
long-haul inter-regional traffic	长途地区间航班

Exercises

Ⅰ. Translate the following terms into Chinese or English.

1. business travel
2. average fare
3. fuel price
4. flight delay
5. 新兴全球航空公司
6. 联程旅客
7. 枢纽城市
8. 大型宽体飞机

Ⅱ. Cloze.

(business travel/large wide-body aircraft/flight delays/connecting passenger)

1. Airlines were in serious trouble even before the events of "9·11", as the start of an economic downturn had already affected negatively the volume of _____ and average fares.

2. Their hub strategies allow them to operate mostly _____, and the location of their hubs

Chapter 1 AIRLINE INDUSTRY OVERVIEW

gives them a geographical advantage over traditional connecting hubs in Europe.

3. To make matters worse, airlines faced deteriorating labor-management relations, aviation infrastructure constraints that led to increasing congestion and _____, and dissatisfied customers due to perceptions of poor service.

4. Dubai (Emirates), Doha (Qatar), Abu Dhabi (Etihad), and Istanbul (Turkish) are _____ with neither origins nor destinations in the hub city.

III. Translate the following sentences into Chinese.

1. At the same time, airline labor costs and fuel prices had been increasing faster than the general rate of inflation for several years.

2. Looking ahead, the combined fleet orders for these four airlines totaled more than 1,000 aircraft at the end of 2013.

IV. Translate the following paragraph into Chinese.

More than three decades after the initial deregulation of US airline markets and the subsequent liberalization of many other markets around the world, the global airline industry remains fragile. Airlines around the world are facing competitive pressures from restructured legacy carriers, new entrant low-cost airlines, and/or emerging global carriers, as already described. The rapid growth of the global airline industry and the continued threat of terrorist attacks make safety and security issues critical to every airline and every airline passenger.

V. Answer the following questions.

1. What's the reason for the high growth rate of emerging airlines?

2. Why the emerging global carriers based in China and South America have been growing at very high rates?

Section 2
Factors Influencing Mode Selections of Low-cost Carriers and a Full-service Airline

Full-service Airline overview Brithish Airways

British Airways(Figure 1-4) is one of the oldest airlines in the world. It is still continue to support that full service model. Brithish Airways is the flag carrier in the UK. It is headquatered in Waterside in its London Heathrow Airport main hub. British Airways remains the largest airline in the UK considering the size of the fleet and international flight destinations. Recently, the airline signed an agreement with Iberia airline from Spain to form the largest carrier in Europe but the deal is awaiting the approval of EU.

Figure 1-4 British Airways

Special Terms

1. Turnaround time: It is the dwell time between arrival and take-off. Airlines can improve aircraft utilization by reducing turnaround time.

转场时间：为航班到站后距再次起飞的停站时间。航空公司通过减少转场时间，可以提高飞机利用率。

2. Code share: Code sharing means that the flight number (i.e. code) of one airline can be used on the flight of another airline, that is, the passenger has a flight in the whole journey or the whole journey takes the flight number of the issuing airline but not the flight carried by the issuing airline.

代码共享：是指一家航空公司的航班号(即代码)可以用在另一家航空公司的航班上，即旅客在全程旅行中，有一段航程或全程航程是乘坐出票航空公司航班号，但非出票航空公司承运的航班。

Text

Annual domestic travelers in Thailand numbered 124,223,700 in 2017 (Airports of Thailand Public Company *Limited* 2017). Thai Airways (Figure 1-5) is the major domestic *Full-Service Airline* (FSA) in Thailand, serving up to twelve domestic destinations with about twenty-five flights a day. The three *Low-cost Carriers* (LCCs) offer services to more than ten domestic destinations with about thirty-eight flights a day.

Figure 1-5 Aircraft of Thai Air Asia

LCCs in Thailand *emerged* in 2004 as a result of the relaxation of air service regulations by the Thai government. The launch of Thai Air Asia, a *joint venture* of Asia Aviation Co., Ltd. and main Asia in Malaysia, has *stimulated momentum* in terms of low-cost growth in Thailand. Today, One-Two-Go, *subsidized* by Orient Thai, and Nok Air, *subsidized* by Thai Airways (TG), have offered domestic services with an *expansion* into international markets, in addition to Thai Air Asia.

Notes 1

❶ Thai Airways is the major domestic Full-service Airline (FSA) in Thailand, serving up to twelve domestic destinations with about twenty-five flights a day.

解释：泰国航空公司(Thai Airways)是泰国主要的国内全服务航空公司(FSA)，每天为12个国内目的地提供25个航班。

语法：serving up 为非谓语结构，表示主动含义。

❷ The launch of Thai Air Asia, a joint venture of Asia Aviation Co., Ltd. and main Asia in Malaysia, has stimulated momentum in terms of low-cost growth in Thailand.

解释：泰国亚洲航空公司(Thai Air Asia)是亚洲航空有限公司(Asia Aviation Co., Ltd.)和马来西亚的亚洲航空公司(main Asia)的合资企业，该公司的成立促进了泰国低成本增长的势头。

The General Characteristics of LCCs

The general *characteristics* of LCCs include high aircraft *utilization*, short *turnaround time*, Internet booking, e-ticketing, minimum *cabin crew*, *one class of seating* to allow more seats per aircraft than that of FSA, simple fare structure and pricing strategy, no *seat allocation*, passengers having to pay for food and drink, *point-to-point services*, and no *connections* offered. While in Thailand, in order to gain and maintain their competitiveness to FSA, a variety of *modifications* by the three LCCs have been made, such as number of seating class, pricing strategy, *on-board food and beverage*, and *seat assignment* (Table 1-1).

Characteristics of LCCs and FSA in Thailand Table 1-1

Item	Full-service Airline (FSA)	Low-cost Carriers (LCCs)		
	Thai Airway (TG)	Air Asia	One-Two-Go	Nok Air
Class	Economy Class and Business Class	Single Class	Single Class	2 Classes: with extra charge (Nok plus class)
Pricing behavior	5 different fare types (Saver, flex saver, flex saver plus, royal silk flexible, royal silk full flexible)	Price change according to quantity of passenger booked	Not change	Price change according to quantity of passenger booked
Distribution	Online, direct booking, and via travel agencies	Online and direct booking	Onlline and direct booking	Online and direct booking
Check-in	Ticketless, IATA ticket contract	Ticketless	Ticketless	Ticketless
Connections	Interlining, code share, globle alliances	Point-to-point	Point-to-point	Point-to-point
Turnaround time	Low turnaround	25 + minutes	25 + minutes	25 + minutes
Onboard food and drink	Serve snack and beverage	Not served but available to purchase	Serve snack and beverage	Not served but available to purchase
Changing flight with the same route	Depends on fare type. For cheapest fare type, changing is permitted before ticket expiration with 500 THB charge and 7% VAT	48 hours in advance with 500 THB charge and 7% VAT	24 hours with 500 THB charge and 7% VAT	24 hours with 500 THB charge and 7% VAT
Changing passenger name	Depends on fare type. Cheapest fare type does not permit name change	Can change with 500 THB + 7% VAT	Can not	Can not
Seating	Seat assignment	No assignment	Offers seat assignment	Offers seat assjgnment
Aircraft	Boeing 737-300	Boeing 737-300	Boeing 757/747	Boeing 737-400

Notes 2

① The general characteristics of LCCs include high aircraft utilization, short turnaround time, Internet booking, e-ticketing, minimum cabin crew, one class of seating to allow more seats per aircraft than that of FSA, simple fare structure and pricing strategy, no seat allocation, passengers having to pay for food and drink, point-to-point services, and no connections offered.

解释：低成本航空公司的一般特点包括：飞机利用率高、转场时间短、互联网预订、电子客票、最少客舱乘务员、每架飞机可容纳比全服务航空公司（FSA）更多座位的单一等级座位、简单的票价结构和定价策略、无座位分配、乘客必须支付餐饮费用、点对点服务，而且不提供任何联程。

❷ While in Thailand, in order to gain and maintain their competitiveness to FSA, a variety of modifications by the three LCCs have been made, such as number of seating class, pricing strategy, on-board food and beverage, and seat assignment.

解释：在泰国，为了获得并保持其对全服务航空公司的竞争力，三家低成本航空公司已经做出了各种修改，如座位等级的数量、定价策略、机上食品和饮料以及座位分配。

Factors Influencing Mode Selections

It may be said that LCCs attract lower income travelers, as expected, in *comparison* with FSA passengers. The distribution of *occupation* of both modes also differs from each other. In terms of *characteristics* of the journey such as trip purpose, reason to choose the mode, ease of ticket buying, and means of travel before LCCs was in service, those of LCCs are different from FSAs.

Overall, passengers have higher satisfaction levels on FSAs as compared to LCCs. One issue reflecting the most FSA passenger satisfaction is *punctuality*, which was the weakness of LCCs, while the issue causing the most dissatisfaction for FSAs is fare, which is the strength of LCCs, and *vice versa*.

The five significant factors influencing mode selection are 1) group size, 2) fare *deviation* to income ratio, 3) waiting time *deviation* multiplied by income, 4) satisfaction level on *punctuality*, and 5) satisfaction level on safety.

Considering effects on number of passengers due to changes of factors influencing mode selection, decreasing income is likely to have significant effects on number of passengers as compared to increasing income. In terms of fare, when the fare of a mode increases, travelers would shift to another mode and *vice versa*. It can be stated that if LCCs improve their *punctuality* to the same level as FSAs, travelers would select LCCs about 40 percent more. In other words, if the *punctuality* of FSAs and LCCs are the same and LCCs' fares increased by 37 percent, the number of passengers will remain the same. If *punctuality* of both modes is the same, FSA may have to reduce their price by about 23 percent to maintain their competitiveness in terms of number of passengers.

If FSAs want to increase number of passengers, airlines may consider offering fare promotions for selected flights, times, and *occupations* (such as student). They may also offer a reduced fare for group traveling. On the other hand, if LCCs are keen on increasing the number of passengers, *punctuality* should be the issue of concern. Although *punctuality* improvement of LCCs may be *tedious* to achieve due to its intensive use of air fleet, its achievement would significantly increase number of passengers.

Notes 3

❶ In terms of characteristics of the journey such as trip purpose, reason to choose the mode, ease of ticket buying, and means of travel before LCCs was in service, those of LCCs are different from FSAs.

解释:就旅行目的、选择出行方式的原因、购票的便利性以及低成本航空公司出现前的旅行方式等旅行特点而言,低成本航空公司与全服务航空公司有所不同。

❷ Considering effects on number of passengers due to changes of factors influencing mode selection, decreasing income is likely to have significant effects on number of passengers as compared to increasing income.

解释:考虑到影响模式选择的因素变化对乘客数量的影响,与收入增加相比,收入减少可能对乘客数量产生显著影响。

❸ If FSAs want to increase number of passengers, airlines may consider offering fare promotions for selected flights, times, and occupations (such as student). They may also offer a reduced fare for group traveling.

解释:如果全服务航空公司想增加乘客数量,航空公司可以考虑为选定的航班、时间和职业(如学生)提供票价促销。他们还可以为团体旅行提供优惠票价。

语法:if 引导条件状语从句。

Further Reading

"Multi Brand" Strategy of Airlines

Singapore Airlines, which has always been famous for its high-quality service and high-end positioning, broke the conservative corporate culture and set up a low-cost airline mid-2012. Scoot started in mid-2012: it has been operating for 4 years, and has developed into a medium and long-range low-cost airline with 11 Boeing 787 aircraft and mainly flying to Oceania, Southeast Asia, Northeast Asia and South Asia. As the world's top airlines, SIA has grown from a single full-service aviation brand to an aviation group with multi brand positioning covering "long-range regional full-service aviation, short, medium and long-range low-cost aviation" (Figure 1-6).

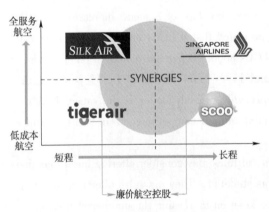

Figure 1-6 "Multi brand" strategy

Chapter 1　AIRLINE INDUSTRY OVERVIEW

New Words

limited	[ˈlɪmɪtɪd]	adj. 有限的；受(……的)限制	
emerge	[ɪˈmɜːdʒ]	v. 浮现；显现	
stimulate	[ˈstɪmjuleɪt]	vt. 促进；激发	
momentum	[məˈmentəm]	n. 推进力；动力	
subsidize	[ˈsʌbsɪdaɪz]	v. 补贴；资助	
expansion	[ɪkˈspænʃən]	n. 膨胀；扩张	
characteristics	[ˌkærɪktəˈrɪstɪks]	n. 特征；特点	
utilization	[ˌjuːtəlaɪˈzeɪʃən]	n. 利用；应用	
connection	[kəˈnekʃən]	n. (两种事实、观念等的)联系，关联	
modification	[ˌmɒdɪfɪˈkeɪʃən]	n. 修改；改进	
comparison	[kəmˈpærɪsn]	n. 比较；对比	
occupation	[ˌɒkjʊˈpeɪʃən]	n. 工作；占领	
punctuality	[ˌpʌŋktjʊˈælɪti]	n. 准时；严守时间	
vice versa	[ˌvaɪs ˈvɜːsə]	adv. 反过来也一样；反之亦然	
deviation	[ˌdiːvɪˈeɪʃən]	n. 偏离；偏差	
tedious	[ˈtiːdɪəs]	adj. 乏味的；冗长的	

Phrases & Expressions

full-service airline (FSA)	全服务航空公司
low-cost carrier (LCC)	低成本航空公司
joint venture	合资企业
turnaround time	转场时间
cabin crew	机组人员
one class of seating	单一舱位座位
seat allocation	座位分配
point-to-point service	点对点服务
on-board food and beverage	机上餐饮
seat assignment	座位分配

Exercises

Ⅰ. **Translate the following terms into Chinese or English.**

1. seat allocation
2. turn around time
3. industry-level
4. LCC

5. 转场时间

6. 低成本航空公司

7. 全服务航空公司

8. 机组人员

Ⅱ. Cloze.

(seat allocation/turn around time/on-board food and beverage/point-to-point services)

1. While in Thailand, in order to gain and maintain their competitiveness to FSA, a variety of modifications by the three LCCs have been made, such as number of seating class, pricing strategy, _____, and seat assignment.

2. The general characteristics of LCCs include high aircraft utilization, short _____, Internet booking, e-ticketing, minimum cabin crew, one class of seating to allow more seats per aircraft than that of FSA, simple fare structure and pricing strategy, no _____.

3. The general characteristics of LCCs include high aircraft utilization, short turnaround time, Internet booking, e-ticketing, minimum cabin crew, one class of seating to allow more seats per aircraft than that of FSA, simple fare structure and pricing strategy, no seat allocation, passengers having to pay for food and drink, _____, and no connections offered.

Ⅲ. Translate the following sentences into Chinese.

1. In other words, if the punctuality of FSAs and LCCs are the same and LCCs' fares increased by 37 percent, the number of passengers will remain the same.

2. One issue reflecting the most FSA passenger satisfaction is punctuality, which was the weakness of LCCs, while the issue causing the most dissatisfaction for FSAs is fare, which is the strength of LCCs, and vice versa.

Ⅳ. Translate the following paragraph into Chinese.

Success will hinge on a number of factors: large size will be an advantage because of the marketing benefits it creates; low fares will be important, but it is the combination of fare levels and brand that will be key. That is how each airline positions and brands itself in terms of product and service quality. Lower service levels may be acceptable to passengers if combined with very low fares. LCCs must provide value for money.

V. Answer the following questions.

1. What are the general characteristics of LCCs?

2. What are the five significant factors influencing LCCs' mode selection?

Section 3
Introduction of ICAO and IATA

Lead in

IATA Travel Pass Initiative

To re-open borders without quarantine and restart aviation governments need to be confident that they are effectively mitigating the risk of importing COVID-19. This means having accurate information on passengers' COVID-19 health status (Figure 1-7).

Figure 1-7 IATA Travel Pass Initiative

Special Terms

1. ICAO: *International Civil Aviation Organization.* The International Civil Aviation Organization (ICAO), a specialized agency of the United Nations, was established in 1944 to promote the safe and orderly development of civil aviation around the world.

国际民用航空组织:是联合国的一个专门机构,于1944年为促进全世界民用航空安全、有序地发展而成立。

2. *Chicago Convention*: The International Civil Aviation Organization adopted *the Convention on International Civil Aviation* on December 7, 1944. Because it was signed in the American city of Chicago, it is also called the *Chicago Convention*.

《芝加哥公约》:国际民用航空组织于1944年12月7日通过《国际民用航空公约》,因其在美国城市芝加哥签订,故又称为《芝加哥公约》。

Text

ICAO

The Convention on International Civil Aviation, *drafted* in 1944 by 54 nations, was established to *promote cooperation* and "create and preserve friendship and understanding among the nations and people of the world" (Figure 1-8).

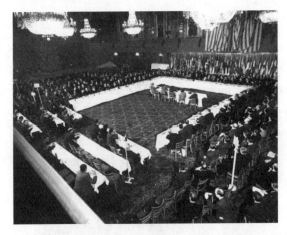

Figure 1-8　International Civil Aviation Conference in Chicago in 1944

Known more commonly today as the "Chicago Convention", this landmark agreement established the core principles permitting international transport by air, and led to the creation of the specialized agency which has overseen it ever since-the International Civil Aviation Organization (ICAO).

Notes 1

❶ The Convention on International Civil Aviation, drafted in 1944 by 54 nations, was established to promote cooperation and "create and preserve friendship and understanding among the nations and people of the world."

解释:《国际民用航空公约》于1944年由54个国家起草,旨在促进合作和"在世界各国和人民之间建立和维护友谊与理解"。

Chapter 1 AIRLINE INDUSTRY OVERVIEW

语法：drafted in 1944 by 54 nations 为非谓语结构，表示被动含义。

❷ Subsequent to several studies initiated by the United States, as well as various consultations it undertook with its Major Allies, the U. S. government extended an invitation to 55 States to attend an International Civil Aviation Conference in Chicago in 1944.

解释：在发起几项研究以及与主要盟国进行各种磋商之后，美国政府向55个国家发出邀请，邀请他们参加1944年在芝加哥举行的国际民用航空会议。

语法：major ally 意为主要盟友。

Known then and today more commonly as the *Chicago Convention*, this landmark agreement laid the foundation for the *standards* and procedures for peaceful global *air navigation*. It set out as its prime objective the development of international civil aviation "in a safe and orderly manner", and such that air transport services would be established "on the basis of equality of opportunity and operated soundly and economically".

The "Chicago Convention" also formalized the expectation that a specialized International Civil Aviation Organization (ICAO) would be established, in order to organize and support the intensive international co-operation which the fledgling global air transport network would require.

Notes 2

❶ Known then and today more commonly as the *Chicago Convention*, this landmark agreement laid the foundation for the standards and procedures for peaceful global air navigation.

解释：今天，其被更普遍地称为《芝加哥公约》，这一划时代的协议奠定了全球航空导航和平发展的标准和程序。

语法：Known then and today more commonly as the "Chicago Convention" 为非谓语结构，表示被动含义。

❷ It set out as its prime objective the development of international civil aviation "…in a safe and orderly manner", and such that air transport services would be established "on the basis of equality of opportunity and operated soundly and economically."

解释：它提出的首要目标是"以安全和有序的方式"发展国际民用航空，以便"在机会平等的基础上，建立健全经济型的航空运输服务"。

ICAO's Strategic Objectives

ICAO has established five comprehensive Strategic Objectives：

- Safety.

Enhance global *civil aviation safety*. This Strategic Objective is focused primarily on the State's regulatory oversight capabilities.

- Air Navigation Capacity and Efficiency.

Increase the capacity and improve the efficiency of the global civil aviation system. Although functionally and organizationally interdependent with Safety, this Strategic Objective is focused primarily on upgrading the air navigation and *aerodrome infrastructure* and developing new procedures to optimize aviation system performance.

- Security & Facilitation.

Enhance global civil aviation security and facilitation. This Strategic Objective reflects the need for ICAO's leadership in aviation security, facilitation and related border security matters.

- Economic Development of Air Transport.

Foster the development of a sound and economically-viable civil aviation system. This Strategic Objective reflects the need for ICAO's leadership in harmonizing the air transport framework focused on economic policies and supporting activities.

- Environmental Protection.

Minimize the adverse environmental effects of civil aviation activities. This Strategic Objective fosters ICAO's leadership in all aviation-related environmental activities and is consistent with the ICAO and UN system environmental protection policies and *practices*.

Notes 3

❶ Increase the capacity and improve the efficiency of the global civil aviation system. Although functionally and organizationally interdependent with Safety, this Strategic Objective is focused primarily on upgrading the air navigation and aerodrome infrastructure and developing new procedures to optimize aviation system performance.

解释：提高全球民航系统的容量和效率。尽管在功能和组织上与安全相互依赖，但该战略目标主要集中于升级空中导航和机场基础设施，并制定新程序以优化航空系统性能。

❷ This Strategic Objective reflects the need for ICAO's leadership in harmonizing the air transport framework focused on economic policies and supporting activities.

解释：该战略目标反映了国际民航组织的领导作用，主要体现在协调航空运输的经济政策框架，以及提供相应的支持。

语法：focused on economic policies and supporting activities 为非谓语结构。

❸ This Strategic Objective fosters ICAO's leadership in all aviation-related environmental activities and is consistent with the ICAO and UN system environmental protection policies and practices.

解释：该战略目标巩固了国际民航组织在所有航空相关环境活动中的领导地位，并与国际民航组织和联合国系统的环境保护政策和做法相一致。

IATA

IATA (*International Air Transport Association*) was *founded* in Havana, Cuba, on 19 April 1945. It is the prime vehicle for inter-airline cooperation in promoting safe, reliable, secure and economical air services. The international *scheduled air transport industry* is more than 100 times larger than it was in 1945. Few industries can match the *dynamism* of that growth, which would have been much less *spectacular* without the standards, practices and procedures developed within IATA.

At its founding, IATA had 57 members from 31 nations, mostly in Europe and North America. Today it has some 290 members from 120 nations in every part of the globe.

Notes 4

❶ It is the prime vehicle for inter-airline cooperation in promoting safe, reliable, secure and economical air services.

解释:它是航空公司间合作的主要媒介组织,以促进安全、可靠和经济的航空服务。prime vehicle 意为主要媒介手段。

❷ Few industries can match the dynamism of that growth, which would have been much less spectacular without the standards, practices and procedures developed within IATA.

解释:几乎没有哪个行业能与这种增长的活力相媲美,如果没有国际航空运输协会制定的标准、做法和程序,这种增长就不会那么引人注目。

语法:which 为非限制定语从句。

IATA's early aims:
- To promote safe, regular and economical air transport for the benefit of the peoples of the world, to *foster* air commerce, and to study the problems connected therewith;
- To provide means for *collaboration* among the air transport *enterprises engaged* directly or indirectly in international air transport service;
- To cooperate with the newly created International Civil Aviation Organization and other international organizations.

Notes 5

❶ The most important tasks of IATA during its earliest days were *technical*, because safety and reliability are *fundamental* to airline operations.

解释:IATA 早期最重要的任务是技术性的,因为安全性和可靠性是航空公司运营的基础。

❷ By 1949, the drafting process was largely complete and reflected in "Annexes" to the *Chicago Convention*, the treaty which still governs the conduct of international civil aviation.

解释:到1949年,起草过程基本完成,并反映在《芝加哥公约》的"附件"中,该条约仍然管辖国际民用航空的行为。

语法:which 为定语从句,先行词为 the treaty。

While the 20th century saw the creation and rapid growth of the air transport industry, the beginning of the 21st century was marked by great challenges met with major transformations.

Over the last decade, the industry has been rocked by a series of successive crises and shocks. These include terrorism, pandemic threats, volcanic eruptions, global economic upheavals and an unprecedented rise in the cost price of fuel. Between 2000 and 2010, airlines posted a *net loss* of $30 billion.

IATA also strengthened its position as the voice of the industry, with firm advocacy and lobbying to focus governments on the long term issues for viability of aviation, such as liberalization, environment and taxation.

Notes 6

❶ While the 20th century saw the creation and rapid growth of the air transport industry, the beginning of the 21st century was marked by great challenges met with major transformations.

解释:虽然20世纪见证了航空运输业的创立和快速发展,但21世纪初的特点是巨大的挑战和重大的变革。

语法:while 为让步状语从句,意思为尽管。

❷ Over the last decade, the industry has been rocked by a series of successive crises and shocks. These include terrorism, pandemic threats, volcanic eruptions, global economic upheavals and an unprecedented rise in the cost price of fuel. Between 2000 and 2010, airlines posted a net loss of $30 billion.

解释:在过去十年中,该行业遭遇到一系列连续的危机和冲击。其中包括恐怖主义、流行病威胁、火山爆发、全球经济动荡和燃料价格空前上涨。2000—2010年,航空公司净亏损300亿美元。

❸ IATA also strengthened its position as the voice of the industry, with firm advocacy and lobbying to focus governments on the long term issues for viability of aviation, such as liberalization, environment and taxation.

解释:国际航空运输协会还加强了其作为航空业代言人的地位,进行了坚定的宣传和游说,使各国政府关注航空业生存的长期问题,如自由化、环境和税收。

Further Reading

IATA's Mission

IATA's mission is to represent, lead, and serve the airline industry (Figure 1-9).

Representing the airline industry

We improve understanding of the air transport industry among decision makers and increase awareness of the benefits that aviation brings to national and global economies.

Leading the airline industry

Our aim is to assist airlines by simplifying processes and increasing passenger convenience while reducing costs and improving efficiency.

Chapter 1 AIRLINE INDUSTRY OVERVIEW

Serving the airline industry

We help airlines to operate safely, securely, efficiently, and economically under clearly defined rules. Professional support is provided to all industry stakeholders with a wide range of products and expert services.

Figure 1-9 IATA mission manual

New Words

found	[faʊnd]	vt. 创立;建立;创办	
cooperation	[kəʊˌɒpəˈreɪʃn]	n. 合作;协作	
promote	[prəˈməʊt]	vt. 促进;提升;推销	
dynamism	[ˈdaɪnəmɪzəm]	n. 活力;动态;推动力	
spectacular	[spekˈtækjələ(r)]	adj. 壮观的;惊人的	
standard	[ˈstændəd]	n. 标准;水准;	
practice	[ˈpræktɪs]	n. 实践;练习;惯例	
		v. 练习	
infrastructure	[ˈɪnfrəstrʌktʃə(r)]	n. 基础设施	
foster	[ˈfɒstə(r)]	v. 促进	
collaboration	[kəˌlæbəˈreɪʃn]	n. 合作	
enterprises	[ˈentəpraɪzɪz]	n. [经] 企业(enterprise 的复数)	
engage	[ɪnˈɡeɪdʒ]	vt. 吸引;占用;使参加	
technical	[ˈteknɪkl]	adj. 工艺的;科技的	
fundamental	[ˌfʌndəˈmentl]	adj. 基本的;根本的	
		n. 基本原理;基本原则	
draft	[drɑːft]	vt. 起草;制定;征募	

Phrases & Expressions

scheduled air transport industry	定期航空运输业
air navigation	空中导航
International Civil Aviation Organization	国际民航组织
net loss	净损失
civil aviation safety	航空安全
International Air Transport Association	国际航空运输协会
air transport industry	航空业
Chicago Convention	芝加哥公约
aerodrome infrastructure	机场基础设施

Exercises

Ⅰ. Translate the following terms into English or Chinese.

1. 芝加哥公约
2. 航空业
3. 国际航空运输协会
4. 机场基础设施
5. civil aviation safety
6. net loss
7. scheduled air transport
8. International Civil Aviation Organization

Ⅱ. Cloze.

(Chicago Convention/ air navigation / scheduled air transport/net loss)

1. Enhance global _____. This Strategic Objective is focused primarily on the State's regulatory oversight capabilities.

2. Objective is focused primarily on upgrading the _____ and aerodrome infrastructure and developing new procedures to optimize aviation system performance.

3. The international _____ industry is more than 100 times larger than it was in 1945.

4. Between 2000 and 2010, airlines posted a _____ of $30 billion.

Ⅲ. Translate the following sentences into Chinese.

1. While the 20th century saw the creation and rapid growth of the air transport industry, the beginning of the 21st century was marked by great challenges met with major transformations.

2. The most important tasks of IATA during its earliest days were technical, because safety and reliability are fundamental to airline operations.

IV. Translate the following paragraph into Chinese.

Representing the airline industry

We improve understanding of the air transport industry among decision makers and increase awareness of the benefits that aviation brings to national and global economies.

Leading the airline industry

Our aim is to assist airlines by simplifying processes and increasing passenger convenience while reducing costs and improving efficiency.

Serving the airline industry

We help airlines to operate safely, securely, efficiently, and economically under clearly defined rules. Professional support is provided to all industry stakeholders with a wide range of products and expert services.

V. Answer the following questions.

1. What is ICAO's five comprehensive strategic objectives?

2. What is IATA's early aim?

Chapter 2
MARKETING

Section 1
Passenger Air Fare

Lead in

Brand Fares in the Civil Aviation Industry

Figure 2-1 Air Canada

Brand Fares appeared in the *civil aviation* industry for the first time in 2008. Air Canada took the lead in applying the *innovative* concept of brand fares to air *route network marketing*, it is called "*Fare Family*" (Figure 2-1). Just as its name implies, it divided the fares into different groups. Air Canada divided the brands into Tango, Tango Plus, Latitude and Executive class according to the level of rights and interests.

Special Terms

1. Benchmark price: Based on civil aviation transport costs and social affordability, make a price that can be measured and use as a standard that other prices can be compared.

基准价:根据民航运输成本和社会承受能力,制定一个可以衡量的价格,作为其他价格可以比较的标准。

2. Open date segment: Segments without booked flights, dates and seats.

不定期航段:没有定妥航班、日期和座位的航段。

Text

Domestic Passenger Air Fares

1. Benchmark Price

In order to further activate market vitality and deepen the reform of *civil aviation*, *Civil Aviation* Administration of China took the lead in implementing market pricing for business class and first class in 2010, meaning that the pricing for business class and first class is completely determined by air carriers according to the market.

In 2017, National Development and Reform Commission and *Civil Aviation* Administration of China jointly issued the Notice on Further Improving *Domestic* Air Transport Pricing Policy of *Civil Aviation*. By the end of 2018, there had been 1,088 *route* market adjustment prices formulated by carriers, accounting for 35.5% of total *routes* and 77.4% of total passenger transportation, respectively. At the same time, it is stipulated that government-guided price *routes* have 25% of floating pricing space on *benchmark price* without lower limit. With further de*regulation* of pricing, airlines have greater power to make their independent pricing, and different *benchmark* prices can be formulated with different *routes*, markets and seasons.

Notes 1

❶ In order to further activate market vitality and deepen the reform of civil aviation, Civil Aviation Administration of China took the lead in implementing market pricing for business class and first class in 2010, meaning that the pricing for business class and first class is completely determined by air carriers according to the market.

解释：为了进一步激发市场活力，深化民航改革，中国民用航空局在2010年带头实施了商务舱和头等舱的市场化定价，这意味着商务舱和头等舱的价格是完全由航空公司根据市场决定的。

语法：in order to 的用法。

in order to 意为"为了……"，表示目的；在用法和意义上相当于 so as to 结构，但是 in order to 结构可以用于句首、句中，而 so as to 多用于句中。其否定式分别为：in order not to 和 so as not to。

❷ In 2017, National Development and Reform Commission and Civil Aviation Administration of China jointly issued the Notice on Further Improving Domestic Air Transport Pricing Policy of Civil Aviation.

解释：2017年，国家发展与改革委员会与中国民用航空局联合发布了《关于进一步完善民航国内航空运输价格政策的通知》。

❸ By the end of 2018, there had been 1,088 route market adjustment prices formulated by carriers, accounting for 35.5% of total routes and 77.4% of total passenger transportation, respectively.

解释：截至2018年底，承运人制定的航线市场调节价已达1,088条，分别占总航线的35.5%和客运总量的77.4%。

语法：By +过去的时间，这是过去完成时的标志，主句要用过去完成时；By +现在的时间，是现在完成时标志，主句要用现在完成时。

❹ With further deregulation of pricing, airlines have greater power to make their independent pricing, and different benchmark prices can be formulated with different routes, markets and seasons.

> **解释**：随着价格进一步的放开,航空公司自主定价的权力越来越大,可以结合不同航线、不同市场、不同季节,制定不同的基准价。
>
> **语法**：比较级单词的变化 greater power；复合句：
> - 一般在词尾加-er, great-greater；
> - 以不发音字母 e 结尾的只加 r,如：close-closer；
> - 以辅音字母加 y 结尾的,先把 y 改为 i 再加-er,如：happy-happier；
> - and 的复合句,两个主语,两个动词。

2. Service Level Fare

Service Level refers to the level of service provided for passengers, charging different fares according to levels of service provided. Passenger fares are generally divided into three service grade fares: first class fare (F), business class fare (C), economy class fare (Y).

First class seats are wider and more comfortable than economy class seats, and the standards of free meals on board and ground meals are higher than economy class; special check-in counters and waiting rooms provide higher quality and faster services for first class passengers; normal fares for first class on domestic routes were originally about 150% of economy normal class fare, but now different airlines may have different first class prices on the same route.

The airlines can provide business class seats to passengers on domestic flights with business class layout. Business class seats are narrower than first class seats, and dining and ground *accommodation* standards are lower than first class but higher than economy class. The normal fare of business class on *domestic* routes was originally 130% of the normal economic class fare, but the changes are the same as those of first class prices. The prices of business class by different airlines are different on the same route, which are lower than first class and higher than economy class.

Economy class normal fare is the benchmark price of passenger air fare, which is the most expensive price of all economy class fare.

3. Multi-level Fare System

Airlines sell at different prices by designing different sub-class seats (Figure 2-2). The *cabin* seats of the aircraft are the product of airlines, and the type number of *cabin* seats is the number of the airline products. In the marketing of airlines, in addition to determining first class, business class and economy class according to service class, airlines also enrich their products to meet different market demand with different charges, by formulating a number of progressively reduced *cabin* rates based on service, with additional *restrictions* such as *endorsement*, reservation change, refund, ticket confirmation and payment deadline.

For example, in the rear of economy class, that is, Y *cabin*, there are sub-*cabins*: K, B, E, H, L, M, N, R, S, T, etc., the comfort level of all these sub-*cabins* seats and the standard of meals are basically the same as the Y class, and the so-called "class" refers only to the rate difference and the level of *restrictions* on the selling and use of tickets related to the rate.

航空代码	票号	9.0折	8.5折	8.0折	7.5折	7.0折	6.5折	6.0折	5.5折	5.0折	4.5折	4.0折	3.5折	3.0折	特殊	中转	来回
南航 CZ	784	T	K	H	M	G	S	L	Q	E	V	X			N/R	B	N
东航 MU	781	B	E	H	L	M	N	R	S	Y	T	W	G		X	Q	E
国航 CA	999	B	M	H	K	L	L1	Q	Q1	G	V	V1			E	W	T
上航 FM	774	B	E	H	L	M	N	R	S	V	T	W	G		X	Q	E
川航 3U	876	T	T1	H	M	G	S	L	Q	E	V	R	K	I	N/Z	B	W
山航 SC	324	B	M	H	K	L	P	Q	G	V	U	Z	R		E	W	T
厦航 MF	731	B	H	K	L	M	N	Q	T	V	X	R					I
海航 HU	880	B	H	K	L	M	M1	Q	Q1	X	U	E			Z/T	V	J
西部 PN	874	B	H	K	L	M	M1	Q	Q1	X	U	E			Z/T	V	J
首都 JD	898	B	H	K	L	M	M1	Q	Q1	X	U	E			Z/T/N	V/W/R	J
天津 GS	826	B	H	K	L	M		Q		X	U	E			Z/T		
祥鹏 8L	859	B	H	K	L	M	M1	Q		X	U	E			N/T	V	J
深航 ZH	479	B	M	H	K	L	J	Q	Z	G	V				E/T/W	S	T
昆明 KY	833	B	M	H	K	L	P	Q			G	V	Z		E/W	W/J	
联合 KN	822	B	E	H	L	M	N	R	S	V	T	W			G	X	Q
河北 NS	836	T		H	M	G	S	L	Q	E	V	R					

Figure 2-2 Sub-class seats

Notes 2

❶ Service Level refers to the level of service provided for passengers, charging different fares according to levels of service provided. Passenger fares are generally divided into three service grade fares: first class fare (F), business class fare (C), economy class fare (Y).

解释：服务等级是指为旅客提供服务的等级,按照提供服务的等级不同来收取不同的票价。客运价一般分为三个服务等级票价：头等舱票价(F)、公务舱票价(C)、经济舱票价(Y)。

语法：provide for 侧重于指直接性的为对方提供支持与帮助。

❷ The airlines can provide business class seats to passengers on domestic flights with business class layout. Business class seats are narrower than first class seats, and dining and ground *accommodation* standards are lower than first class but higher than economy class.

解释：航空公司可以为国内航班的乘客提供商务舱座位。商务舱的座位比头等舱窄,餐饮和地面住宿标准低于头等舱,但高于经济舱。

语法：比较级 narrower than, higher than 表示"比……更",用形容词比较级 + than + 比较成分,than 后主语的述语动词往往省略。
- 非正式用法的 than 后的人称代词可用所有格。
- 表示"较……低；不及……",用 less + 形容词原级 + than + 比较成分。
- 表示两者之中"较……",用 the + 比较级 + of the two。
- 定冠词或指示形容词 + 比较级 + 名词表示比较。

International Passenger Air Fare

1. IATA Normal Fares

This kind of fare is commonly known as "no discounted fare", which is characterized by expensive prices, but there are no *restrictions* on refund or reservation change, mainly applicable to business class passengers, because their itineraries are more liable to change and they are not so sensitive to ticket price. Generally speaking, first class booking seats are F and P, Business Class C and J, Economy Class Y and S.

2. IATA Special Fares

This kind of fare may also be called "*promotional fare*" or "discounted fare". It is characterized by cheaper prices than a normal fare, but with more usage *restrictions*. It is mainly applicable to casual passengers, who are extremely sensitive to the level of price. For the two factors of "price" and "*restrictions*", they would first consider price as their priority. Common *restrictions* include (Figure 2-3):

- The minimum and maximum stay, the maximum stay is also known as validity.
- Number of transfer or stopover points.
- Limitations on booking, payment, and issue.
- Limit on travel dates and time periods.
- *Eligibility* (user limitation).
- *Restriction*s on *ticket refunds and changes*.

```
> XS FSN1/3/6/18
FSN 001/01DEC09 6778/UA/003/IPRP/ATP/29
01DEC09 * 01DEC09/UA BJSLAX/PA/ADT/TPM 6237/MPM 7484/CNY
01 LAPCN/ADVP 45D/5000/L/SU. 3M//6778R
03. SEASONALITY
NO SEASONAL TRAVEL RESTRICTIONS
06. MINIMUM STAY
TRAVEL FROM LASST STOPOVER MUST COMMENCE NO EARLIER THAN
THE FIRST SUN AFTER DEPARTURE OF THE OUTBOUND
TRANSATLANTIC SECTOR
18. TICKET ENDORSEMENT
THE ORIGINAL AND THE REISSUED TICKET MUST BE ANNOTATED –
NONREF FARE/CHANCE FEE – AND – VALID ON UA ONLY – IN THE
+ ENDORSEMENT BOX
* * * * * * * END * * * * * * *
AFPDEMO/1E/DB1/PAGE 1/1
```

Figure 2-3　Example of special fares restrictions

Because of different fare levels and *restrictions*, special fares can be divided into the following different types suitable for the public:

- Advance purchase Tour Fare: purchase the ticket and book the seat before travel, *open date segment* is not allowed, charges applicable for change and cancellation. Code of this type is AP or APEX.

● Instant purchase Tour Fare: also known as the purchase fare, such fare is not required to buy in advance, but need to book seats and make payment before travel, open date segment is not allowed, charges applicable for change and cancellation, and the code is PX or PEX;

● Excursion Tour Fare: this rate is a higher category of special rate, generally allow open date, do not limit the dates of reservation change and cancellation. The rate code is EE.

3. *Carries Fares*

A carrier fare which is determined individually based on each airline's judgement or is jointly determined by the cooperation of a group of allied airlines. Carrier fare usage has grown rapidly in recent years because of *liberalization*. Under the same *restrictions*, these fares are generally lower than the normal and special fares, but there are also many *restrictions*, such as those on refund and reservation change.

Notes 3

❶ Common restrictions include: The minimum and maximum stay, the maximum stay is also known as validity; Number of transfer or stopover points; Limitations on booking, payment, and issue; Limit on travel dates and time periods; Eligibility (user limitation); Restrictions on ticket refunds and changes.

解释:常见的限制包括:最短停留时间和最长停留时间,最长停留时间也称为有效期;中转点或中途分程点数目;预订、支付和出票方面的限制;限制旅行日期和时间;资格(用户限制);机票退改限制。

语法:be known as 表示"作为……而闻名",后接称号或表示身份的词。

❷ Advance purchase Tour Fare: purchase the ticket and book the seat before travel, open date segment is not allowed, charges applicable for change and cancellation. Code of this type is AP or APEX.

解释:预购游览票价:在出发前购票定座,不允许不定期航段,更改和取消需收取相应费用。该类型的代码为 AP 或 APEX。

语法:open date segment 是主语,is not allowed 是被动式谓语。
Be 动词加动词的过去分词是被动语态的形式。

❸ This fare applies to the airlines issuing it, which is exclusive, not allowed to be used by other airlines. Under the same restrictions, these fares are generally lower than the normal and special fares, but there are also many restrictions, such as those on refund and reservation change.

解释:航空公司运价具有排他性,其他航空公司不得使用,在同等的限制条件下,票价一般低于航协普通运价和特殊运价,但同样有诸多限制条件,如退改签等。

语法:which is exclusive, not allowed to be used by other airlines 非限制性定语从句,修饰前面 This fare applies to the airlines issuing it 整件事。

not allowed to be used by other airlines 可以看成同位语,对前面的 is exclusive 进行进一步解释说明,其他航空公司都不允许用,更加显示 exclusive.

Low-cost Airlines Fares

Over the years, airlines have suffered from *homogenization competition*, with the root cause of the low *differentiation* of air products. How to provide different products? It was not until low-cost airlines appeared that many airlines seemingly found a *feasible* path. The practice of low-cost airline can be simply summarized as "unbundling", which finely divides the *tangible* and intangible products and services included in traditional air fares, and divides them one by one in terms of ticket change and cancellation, seat selection, *free baggage allowance*, catering, boarding order, *cabin* promotion service and mileage *accumulation*. This product model is first to educate the majority of passengers that air tickets no longer contain all the segments, which are defined as additional products. Low-cost airlines can offer cheaper fares, but only if passengers sacrifice part of or even most of the additional interests.

Airlines Brand Fares

The brand fare portfolio was first introduced by Air Canada in 2008, and then the *innovative* concept was widely applied to marketing across the entire *route* network and became one of the leading practicing in the field (Table 2-1). It is understood that of the world's 30 largest airlines, 20 have implemented the Brand Fare practice of economy class. The so-called brand fares mean splitting the ticket and its additional rights and interests, reorganizing them, and presenting the prices in the forms of products, in order to meet differentiated needs of different passengers, and thus realizes the transformation from price-centered marketing to product-centered marketing model.

Air Canada Tango fare family   Table 2-1

Tango	Tango Plus	Latitude	Executive Class
①The lowest product price; ②Not refundable; ③Reed charge; ④Advance seat selection is not included; ⑤No on-board meals are included; ⑥Frequent passenger mileage is deducted	① The product price is slightly higher; ②Not refundable; ③ The replacement charge is low; ④The seat can be selected in advance; ⑤ No on-board meals are included; ⑥Full mileage of regular passengers	①High prices is high; ②Full refund is allowed; ③No charge for the replacement period; ④The seat can be selected in advance; ⑤Incltains onboard meals; ⑥Additional mileage for regular passengers	①Product prices are very high; ②Business class alone; ③Airport lounge; ④Full refund is allowed; ⑤No charge for the replacement period; ⑥ The seat can be selected in advance; ⑦Incltains onboard meals; ⑧Additional on-board drinks; ⑨Additional mileage for regular passengers

Through brand fare pricing, combined with item pricing sales and split service, airlines can separate service items included in the original ticket one by one, allowing passengers to combine personal preferences and travel needs by choosing additional fixed "package" services, giving them more choices, with relatively *customized* travel experience called "unbundling" and "*bundling*".

Notes 4

❶ Over the years, airlines have suffered from homogenization competition, with the root cause of the low differentiation of air products.

解释：多年来，航空公司遭遇同质化竞争的根本原因是航空产品差异化低。

语法：over the years 的意思是"这么多年来""经过这么多年之后"，它指的是一种从几年前持续到现在的一种情况，因此通常与现在完成时连用。Have suffered from 是现在完成时。

❷ The practice of low-cost airline can be simply summarized as "unbundling", which finely divides the tangible and intangible products and services included in traditional air fares, and divides them one by one in terms of ticket change and cancellation, seat selection, free baggage allowance, catering, boarding order, cabin promotion service and mileage accumulation.

解释：低成本航空的做法可以简单地概括为"拆包"，将传统机票价格中包含的有形产品和无形产品及服务进行精细划分，并在机票改签、选座、免费行李限额、餐饮、登机顺序、客舱优惠服务及里程累积等。

语法：included 是过去分词形式的形容词，在表示"包括……在内"时常放在被修饰的名词或代词之后，起着补充说明的作用。

❸ The so-called brand fares mean splitting the ticket and its additional rights and interests, reorganizing them, and presenting the prices in the forms of products, in order to meet differentiated needs of different passengers, and thus realizes the transformation from price-centered marketing to product-centered marketing model.

解释：所谓品牌运价，即把机票及其附加权益进行拆分，再进行重新组合，将机票价格以产品的形式进行呈现，满足不同旅客对机票的差异化需求，进而实现从价格为中心到以产品为中心的机票营销模式。

Further Reading

IATA YY Fares will Be Abolished

Starting October 31, 2018. IATA YY fares will be abolished.

What is a YY fares? It was born in the first conference of IATA in 1945, and established the original international interline transfer ticket settlement system with YY ticket. The fare of city pairs was suitable for all carriers, which greatly promoted the rapid development of the interline transfer business in the global air industry.

However, with the emergence of a series of problems such as the rise of airline alliance, the intensified competition of non-alliance airlines, the rise of low-cost airlines, the suspected violation of relevant international laws, and the diversification of ticket price products after the rise of the Internet, the YY ticket system encountered unprecedented challenges and finally withdrew from the stage of history. It announces the end of the era of IATA unified global fare system, and truly reflects the demands of international airlines for the personalized, liberal and differentiated interline transfer fare system that more meets the requirements of *consumer* demands, the demands of partners and sales channels.

New Words

civil	[ˈsɪvl]	adj.	公民的;民间的;根据民法
aviation	[ˌeɪviˈeɪʃən]	n.	航空;飞行术;飞机制造业
domestic	[dəˈmestɪk]	adj.	国内的;家庭的;驯养的
		n.	国货
regulation	[ˌregjuˈleɪʃən]	n.	法规,规章;调节
		adj.	规定的;平常的
cabin	[ˈkæbɪn]	n.	小屋;客舱;船舱;机舱
route	[ruːt]	n.	路线,航线;道路,公路
benchmark	[ˈbentʃmɑːk]	n.	基准(价);标准检查程序
itinerary	[aɪˈtɪnərəri]	n.	旅程,路线;旅行日程 (pl. -ies)
eligibility	[elɪdʒəˈbɪləti]	n.	适任,合格
endorsement	[ɪnˈdɔːsmənt]	n.	认可,支持
accommodation	[əˌkɒməˈdeɪʃən]	n.	住处;膳宿;预订铺位
promotional	[prəˈməʊʃənl]	adj.	促销的;增进的;奖励的
restriction	[rɪˈstrɪkʃən]	n.	限制;限制条件;约束;束缚
homogenization	[həʊmədʒənaɪˈzeɪʃ(ə)n]	n.	同质化;均匀化;均质化
differentiation	[ˌdɪfəˌrenʃɪˈeɪʃən]	n.	变异,[生物] 分化;区别;差异化
feasible	[ˈfiːzəbl]	adj.	可行的;行得通;切实可行的
bundling	[ˈbʌndlɪŋ]	n.	捆扎;集束
tangible	[ˈtændʒəbl]	adj.	有形的;切实的;可触摸的
liberalization	[ˌlɪbrəlaɪˈzeɪʃən]	n.	自由化;自由主义化;放宽限制
accumulation	[əˌkjuːmjəˈleɪʃən]	n.	积累,累积;堆积物
innovative	[ˈɪnəveɪtɪv]	adj.	革新的,创新的;新颖的;有创新精神的
customized	[ˈkʌstəmaɪzd]	adj.	定制的;用户化的
consumer	[kənˈsjuːmə(r)]	n.	消费者

Phrases & Expressions

fare family	品牌运价
homogenization competition	同质化竞争
free baggage allowance	免费行李额
ticket refunds and changes	退票和更改

route network marketing	航线网络营销
brand fares	品牌运价
benchmark price	基准价格
multi-level fare system	多等级运价制度
IATA Normal Fares	国际航空运输协会普通运价
IATA Special Fares	国际航空运输协会特殊运价
promotional fare	促销票价
open date segment	不定期的航段
carries fares	航空公司运价

 Exercises

Ⅰ. Translate the following terms into Chinese or English.

1. 服务等级票价
2. 多等级运价制度
3. 低成本航空公司票价
4. 航空公司运价
5. 国际航空运输协会普通运价
6. benchmark price
7. passenger air fare
8. brand Fare
9. restrictions
10. special Fares

Ⅱ. Cloze.

(civil/aviation/route/*itinerary*/restriction/feasible/bundling/tangible)

1. The prices of business class by different airlines are different on the same _____, which are lower than first class and higher than economy class.

2. For the two factors of "price" and "_____", they would first consider price as their priority.

3. In 2017, National Development and Reform Commission and _____ Aviation Administration of China jointly issued the Notice on Further Improving Domestic Air Transport Pricing Policy of Civil _____.

4. The practice of low-cost airline can be simply summarized as "unbundling", which finely divides the _____ and intangible products and services included in traditional air fares, and divides them one by one in terms of ticket change and cancellation, seat selection, free baggage allowance, catering, boarding order, cabin promotion service and mileage accumulation.

5. This kind of fare is commonly known as "no discounted fare", which is characterized by expensive prices, but there are no restrictions on refund or reservation change, mainly applicable

to business class passengers, because their _____ are more liable to change and they are not so sensitive to ticket price.

III. Translate the following sentences into Chinese.

1. Brand Fares appeared in the civil aviation industry for the first time in 2008. Air Canada took the lead in applying the innovative concept of brand fares to air *route network marketing*, it is called "Fare Family".

2. First class seats are wider and more comfortable than economy class seats, and the standards of free meals on board and ground meals are higher than economy class.

IV. Translate the following paragraph into Chinese.

Starting October 31, 2018. IATA YY fares will be abolished. What is a YY fares? It was born in the first conference of IATA in 1945, and established the original international interline transfer ticket settlement system with YY ticket. The fare of city pairs was suitable for all carriers, which greatly promoted the rapid development of the interline transfer business in the global air industry.

V. Answer the following questions

1. What is Benchmark price?

2. Over the years, airlines have suffered from homogenization competition, with the root cause of the low differentiation of air products. How to provide different products?

Section 2
Global Distribution System

Lead in

Sabre: Remove Air India from GDS

Texas, USA - on January 3, 2020. Sabre, a company providing software and technology for the global tourism industry, issued an *announcement* on its *relationship* with Air India today. The following is the view of Kristin Hays, the vice president of global communication of Sabre: after 20 years of *cooperation*, Sabre was forced to remove the content of Air India from its GDS. Therefore, the travel agencies cooperating with Sabre can no longer use the content of Air India, effective today (Figure 2-4).

Figure 2-4　Air India

Special Terms

1. CRS: *Computer Reservation System*, it is the computer system by which the sales agent booked and sold flight seats and other tourism products.

计算机定座系统:是销售代理人据此进行航班座位及其他旅游产品预订和销售活动的电脑系统。

2. ICS: *Inventory Control System*, it is the airline reservation system used by airline personnel. ICS is a centralized, multi-airline system. Each airline has its own independent database, independent user base, independent control and management methods, various operations can be personalized, including flight schedule, seat control, freight rate and income management, air alliance, sales control parameters and other information and a complete set of booking function engines.

航班座位控制系统:即航空公司人员使用的航空公司定座系统。ICS是一个集中式、多航空公司的系统。每个航空公司享有自己独立的数据库、独立的用户群、独立的控制和管理方式,各种操作均可以加以个性化,包括航班班期、座位控制、运价及收益管理、航空联盟、销售控制参数等信息和一整套完备的定座功能引擎。

3. PSS: *Passenger Service System*, it is the underlying system of the CRS, ICS, DCS (*Departure Control System*), carrying the business application of airlines from all aspects involving passenger travel, such as flight management, flight ticket booking and departure system (Figure 2-5).

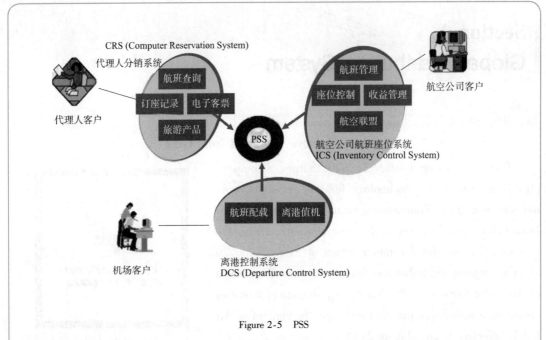

Figure 2-5　PSS

旅客服务系统：是民航客运商务体系代理人分销系统（CRS）、航空公司航班座位控制系统（ICS）、离港控制系统（DCS）的底层系统，承载着航空公司在航班管理、机票预订、离港系统等涉及旅客出行的各个方面的业务应用。

What Is the GDS?

GDS is short for Global Distribution System. It is a technology provider that replaces airlines to provide *unified* access and query services. Airlines can distribute flight information and *inventory* status to all sales channels through GDS (Figure 2-6).

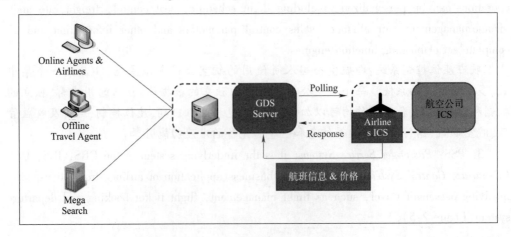

Figure 2-6　Introduction to the GDS system

Function of the GDS

International GDS, was developed based on the Computer *Reservation* System (CRS), which dates back to a database established for itself by major international airlines in the 1960s. GDS, not only connects the databases of major airlines to sells neutral tickets from multiple airlines, but has expanded its business from airline to travel bookings. Compared with a single tourism reservation system, GDS has obvious advantages: first, the perfect functions, the products include all tourism product types, and tourists can book their special service products through GDS; secondly, the *numerous* networks, covering the world, rich *information* and fast service. From the development process of GDS, GDS is a travel service-oriented system diverted from the airline booking system due to the rapid development of tourism.

Today, GDS has developed into an industry serving the entire tourism industry, in addition to the original air transport industry, hotels, car rental, tourism companies, railway companies and so on have also joined the GDS(Figure 2-7). With evolving technology and business, GDS has been able to provide travelers with timely, accurate and *comprehensive* information services and can meet the full range of needs for consumer travel, including transportation, accommodation, entertainment, payment and other subsequent services. Because of the *aviation* reservation, the GDS system is still controlled by major Western airlines, but the system itself operates in the form of *enterprise* and is constantly expanding the network to gain benefits.

Figure 2-7 GDS serve the entire tourism industry

Notes 1

❶ International GDS, was developed based on the Computer Reservation System (CRS), which dates back to a database established for itself by major international airlines in the 1960s.

解释：国际全球分销系统是在计算机定座系统(CRS)的基础上发展起来的,该系统可以追溯到20世纪60年代主要国际航空公司为自己建立的数据库。

语法：非限制性定语从句起补充说明作用,是先行词的附加说明,去掉了也不会影响主句的意思,它与主句之间通常用逗号分开。

❷ With evolving technology and business, GDS has been able to provide travelers with timely, accurate and comprehensive information services and can meet the full range of needs for consumer travel, including transportation, accommodation, entertainment, payment and other subsequent services.

解释：随着技术和业务的不断发展，GDS 已经能够为旅行者提供及时、准确、全面的信息服务,能够满足消费者出行的全方位需求,包括交通、住宿、娱乐、支付等后续服务。

语法：with 是介词,后边不能直接加动词,可以加非谓语如名词、动名词、不定式、分词等。With 加上动词 ing 形式,一般来说做的是伴随状语,表示伴随的事正在发生。

❸ Because of the aviation reservation, the GDS is still controlled by major Western airlines, but the system itself operates in the form of enterprise and is constantly expanding the network to gain benefits.

解释：由于航空预订,GDS 仍由西方各大航空公司控制,但系统本身以企业的形式运作,并不断扩大网络以获取效益。

语法：Because of 是复合介词,后面可接名词、代词、动名词以及由关系代词 what 所引导的从句,但是不能跟 that 从句。

GDS Companies

Currently, the following four major GDS companies account for more than 90% of the global *reservation distribution market* (Table 2-2).

Four GDS companies　　　　　　　　　　　　　　　　Table 2-2

GDS Companies	Codes	GDS System	Major Service Areas	Features
AMADEUS	1A	AMADEUS	Europe	It is currently the world leader in market share and the largest ICS/PSS supplier to airlines
SABRE	1S	SABRE ABACUS	America, Asia-Pacific	Traditional GDS supplier, leading market share in North America
TRAVELPORT	1G	GALILEO APOLLO WORLDSPAN	Europe, America, Asia-Pacific	Top reservation, widest service area, but no ICS products
TRAVELSKY	1E	TRAVELSKY	China	—

Charging Mechanism

Each GDS is charged by *transaction* (Figure 2-8). The booking *fee* is usually 2%~4% of the ticket price, which is about 20% if it is a hotel reservation. Thus, by paying a percentage of the booking price, airlines can reach a global network of travel sellers consisting of travel agents and *OTA* (*Online Travel Agent*). The airline also pays additional fees for GDS's system access and consulting services.

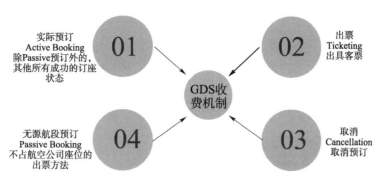

Figure 2-8 GDS charging mechanism

In recent years, *disputes* have begun between some airlines and GDS. According to the information disclosed in a *lawsuit* involving American Airways, some airlines would pay different transaction fees according to their contracts with GDS. Some airlines pay as much as $16 per deal.

If given that over 10 million flights are booked each year, the amount of fees involved is huge, Travelport earned $650.8 million in the first quarter of 2017 and airlines paid $310.4 million.

Notes 2

❶ In recent years, disputes have begun between some airlines and GDS.

解释:近年来,一些航空公司和全球分销系统之间的争端已经开始。

语法:in recent years 通常多与现在完成时连用,但有时也可根据具体情况,用于一般现在时、一般过去时或完成进行时等。

❷ If given that over 10 million flights are booked each year, the amount of fees involved is huge, Travelport earned $650.8 million in the first quarter of 2017 and airlines paid $310.4 million.

解释:如果考虑到每年超过1,000万次航班的预订,涉及的费用数额是巨大的,Travelport在2017年第一季度赚了6.508亿美元,航空公司支付了3.104亿美元。

语法:完整的是 if it was given,该句是虚拟从句,从句省略了 it was。

Further Reading

Take Online Direct Selling as a Strategy

The so-called online direct selling of airlines, is through their own official website, APP, WeChat small program and Tik-tok number and other information means, to directly sell the air tickets to passengers. The traditional air ticket sales channels refer to being distributed to agents at all levels through the GDS system. At present, the official websites of the major airlines have carried out direct ticket sales business. Growth has remained at 50% in recent years. In the development plan of Eastern Airlines, it is clear that IT investment should be increased, and an important strategy of the company is the construction of direct selling channel, while Spring

Airlines completely adopts 100% direct sales, reducing the cost to the greatest extent.

In addition to direct tickets on their official website, airlines also started opening "*flagship stores*" online. In Taobao's airline flagship store, all air tickets will be directly provided by airlines, and passengers can refund and change air tickets, check in, choose seats and other services on Taobao without leaving home (Figure 2-9).

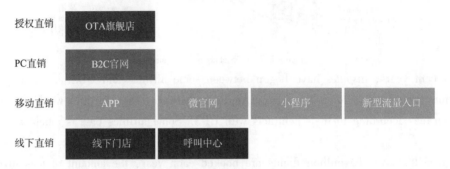

Figure 2-9　Diagram of an airline global distribution system

New Words

announcement	[əˈnaʊnsmənt]	n. 公告;宣告;发表;通告
unified	[ˈjuːnɪfaɪd]	adj. 统一的
		v. 统一;使一致(unify 的过去分词)
inventory	[ˈɪnvəntrɪ]	n. 存货清单;详细目录;财产清册
		vt. 给……开列清单
numerous	[ˈnjuːmərəs]	adj. 许多的,很多的
aviation	[ˌeɪvɪˈeɪʃən]	n. 航空;飞行术;飞机制造业
enterprise	[ˈentəpraɪz]	n. 企业;事业;进取心;事业心
transaction	[trænˈzækʃən]	n. 交易;事务;办理;会报,学报
dispute	[dɪˈspjuːt; ˈdɪspjuːt]	n. 辩论;争吵;意见不同
		v. 辩论
lawsuit	[ˈlɔːsuːt; ˈlɔːsjuːt]	n. 诉讼(尤指非刑事案件);诉讼案件
fee	[fiː]	n. 费用;专业服务费;
reservation	[ˌrezəˈveɪʃən]	n. 预订;预约;
information	[ˌɪnfəˈmeɪʃən]	n. 信息;消息;
relationship	[rɪˈleɪʃənʃɪp]	n.关系;(人、团体、国家之间的)联系
cooperation	[kəʊˌɒpəˈreɪʃən]	n. 合作;协作;协助;配合
comprehensive	[ˌkɒmprɪˈhensɪv]	adj. 综合的;全部的

Chapter 2 MARKETING

Phrases & Expressions

GDS(Global Distribution System)	全球分销系统
distribution market	分销市场
Asia-Pacific	亚太
flagship stores	旗舰店
PSS(Passenger Service System)	旅客服务系统
ICS(Inventory Control System)	航班座位控制系统
CRS(Computer Reservation System)	计算机定座系统
DCS(Departure Control System)	离港控制系统
OTA(online travel agent)	线上旅游代理

Exercises

I. Translate the following terms into Chinese or English.

1. 实际预订
2. OTA
3. 旗舰店
4. Passenger Service System
5. 全球分销系统
6. 航班座位控制系统
7. CRS
8. 离港控制系统

II. Cloze.

(issue/unified /GDS/ICS/numerous/aviation/enterprise/dispute/lawsuit)

1. Airlines can distribute flight information and inventory status to all sales channels through _____.

2. In recent years, _____ have begun between some airlines and GDS.

3. Because of the _____ reservation, the GDS system is still controlled by major Western airlines, but the system itself operates in the form of enterprise and is constantly expanding the network to gain benefits.

4. secondly, the _____ network, covering the world, rich information and fast service.

5. According to the information disclosed in a _____ involving American Airways, some airlines would pay different transaction fees according to their contracts with GDS.

III. Translate the following sentences into Chinese.

1. In recent years, disputes have begun between some airlines and GDS. According to the information disclosed in a lawsuit involving American Airways, some airlines would pay different transaction fees according to their contracts with GDS.

2. Some airlines pay as much as $16 per deal.

IV. Translate the following paragraph into Chinese.

The so-called online direct selling of airlines, is through their own official website, APP, WeChat small program and Tik-tok number and other information means, to directly sell the air tickets to passengers. The traditional air ticket sales channels refer to being distributed to agents at all levels through the GDS. At present, the official websites of the major airlines have carried out direct ticket sales business. Growth has remained at 50% in recent years. In the development plan of Eastern Airlines, it is clear that IT investment should be increased, and an important strategy of the company is the construction of direct selling channel, while Spring Airlines completely adopts 100% direct sales, reducing the cost to the greatest extent.

V. Answer the following questions.

What are the names of the world's four largest GDS?

Section 3
Electronic Ticket

Industry Bids Farewell to Paper Ticket

According to the unified deployment of the global *implementation* of e-tickets by the International Air Transport Association, global ticket agencies, including China, will stop selling paper tickets from June 1 this year (Figure 2-10). IATA began to implement e-tickets in June 2004. When the plan was launched, only 18% of the world's tickets were e-tickets. While the global *penetration* rate of e-tickets has exceeded 93% *at present*. This plan will help the aviation industry save

$6.5 billion each year.

Figure 2-10 Paper ticket retired

Special Terms

1. Host-based Ticket: A ticket for airline direct sales, blank ticket with the airline ticket settlement code, airline name and other information, the word "ARL" on the electronic ticket.

航空公司本票:一种供航空公司直销使用的客票,空白客票上有出票航空公司票证结算代号、航空公司名称等信息,电子客票上有 ARL 字样。

2. BSP(Billing and Settlement Plan): It is a *neutral* ticket sales and settlement system established by IATA according to the requirements of member airlines of the association in order to adapt to the rapid development of international air transportation, expand the sales network and *standardize* the behavior of sales agents.

开账与结算计划:是 IATA 根据协会会员航空公司的要求,为适应国际航空运输的迅速发展,扩大销售网络和规范销售代理人的行为而建立的一种供销售代理人使用中性客票销售和结算的系统。

3. IET(Interline E-Ticketing): Interline Electronic Ticketing is the ability for an airline to sell and report usage on an electronic ticket when part or all of the itinerary is provided by another operating carrier.

联运电子客票:指航空公司在另一家运营商提供的部分或全部行程时销售和报告电子票使用情况的能力。

Text

What Is the Electronic Ticket?

Electronic ticket is an electronic *substitute* product of ordinary paper ticket. It stores the ticket information of ordinary paper ticket in the electronic ticket database of the booking system, which is the electronic form of paper ticket.

Advantages of Electronic Ticket

Electronic ticket stores the ticket information in the booking system, which can *execute* ticketing, cancellation, refund, exchange and other operations like a paper ticket.

For passengers, the use of electronic tickets can get the following benefits:

• Ticket is convenient and fast. Electronic ticket booking, *endorsement*, change and refund can be realized directly through the Internet or through the *call center*.

• Take the opportunity to save time. In the United States, electronic tickets cut passenger waiting time from the past 2 hours to 10 minutes, with significant time savings.

• Price discount. Electronic tickets because they save the cost of ticket marketing, passengers can buy at a better price.

• Identity confirmation is easy. Once the traditional ticket is lost or not carried with you, it will not be able to take the plane. The passengers who buy electronic tickets only need to provide identity documents to obtain identification, which brings great convenience for the passengers.

For airlines, the value created by electronic word tickets is obvious, reflected in:

• The marketing cost is significantly reduced, and because the electronic ticket reduces the cost of intermediate links and *artificial services*, the marketing cost of the passenger ticket drops significantly, creating a greater profit space for the airlines.

• Settlement efficiency is greatly improved, electronic ticket makes traditional sales ticket flow into electronic data flow, not only improve the speed of ticket sales capital return, effectively *eliminate* the possibility of illegal *interception*, misappropriation, loss, and greatly improve the efficiency of capital settlement, improve the economic benefits of airlines.

• Easy for customer management. A wide variety of passenger information about buying electronic tickets is kept in the airline's dedicated database to facilitate the airlines to effectively manage their customers.

• Improve the ability and level of customer service. With electronic tickets, there is a more direct and convenient communication between airlines and passengers. Airlines can provide more targeted services for passengers, which will inevitably effectively improve customer satisfaction and loyalty.

Notes 1

❶ Settlement efficiency is greatly improved, electronic ticket makes traditional sales ticket flow into electronic data flow, not only improve the speed of ticket sales capital return, effectively eliminate the possibility of illegal interception, misappropriation, loss, and greatly improve the efficiency of capital settlement, improve the economic benefits of airlines.

解释：结算效率大大提高,电子客票使传统的销售客票流变成了电子数据流,不仅提高了客票销售资金回流的速度,有效地消除了非法截取、挪用、损失的可能性,大大提高了资金结算的效率,提高航空公司的经济效益。

❷ With electronic tickets, there is a more direct and convenient communication between airlines and passengers. Airlines can provide more targeted services for passengers, which will inevitably effectively improve customer satisfaction and loyalty.

解释：有了电子机票，航空公司和乘客之间的沟通更加直接和方便。航空公司可以为乘客提供更有针对性的服务，这必然会有效提高顾客的满意度和忠诚度。

语法：greatly 词性本来就是副词，用法是加在动词或形容词后起修饰作用。

❸ A wide variety of passenger information about buying electronic tickets is kept in the airline's dedicated database to facilitate the airlines to effectively manage their customers.

解释：有关购买电子机票的各种乘客信息都保存在航空公司的专用数据库中，以方便航空公司有效地管理他们的客户。

语法：a wide variety of 的释义为各种各样的；种类繁多的；多种多样的；很多的；种种。其用法为指各式各样的事物，作此解时用单数形式。且后常接名词复数或集合名词。若要强调有多种人或事物，可在 variety 前加 great 或 wide。

Classification of E-ticket

In terms of purposes, electronic tickets can be divided into three types：

- Host-based E-Ticketing：to support airline direct selling channel model.
- BSP E-Ticketing：used to support distribution channels such as agents and travel agencies.
- IET, interline E-Ticketing：used to support the sales model of interline airlines.

The function of BSP electronic tickets is mainly to support the marketing activities of agents and travel agencies, which belongs to the distribution model. But BSP E-ticket does not help airlines improve the existing sales process, let alone help airlines develop new sales channels. What's more, using BSP E-ticket still has to pay agent's commission, reservation fee, including CRS fee and ICS fee. The cost has not been reduced at all, and the payment collection cycle has not been shortened much.

Therefore, it is a future trend to vigorously develop airline direct sales to promote the development of airline e-commerce.

Notes 2

❶ What's more, using BSP E-ticket still has to pay agent's commission, reservation fee, including CRS fee and ICS fee.

解释：此外，使用 BSP 电子机票仍需支付代理商佣金、预订费，包括 CRS 费和 ICS 费。

语法：表示递进，译为而且。用法：在陈述了一个理由之后，用 what's more 连接另一个递进的理由。

CONTENTS OF E-TICKET

When a reservation is confirmed, the airline keeps a record of the booking in computer reservations system (Figure 2-11).

```
◎ DETR:TN/999-2406341848
  ISSUED BY:AIR CHINA        ORG/DST:PEK/SHA      ISI:SITI   ARL-D
  TOUR CODE:
  PASSENGER:王明
  EXCH:                      CONJ TKT:
  O FM:1PEK CA  1855 B  5JAN  1755 OK  Y90        20K   OPEN FOR USE
             RL:BQH3Q    / QZ80B 1E
   TO:SHA
  FC:25JAN08PEK CA SHA1020.00Y90CNY1020.00END
  FARE:         CNY 1020.00 | FOP:CASH(CNY)
  TAX:          CNY 50.00CN | OI:
  TAX:          CNY 100.00YQ |
  TOTAL:        CNY 1170.00|TKTN:999-2406341848
```

Figure 2-11 An electronic ticket stored in the computer reservation system

An e-ticket contains:

• An official ticket number (including the airline's 3-digit *ticket settlement code*, a 10-digit serial number, and sometimes a check digit).

• Passenger name, segment, flight, booking and ticket usage status.

• *Fare* and tax details, including *fare* calculation details and some additional data such as tour codes. The exact cost might not be stated, but a "*fare basis*" code will always *identify* the *fare* used.

• A short summary of fare restrictions, usually specifying only whether change or refund are permitted but not the penalties to which they are subject to.

• Form of payment.

• Baggage allowance.

The emergence of electronic tickets has brought a great revolution to the operation mode of civil aviation business with paper tickets as vouchers for a long time. Whether it is the processing process of *civil aviation* business or the consumption habits of passengers, as well as the traditional financial system with paper bills as *reimbursement credentials*, it will undergo fundamental changes.

Notes 3

❶ A short summary of fare restrictions, usually specifying only whether change or refund are permitted but not the penalties to which they are subject to.

解释：对票价限制的简短总结，通常只说明是否允许更改或退款，但不说明他们所受到的处罚。

❷ Whether it is the processing process of civil aviation business or the consumption habits of passengers, as well as the traditional financial system with paper bills as reimbursement credentials, it will undergo fundamental changes.

解释：无论是民航业务的处理流程，还是旅客的消费习惯，以及传统的以纸质票据作为报销凭证的财务体系，都将发生根本性的变化。

语法：whether 和 if 都可以表示"是否"，引导宾语从句。

Electronic Ticket Itinerary

The Itinerary of Electronic Ticket for Air Transportation is *supervised* by the State Administration of Taxation and incorporated into the *invoice* management of the taxation authorities in accordance with the Measures for the Administration of Invoices of the People's Republic of China, and is a proof of payment and *reimbursement* for the purchase of electronic tickets by passengers (Figure 2-12). Passengers who purchase an electronic ticket should *obtain* an "Itinerary" from the ticket issuer after making payment; the "Itinerary" is a single ticket and cannot be replaced if lost; the "Itinerary" is not used as a proof of boarding, but passengers must present the original "Itinerary" when changes occur; when refunding a ticket, passengers must apply to the original ticketing department with the original "Itinerary".

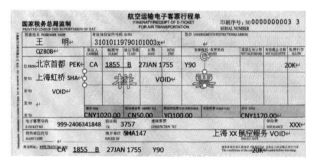

Figure 2-12　E-ticket Itinerary/Receipt

New Words

implementation	[ˌɪmplɪmenˈteɪʃən]	n.	[计] 实现；履行；安装启用
penetration	[ˌpenəˈtreɪʃ]	n.	渗透；突破；侵入；洞察力
standardize	[ˈstændədaɪz]	vt.	使标准化；用标准检验
neutral	[ˈnjuːtrəl]	adj.	中立的，中性的；中立国的；非彩色的
substitute	[ˈsʌbstɪtjuːt, -tuːt]	n.	代用品；代替者
execute	[ˈeksɪkjuːt]	vt.	实行；执行；处死
eliminate	[ɪˈlɪmɪneɪt]	vt.	消除；排除

baggage	[ˈbægɪdʒ]	n. 行李;[交] 辎重(军队的)
credentials	[krəˈdenʃlz]	n. [管理] 证书;文凭;信任状(credential 的复数)
identify	[aɪˈdentɪfaɪ]	vt. 识别;鉴定;确认
supervise	[ˈsuːpəvaɪz]	v. 监督;管理;指导;主管
invoice	[ˈɪnvɔɪs]	n. 发票;(发货或服务)费用清单
reimbursement	[ˌriːɪmˈbɜːsmənt]	n. 报销;偿付;补偿;赔偿
obtain	[əbˈteɪn]	v. 获得;(尤指经努力)赢得

Phrases & Expressions

e-ticket	电子客票
ticket endorsement	客票签转
call center	呼叫中心
civil aviation	民用航空
ticket settlement code	客票结算代码
fare basis	票价级别
at present	目前,现在
artificial services	人工服务
reimbursement credential	报销凭证

Exercises

I. Translate the following terms into Chinese or English.

1. Baggage allowance
2. ticket settlement code
3. ticket endorsement
4. BSP
5. 人工服务
6. 民用航空
7. 票价级别
8. 电子客票

II. Cloze.

(electronic ticket/penetration/fare/interception/civil/BSP/*credentials*)

1. _____ is an electronic substitute product of ordinary paper ticket.

2. The function of _____ electronic tickets is mainly to support the marketing activities of agents and travel agencies, which belongs to the distribution model.

3. The emergence of electronic tickets has brought a great revolution to the operation mode of _____ aviation business with paper tickets as vouchers for a long time.

4. Whether it is the processing process of civil aviation business or the consumption habits of passengers, as well as the traditional financial system with paper bills as reimbursement _____, it will undergo fundamental changes.

5. _____ and tax details, including fare calculation details and some additional data such as tour codes.

III. Translate the following sentences into Chinese.

1. Settlement efficiency is greatly improved, electronic ticket makes traditional sales ticket flow into electronic data flow, not only improve the speed of ticket sales capital return, effectively eliminate the possibility of illegal interception, misappropriation, loss, and greatly improve the efficiency of capital settlement, improve the economic benefits of airlines.

2. Easy for customer management. A wide variety of passenger information about buying electronic tickets is kept in the airline's dedicated database to facilitate the airlines to effectively manage their customers.

IV. Translate the following paragraph into Chinese.

The Itinerary of Electronic Ticket for Air Transportation is a proof of payment and reimbursement for the purchase of electronic tickets by passengers. Passengers who purchase an electronic ticket should obtain an "Itinerary" from the ticket issuer after making payment; the "Itinerary" is a single ticket and cannot be replaced if lost; the "Itinerary" is not used as a proof of boarding, but passengers must present the original "Itinerary" when changes occur; when refunding a ticket, passengers must apply to the original ticketing department with the original "Itinerary".

V. Answer the following questions.

1. What is the meaning of electronic passenger tickets?

2. What are the several types of electronic passenger tickets?

Section 4
Code-Sharing and Airline Alliances

Lead in

China Southern Withdraw from Sky Team

The decision to withdraw from Sky Team was announced on 15 November 2018, and after the withdrawal transition period in 2019 (Figure 2-13). China Southern will discontinue its frequent flyer partnership with China Eastern Airlines in the Sky Team alliance, replacing Sky Team *Priority* with China Southern CZ Priority. Frequent *flyer miles* and code share flights with Delta, Xiamen Airlines, Korean Air, China Airlines, Air France, KLM Royal Dutch Airlines, Alitalia and Aeroflot will remain unchanged.

Figure 2-13　China Southern Airlines withdraw from Sky Team

Special Terms

1. *Operating carrier*: The carrier having operational control of the aircraft used for a designated Code-share Flight.

运营承运人：对用于指定代码共享飞行的飞机具有操作控制权的承运人。

2. *Marketing carrier*: The carrier whose code is shown in the carrier designator box of a flight coupon for a designated Code-sharing flight but which is not operating the flight.

销售承运人：其代码显示在指定代码共享航班的乘机联中的承运人代号栏上，但不运行该航班的承运人。

3. *Frequent-flyer programme*: The *frequent flyer program* is a *reward* programme offered by many airlines to loyal passengers, and is commonly available in the form of a programme whereby passengers accumulate their own miles and use them to *redeem* free tickets, goods and services and other privileges such as VIP lounges or class upgrades.

> 飞行常旅客计划:是许多航空公司给忠实乘客的一种奖励方案,普遍的形式是:乘客们通过这个计划累计自己的飞行里程,并使用这些里程来兑换免费的机票、商品和服务以及其他类似贵宾休息室或舱位升等之类的特权。

Text

Code-Sharing

1. What Is Code-Sharing?

According to the general rules, we usually use the description as "Code-sharing" means where one airline assigns its code to a flight operated by the other airline and that other airline continues to use its own on that flight (Figure 2-14).

Figure 2-14　AY and CA code-sharing

This is not only for airlines to improve the route network and expand market share without investing in costs, but also beyond the barriers to some relatively closed aviation markets. For passengers, they can enjoy more convenient and rich services, such as many flights and moment choices, integrated transfer services, more discounted fares, and frequent passenger programme and so on. Because code-sharing optimized the resources of airlines and benefited passengers a lot, it became the most popular way of cooperation in the global air transport industry in the 1970s and become the most popular after it was born in the domestic market in the 1970s.

The airlines involved in bilateral agreements generally have two roles, the operating carrier and the marketing carrier.

Notes 1

① According to the general rules, we usually use the description as "Code-sharing" means where one airline assigns its code to a flight operated by the other airline and that other airline continues to use its own on that flight.

解释:根据一般规则,我们通常使用"代码共享"的描述,即一家航空公司将其代码分配给其他一家航空公司运营的航班,而其他航空公司继续在该航班上使用自己的代码。

语法:where 引导定语从句。

where 引导定语从句时,其先行词是表示地点的名词,它在定语从句中作地点状语,此时 where 相当于 at/in/on 加 which。

❷ This is not only for airlines to improve the route network and expand market share without investing in costs, but also beyond the barriers to some relatively closed aviation markets.

解释:这不仅有利于航空公司在不投入成本的情况下改善航线网络、扩大市场份额,而且还可以突破一些相对封闭的航空市场的壁垒。

语法:not only…but also…表示"不仅……而且""既……又",用于连接两个性质相同的词、短语或分句。连接对等的成分。

❸ The airlines involved in bilateral agreements generally have two roles, the operating carrier and the marketing carrier.

解释:参与双边协议的航空公司通常有两个角色,运营承运人和营销承运人。

语法:and 表示并列或对称的关系,用来连接语法作用相同的词、短语或句子。

2. The Form of Code-Sharing

- *Free Sell*: marketing carrier and operating carriers sell the same flight with their flight number without limiting the number of seats.

- *Block Seats Sell*: refers to the cooperation agreement between a marketing carrier and operating airline to *purchase* the number of fixed seats for a flight of the carrier, and the marketing airline can only sell with its own flight number within this scope.

Chinese airlines have signed code sharing agreements with foreign airlines many years ago, amongwhich Air China and Northwest Airlines started the earliest, starting in May 1998, with deep levels of cooperation and a wide range of fields. The two sides not only connected the reservation and departure system, exchanged frequent passenger projects, and joint sales and promotion, but also truly realized the "through boarding" and "seamless" service, passengers can get the boarding card of all the flights on the way when checking in at the departure airport, and the luggage can also be transported directly transported to the *destination*. The "code sharing" approach allows Chinese airlines to directly absorb the experience in the operation and management of advanced foreign airlines, and integrate into the increasingly global and liberalized air transport industry as soon as possible.

Notes 2

❶ Chinese airlines have signed code sharing agreements with foreign airlines many years ago, among which Air China and Northwest Airlines started the earliest, starting in May 1998, with deep levels of cooperation and a wide range of fields.

解释：我国航空公司早在多年前就与外国航空公司签订了代码共享协议，其中，中国国航和西北航空公司最早于1998年5月开始合作，合作层次深、领域广。

语法：among which 是带介词 among 且由 which 引导的定语从句，其后必须要加句子，表示"从……中"、"在……之间"之类的意思。

❷ The two sides not only connected the reservation and departure system, exchanged frequent passenger projects, and joint sales and promotion, but also truly realized the "through boarding" and "seamless" service, passengers can get the boarding card of all the flights on the way when checking in at the departure airport, and the luggage can also be transported directly transported to the destination.

解释：双方不仅对接了订票和出发系统，交换了往来旅客项目，联合销售和推广，还真正实现了"直达登机"和"无缝"服务，旅客在出发机场办理登机手续时即可获得途中所有航班的登机牌，而且行李也可以直接运送到目的地。

语法：not only, but also 可以用来连接主语、连接宾语、连接谓语动词、连接表语、连接宾语补足语、连接状语、连接从句、连接定语、连接句子，用于 it is…that 强调结构。用于连接两个对等的成分，若连接两个成分作为主语，其后谓语动词与靠近的主语保持一致。also 通常可以省略，或换成 too, as well(要置于句末)。

❸ The "code-sharing" approach allows Chinese airlines to directly absorb the experience in the operation and management of advanced foreign airlines, and integrate into the increasingly global and liberalized air transport industry as soon as possible.

解释：通过"代码共享"的方式，中国航空公司可以直接吸收国外先进航空公司的运营管理经验，尽快融入日益全球化、自由化的航空运输业。

语法：as soon as ＋形容词 adj 表示像……一样快。

Airline Alliances

Alliance cooperation is essentially amplified code-sharing cooperation. Alliances allow member airlines to "network" their flights and share revenue from interline travel, allowing airlines to increase capacity and expand their networks without increasing investment or expanding their fleets, as well as *aligning* passengers, marketing, services and products, human resources, industry communications and more. In addition, the alliance expands the joint purchasing power of the companies and enables them to obtain lower prices when purchasing fuel, aircraft components and aircraft, thus reducing airline operating costs.

Notes 3

❶ Alliances allow member airlines to "network" their flights and share revenue from interline travel, allowing airlines to increase capacity and expand their networks without increasing investment or expanding their fleets, as well as aligning passengers, marketing, services and products, human resources, industry communications and more.

> **解释**：联盟允许成员航空公司将其航班"联网"，并分享联盟航线旅行的收入，允许航空公司在不增加投资或扩大机队的情况下增加运力和扩大其网络，以及调整乘客、营销、服务和产品、人力资源、行业通信等。
>
> **语法**：非谓语动词，这里 allowing 与其逻辑主语是主谓关系，所以用 ing 形式。
>
> ❷ In addition, the alliance expands the joint purchasing power of the companies and enables them to obtain lower prices when purchasing fuel, aircraft components and aircraft, thus reducing airline operating costs.
>
> **解释**：此外，联盟扩大了企业的联合购买力，使企业在购买燃油、飞机零部件和飞机时获得更低的价格，从而降低了航空公司的运营成本。
>
> **语法**：in addition to 整个词组相当于一个介词，所以 to 的后面要接宾语。in addition 相当于副词，通常放在从句的句首，后面接完整的句子。

1. Star Alliance

Established in 1997, Star Alliance is a global industry pioneer, providing customers with a worldwide network that offers a complete travel experience. In total, the Star Alliance network offers more than 18,100 flights daily to 1,330 *destinations* in 192 countries around the world. The major airlines are as follows (Figure 2-15).

Logo	中文名称	English Name	Code
AIR CANADA	加拿大航空公司	Air Canada	AC
国航	中国国际航空公司	Air China	CA
AIR NEW ZEALAND	新西兰航空公司	Air New Zealand	NZ
ANA	全日空航空公司	All Nippon Airways	NH
ASIANA AIRLINES	韩亚航空公司	Asiana Airlines	OZ
Lufthansa	德国汉莎航空公司	Deutsche Lufthansa A.G.	LH
SAS Scandinavian Airlines	北欧航空公司	SAS	SK
SINGAPORE AIRLINES	新加坡航空公司	Singapore Airlines	SQ
THAI	泰国国际航空公司	Thai Airways	TG
TURKISH AIRLINES	土耳其航空	Turkish Airways	TK
UNITED	美国联合航空公司（美大陆被并入美联合）	United Airlines	UA

Figure 2-15　Major Alliances of Star Alliance

2. Oneworld

Formally *established* on 1 February 1999. An alliance initiated by five major international airlines in different countries, its member airlines and their *affiliates cooperate* in various areas such as flight times, ticketing, code-sharing, passenger transfers, frequent flyer plans, airport lounges and reduced expenses. The main airlines are as follows (Figure 2-16).

Logo	中文名称	English Name	Code
American Airlines	美国航空公司 (全美航空被并入美国航空公司)	American Airline	AA
BRITISH AIRWAYS	英国航空公司	British Airways	BA
CATHAY PACIFIC	国泰航空公司	Cathay Pacific	CX
(Finnair logo)	芬兰航空公司	Finnair	AY
IBERIA	西班牙国家航空公司	Iberia Airlines of Spain	IB
JAL	日本航空	Japan Airlines	JL
QANTAS	澳洲航空公司	Qantas	QF
ROYAL JORDANIAN	约旦皇家航空公司	Royal Jordanian Airlines	RJ

Figure 2-16 Major Airlines of Oneworld

3. Sky Team

Sky Team is an alliance of airlines founded on 22 June 2000 and headquartered at Amsterdam International Airport. Initially, the alliance was formed by four major international airlines from different countries to strengthen the *competitiveness* of the alliance members by sharing the flight times, ticketing, passenger connections, frequent flyer programs, airport lounges and other hardware and software resources and route networks of the member airlines. The main airlines are as follows (Figure 2-17).

Airline alliances allow individual member airlines to partner on a particular route in a market, using code-sharing and frequent flyer programs to provide a better experience for customers.

KOREAN AIR	大韩航空公司	Korean Air	KE
AIRFRANCE	法国航空公司	Air France	AF
KLM	荷兰皇家航空公司	KLM Royal Dutch	KL
Alitalia	意大利航空公司	Alitalia	AZ
CSA CZECH AIRLINES	捷克航空公司	Czech Airlines	OK
АЭРОФЛОТ Russian Airlines	俄罗斯航空公司	Aeroflot-Russian Airlines	SU
Delta	美国达美航空公司 (美西北航空被并入达美航空公司)	Delta Airlines	DL
中国东方航空 CHINA EASTERN	中国东方航空公司	China Eastern	MU

Figure 2-17 Major Airlines of Sky Team

China Eastern Airlines New Frequent Flyer Membership Programme

A frequent flyer program is a marketing tool to attract business and business passengers and improve the *competitiveness* of airlines by offering frequent flyers a promotional tool based on *mileage accumulation awards.*

Figure 2-18 New frequent flyer programme

On January 9, 2020, China Eastern Airlines announced its new frequent flyer membership programme, which will be implemented in July this year (Figure 2-18).

In summary, there are four major changes in the new Eastern Airlines' Frequent Flyer Membership Programme:

Change 1: Change in membership levels.

Change 2: Grades and upgrades.

Change 3: Flier miles.

Change 4: The number of beneficiaries on Eastern Airlines has changed from the previous 10, with 200 points *deduct*ed for each additional person over 10.

Chapter 2 MARKETING

New Words

align	[əˈlaɪn]	vt.	使结盟;使成一行;匹配
		vi.	排列;排成一行
competitiveness	[kəmˈpetətɪvnəs]	n.	竞争力,好竞争
affiliate	[əˈfɪlieɪt]	v.	(使)附属,隶属;加入,加盟;紧密联系
cooperate	[kəʊˈɒpəreɪt]	vi.	合作,配合;协力
establish	[ɪˈstæblɪʃ]	v.	建立,创立;确立;获得接受;查实,证实
purchase	[ˈpɜːtʃəs]	v./n.	购买;获得,
deduct	[dɪˈdʌkt]	vt.	扣除,减去;演绎
redeem	[rɪˈdiːm]	vt.	赎回;挽回;兑换;履行;补偿;恢复
destination	[ˌdestɪˈneɪʃən]	n.	目的地,终点
reward	[rɪˈwɔːd]	n./v.	报酬;报答;酬谢
priority	[praɪˈɒrəti]	n.	优先事项;最重要的事

Phrases & Expressions

frequent flyer program	飞行常客奖励计划
mileage accumulation awards	里程累积奖励
flyer miles	里程积分
free sell	自由销售
block seats sell	硬包座销售
airline alliance	航空联盟
operating carrier	实际承运人
marketing carrier	销售承运人

Exercises

I. Translate the following terms into Chinese or English.

1. 代码共享
2. 运营承运人
3. 客票成本
4. 销售承运人
5. frequent flyer plans
6. Flyer miles
7. airline alliance
8. block seats sell

II. Cloze.

(code-sharing/airline alliance/purchase/multiple/free sell/operate)

1. According to the general rules, we usually use the description as "Code-sharing" means where one airline assigns its code to a flight _____ by the other airline and that other airline continues to use its own on that flight.

2. _____ is not only for airlines to improve the route network and expand market share without investing in costs, but also beyond the barriers to some relatively closed aviation markets.

3. _____ cooperation is essentially amplified code-sharing cooperation.

4. _____ code-sharing means marketing carrier and operating carriers sell the same flight with their flight number without limiting the number of seats.

III. Translate the following sentences into Chinese.

1. Regular members are divided into 6 levels, ranging from 1 to 6 stars. Silver Elite, Gold Elite Plus and Platinum Elite Plus remain unchanged. So the new frequent flyer program has a total of 9 tiers, going beyond Marriott.

2. Alliances allow member airlines to "network" their flights and share revenue from interline travel, allowing airlines to increase capacity and expand their networks without increasing investment or expanding their fleets, as well as aligning passengers, marketing, services and products, human resources, industry communications and more.

IV. Translate the following paragraph into Chinese.

Formally established on 1 February 1999, an alliance initiated by five major international airlines in different countries, its member airlines and their affiliates cooperate in various areas such as flight times, ticketing, code-sharing, passenger transfers, frequent flyer programs, airport lounges and reduced expenses.

V. Answer the following questions.

1. What are the two types of code-sharing?

2. What are the names of the world's three major aviation alliances?

Chapter 3
PASSENGER SERVICE

Section 1
Self-service Check-in Kiosk—CUSS

Lead in

One ID at Guangzhou Baiyun International Airport

From August 2, passengers taking domestic flights in terminal 2 of Guangzhou Baiyun Aairport can also enjoy the whole process face brushing Travel Service (One ID). Terminal T2 one ID service is jointly launched by Baiyun Airport and China Southern Airlines (Figure 3-1).

It mainly provides whole process face brushing travel services for passengers taking domestic flights of China Southern Airlines. Passengers can register One ID at any official account "Baiyun Airport" or "Baiyun Airport" drop-down menu, "airport pass", self-service check-in and self-service baggage. Then, no need to produce ID card, *boarding pass* or two-dimensional code. Self *baggage check-in*, self service check-in and other businesses can be handled by brush. In case of unidentified face brushing, ticket purchase through passport or unregistered one ID service, passengers can take the flight in the original way (ID card verification).

Figure 3-1 Check-in at Guangzhou Baiyun International Airport

Special Terms

1. Continental Airlines: Continental Airlines, Inc., founded in 1934, is headquartered in Houston, Texas. It is the fourth largest airline in the United States and the fifth largest airline in the world. Now Continental Airlines has completed its merger with United Airlines.

美国大陆航空公司:成立于1934年,总部位于美国得克萨斯州休斯敦市,是美国第四、全球第五大航空公司。现美国大陆航空公司与美国联合航空公司完成合并。

2. Automated Ticket and Boarding pass (ATB): Also known as ATB ticket in civil aviation, it is a kind of transportation document integrating automatic printed ticket and boarding card function.

自动打印售票和登机牌:在民航中又称为ATB票,是一种集自动打印的客票与登机牌功能于一体的运输凭证。

Text

In recent years the airlines have started using *innovative* check-in technologies. The dedicated Self-service Check-in kiosks are now an *integral* part of the airport facility and the new e-ticket also allows the use of the internet for check-in. These processes enable airlines to reduce the time and number of staff required, thus saving *substantial* costs in operations. These changes in the process have allowed airports to handle more passengers in the same space by reducing queues.

Figure 3-2　CUSS

Further to this, IATA is *advoca*ti*ng* CUSS- *Common Use Self-service* (Figure 3-2), similar to standardized ATMs- Automated Trailer Machines at banks.

CUSS-Common Use Self-service kiosks were first introduced by Continental Airlines in 1995 at US airports. Since then the CUSS has become an *integral* part of providing services for passengers. Most schedule airlines now provide the option for Common Use Self-service kiosk check-in at major airports. The cost of check-in through kiosks is just ＄0.16 as against ＄3.68 with normal check-in with an agent. The airports and airlines have understood the importance of the shared facilities.

Notes 1

❶ The dedicated Self-service Check-in kiosks are now an integral part of the airport facility and the new e-ticket also allows the use of the internet for check-in.

解释:专用自助值机柜台现已成为机场设施的一个组成部分,新的电子机票还允许使用互联网办理值机手续。

❷ The cost of check-in through kiosks is just ＄0.16 as against ＄3.68 with normal check-in with an agent.

解释:通过自助值机柜台办理值机手续的费用仅为0.16美元,而通过代理人办理正常值机手续的费用为3.68美元。

The Function of Cuss

This *evolv*ing pattern will enable passengers to obtain *boarding passes*, *check baggage*, and conduct other *transactions* at times and places of their convenience. Passenger check in procedures will gradually shift from check in procedures performed at check in counters, to check in procedures performed at home from the internet, by mobile phone, or through self service check in facilities at the airport such as CUSS. The trend is towards common use equipment which may consist of free standing column type or counter type workstations with built-in *Automated Ticket and Boarding pass* (ATB) printer.

The CUSS will provide ticketed passengers the ability to perform many tasks, not limited to, check-in for flights, select or change a *seat assignment*, and obtain a *boarding pass* for their departures. The CUSS will be used by self-service passengers to check-in, seat allocation, *boarding pass* printing, and *baggage check-in* in a common use environment. The CUSS will be designed for the use of different types of passengers with or without luggage where passengers with luggage could use the new facility of the Common Use Baggage System.

Notes 2

❶ Passenger check in procedures will gradually shift from check in procedures performed at check in counters, to check in procedures performed at home from the internet, by mobile phone, or through self service check in facilities at the airport such as CUSS.

解释：旅客值机手续将逐渐从在值机柜台办理的值机手续转变为通过在家使用互联网或者手机办理值机手续,或者是通过机场自助值机设施(如 CUSS)办理值机手续。

语法：performed 为非谓语结构。

❷ The CUSS will provide ticketed passengers the ability to perform many tasks, not limited to, check-in for flights, select or change a seat assignment, and obtain a boarding pass for their departures.

解释：机场自助值机设施将为持票乘客提供执行多项业务办理的能力,包括办理航班登记、选择或更改座位分配以及获取出发登机牌。

❸ The CUSS will be designed for the use of different types of passengers with or without luggage where passengers with luggage could use the new facility of the Common Use Baggage System.

解释：机场自助值机设施将设计用于不同类型的带或不带行李的乘客,其中带行李的乘客可以使用通用行李系统的新设施。

语法：where 为定语从句,先行词为 luggage。

The Layout of Cuss

With so many kiosk types available and with the changing requirements the *configuration* of the check-in kiosks depends on a large number of factors. The main aspects to be considered in the placement of kiosks are:

- *Visibility*.
- *Accessibility* and movement of passenger traffic.
- Comfort and *privacy* of the passenger.

There are many possible solutions for the layout of kiosks and it has been *observ*ed that for the efficient use of kiosks it is essential to have some *roving* agents to help the customers increase their *transaction* speed. These are steps the procedures of travel using self-service technology at international airports, The new concept of self-service kiosks has divided the check-in process in two parts:
- Getting the *boarding pass*.
- Getting the *bag-tag* to dropping the bags at *bag drop-off*. The passenger arrives at the airport and proceeds to the kiosk, which issues the *boarding pass* based on the information provided by the passenger. The passenger then proceeds to the fast baggage drop-off if he/she has any baggage otherwise can move to the *security check*. The main steps in the check-in process through kiosk are shown in (Figure 3-3).

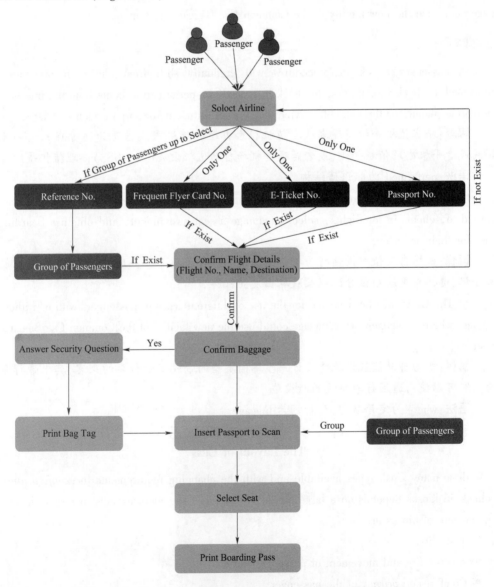

Figure 3-3 How to make check-in procedures through common use self-service

It is easy to follow the instructions on the kiosk and very direct in most of the cases. The speed of checking in depends on the familiarity of the passenger with the kiosks and on the speed of the machine itself in processing the request. The kiosks are also equipped with the passport reader to enable international passenger check-in.

Notes 3

❶ With so many kiosk types available and with the changing requirements the configuration of the check-in kiosks depends on a large number of factors.

解释：由于自助值机类型众多，且需求不断变化，值机柜台的配置取决于许多因素。

❷ The passenger arrives at the airport and proceeds to the kiosk, which issues the boarding pass based on the information provided by the passenger.

解释：乘客到达机场后，前往自助值机，自助值机根据乘客提供的信息签发登机牌。

语法：which 为非限制性定语从句，先行词为 kisok。

❸ The speed of checking in depends on the familiarity of the passenger with the kiosks and on the speed of the machine itself in processing the request.

解释：办理登机手续的速度取决于乘客对自助值机的熟悉程度，以及机器本身处理请求的速度。

Further Reading

Normal Check-in Procedures

The normal check-in time for domestic flight is one hour and a half before the scheduled time of departure (Figure 3-4). For international flights, the check-in time varies according to the type of flight and local CIQ procedures. The normal check-in procedure involves a passenger service agent who checks the passenger's travel document and his or her reservation status. The agent also takes care of the passenger's checked baggage. For some flights the agent also assigns seats to the passengers. When all this has been done, the passenger receives a *boarding pass* that ordinarily shows the flight number, the class and the *seat assignment*. Then the passenger can proceed to the departure gate or to the international departure area.

Figure 3-4 Normal check-in procedures

民航商务英语

New Words

innovative	[ˈɪnəveɪtɪv]	adj. 革新的；创新的
integral	[ˈɪntɪgrəl]	adj. 完整的；不可或缺的
substantial	[səbˈstænʃl]	adj. 大量的
advocate	[ˈædvəkeɪt]	v. 拥护；提倡
integral	[ˈɪntɪgrəl]	adj. 完整的；不可或缺的
evolve	[ɪˈvɒlv]	v. 发展；进化
transaction	[trænˈzækʃən]	n. 交易；处理
configuration	[kənˌfɪgəˈreɪʃən]	n. （计算机的）配置；结构
accessibility	[əkˌsesɪˈbɪlɪtɪ]	n. 可达性，可接近性
privacy	[ˈprɪvəsɪ]	n. 隐私；私密
observe	[əbˈzɜːv]	v. 看到；注意到
roving	[ˈrəʊvɪŋ]	adj. 流动的；漂泊的

Phrases & Expressions

CUSS (Common Use Self-service)	通用自助服务
boarding pass	登机牌
check baggage	托运行李
ATB (Automated Ticket and Boarding pass)	自动打印售票和登机牌
seat assignment	座位安排
baggage check-in	行李托运
bag-tag	行李牌
bag drop-off	行李托运
security check	安检

Exercises

Ⅰ. **Translate the following terms into Chinese or English.**

1. common use self service
2. boarding pass
3. check baggage
4. automated ticket and boarding pass
5. 安检
6. 座位安排
7. 行李牌

II. Cloze.

(boarding pass/bag-tag/security check/automated ticket and boarding pass)

1. Then, no need to produce ID card, _____ or two-dimensional code.

2. Getting the _____ to dropping the bags at bag drop-off. The passenger arrives at the airport and proceeds to the kiosk, which issues the boarding pass based on the information provided by the passenger.

3. The passenger then proceeds to the fast baggage drop-off if he/she has any baggage otherwise can move to the _____.

4. The trend is towards common use equipment which may consist of free standing column type or counter type workstations with built-in _____ printer.

III. Translate the following sentences into Chinese.

1. The kiosks are also equipped with the passport reader to enable international passenger check-in.

2. There are many possible solutions for the layout of kiosks and it has been observed that for the efficient use of kiosks it is essential to have some roving agents to help the customers increase their transaction speed.

IV. Translate the following paragraph into Chinese.

The normal check-in time for domestic flight is one hour and a half before the scheduled time of departure. For international flights, the check-in time varies according to the type of flight and local CIQ procedures. The normal check-in procedure involves a passenger service agent who checks the passenger's travel document and his or her reservation status. The agent also takes care of the passenger's checked baggage. For some flights the agent also assigns seats to the passengers. When all this has been done, the passenger receives a boarding pass that ordinarily shows the flight number, the class and the seat assignment. Then the passenger can proceed to the departure gate or to the international departure area.

V. Answer the following questions.

1. What are the main aspects to be considered in the placement of kiosks?

2. Why are self-service check-in kiosks now an integral part of the airport facility?

Section 2
Travel Information Manual

Lead in

Live Animals in TIM

Living animals (Figure 3-5) transported as checked baggage must have:

1. Valid health certificate (generally rabies immunization certificate);

2. Inspection and quarantine certificate issued by the animal and plant quarantine department (generally the certificate of inspection and disinfection of living animals and their outer packaging);

3. All countries along the route shall consult the documents necessary for transporting living animals (such as entry-exit or transit permits, etc.), and all kinds of documents required by all countries and regions for the entry-exit and entry of living animals shall refer to the latest issue of travel information manual).

Figure 3-5　Living animals

Special Terms

1. *Laissez-Passer*: It is issued by the United Nations to its staff to facilitate their travel to perform official duties, etc.

联合国护照:是联合国发给其工作人员,以方便其旅行去执行公务等。

2. *Seaman Book*: It is a valid identity document for seaman to enter and leave the *country of destination* and travel abroad. It is issued to seaman working on ships sailing international routes.

海员证:海员进出目的国和出国旅行的有效身份证件,发给在国际航线船舶上工作的海员。

Chapter 3 PASSENGER SERVICE

Text

Every year, airline staff and ground handlers use Travel Information *Manual* to check over 700 million passengers. Travel agents of all sizes use the tool to make sure their customers arrive at the airport with a valid passport, the correct visa and the necessary *health documents*.

TIM is a monthly *publication* published by IATA. The *Travel Information Manual* (TIM) (Figure 3-6) was first published in 1963 and today is owned and managed by lATA Netherlands Data *Publication*s TIM is published for the main purpose of providing airlines, their agents and other parties in the travel industry with up-to-date, official information on government travel regulations, procedures and restrictions for air travel to more than 200 countries. Government requirements are listed under the following section headings:

1. Passport;
2. Visa;
3. Health;
4. Airport tax;
5. Customs;
6. *Currency*.

Figure 3-6 Travel Information Manual

Notes 1

❶ Travel agents of all sizes use the tool to make sure their customers arrive at the airport with a valid passport, the correct visa and the necessary health documents.

解释:各种规模的旅行社都使用该手册来确保他们的客户带着有效护照、正确的签证和必要的健康文件抵达机场。

❷ The Travel Information Manual (TIM) was first published in 1963 and today is owned and managed by lATA Netherlands Data Publications TIM is published for the main purpose of providing airlines, their agents and other parties in the travel industry with up-to date, official information on government travel regulations, procedures and restrictions for air travel to more than 200 countries.

解释:《旅行信息手册》(TIM)于1963年首次出版,如今由荷兰数据出版公司所有和管理。TIM 出版的主要目的是向航空公司、其代理人和旅游业的其他各方提供飞往200多个国家的航空旅行程序和限制,以及有关政府旅行法规的最新官方信息。

Passport

An official document issued by a *competent* public authority to nationals or to *alien* resi-dents (mostly stateless persons) of the *issuing country* (Figure 3-7).

Figure 3-7　Types of passports

General: Passengers must hold a passport valid for all the countries to or via which they travel, unless:

1. An *exemption* to that effect is stated on the page of the country(ies) *concerned*;

2. They pass through a country without leaving the airport. A few countries do not allow this, in which case it is stated under 1. Passport on the page of the country *concerned*.

Notes 2

❶ An official document issued by a competent public authority to nationals or to alien residents (mostly stateless persons) of the issuing country.

解释：由主管部门向签发国的国民或外国人(主要是无国籍人)签发的官方文件。

❷ A few countries do not allow this, in which case it is stated under 1. Passport on the page of the country concerned.

解释：少数国家不允许这样做，在这种情况下，相关国家页面上的1. 护照中说明了这一点。

Visa

An entry in a passport or other *travel document* made by a (*consular*) official of a government to indicate that the bearer has been granted authority to enter or re-enter the country *concerned* (Figure 3-8).

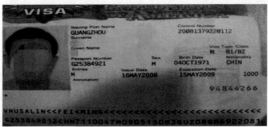

Figure 3-8　Visa

Checking of visa: A visa, *transit visa* or a visa *exemption* for a country does not guarantee admission to that country. The final decision rests with the *competent* authorities at the *port of entry* in the country *concerned*. It is necessary to check carefully the (transit) visas required by the authorities of:

1. The *country of destination*;
2. The *country of departure* (if returning to this country);
3. The *country of residence*;
4. The *transit stations*.

Notes 3

❶ An entry in a passport or other travel document made by a (consular) official of a government to indicate that the bearer has been granted authority to enter or re-enter the country concerned.

解释:一国政府(领事)官员在护照或其他旅行证件上的盖章,表明持证人已被授权进入或重新进入有关国家。

语法:that 引导宾语从句。

❷ The final decision rests with the competent authorities at the port of entry in the country concerned.

解释:最后的决定取决于有关国家入境口岸的主管当局。

Health

Checking of Certificates of *Vaccination*.

It is necessary to check carefully the health regulations of:

1. The country of destination;
2. The country of departure (also for returning if applicable);
3. The transit stations.

Airport Tax

Information is published only about airport tax to be paid by the passenger, mostly upon departure at the airport, in some cases upon arrival at destination. Information on the following kind of taxes is not published in TIM:

1. Taxes collected from a passenger upon purchase of the ticket;
2. Taxes failed to be collected from a passenger (if applicable) at the time of ticket issue, which as a *consequence* thereof will be collected at the *airport of embarkation* (see also appropriate carrier's tariff *publications*);
3. Taxes included in the air fare.

Notes 4

❶ Information is published only about airport tax to be paid by the passenger, mostly upon departure at the airport, in some cases upon arrival at destination.

解释:仅公布了有关乘客应缴纳机场税的信息,主要是在机场离境时,在某些情况下是在到达目的地时。

❷ Taxes failed to be collected from a passenger (if applicable) at the time of ticket issue, which as a consequence thereof will be collected at the airport of embarkation (see also appropriate carrier's tariff publications).

解释:在出票时未能向乘客(如需要的情况下)征税,因此将在登机的机场征税(另见相应承运人的关税出版物)。

语法:which 为非限制性定语从句。

Customs

Customs regulations, including information on *prohibited* articles, are published for import and export of:

- Tobacco products; alcoholic beverages; per- fume; eau-de-Cologne.
- Personal effects are normally not subject to restrictions. (Clothes and toilet requisites such as jewelry and cosmetics, a camera and films, a pair of *binoculars*, a laptop computer a portable radio receiving set, a CD player, a portable musical instrument, a small quantity of foodstuffs and travel souvenirs, insofar as these articles are for personal use).

Customs regulations include other information: pets, baggage clearance, wild fauna and flora, firearms.

> **Notes 5**
>
> Clothes and toilet requisites such as jewelry and cosmetics, a camera and films, a pair of binoculars, a laptop computer a portable radio receiving set, a CD player, a portable musical instrument, a small quantity of foodstuffs and travel souvenirs, insofar as these articles are for personal use.
>
> **解释**：衣服和洗漱用品，如珠宝和化妆品、照相机和胶卷、双筒望远镜、笔记本电脑、便携式收音机、CD播放机、便携式乐器、少量食品和旅游纪念品，只要这些物品是供个人使用的。

Currency

Currency regulations are given for import and export of *currency* based on normal travel and hotel expenses. For regulations concerning current payments and *capital* payments consult the National Bank of the country *concerned*.

> **Notes 6**
>
> For regulations concerning current payments and capital payments consult the National Bank of the country concerned.
>
> **解释**：有关货币付款和资金付款的规定，请咨询相关国家的国家银行。

Example of GHANA in TIM

Ghana

1. Passport: Required, except for holders of:
   a. Laissez-Passer issued by the United Nations;
   b. Seaman Book (travelling on duty) issued by any country;
   c. Travel Certificate issued to nationals of Togo.
2. Visa: Required, except for:

a. Nationals of Ghana;

b. Nationals of: Benin, Burkina Faso, Cape Verde Island, Cote d'lvoire, Cuba (only if holding diplomatic, service or official passports), Gambia, Guinea, Guinea-Bissau, Liberia, Mali, Mauritania, Niger, Nigeria, Senegal, Sierra Leone, Togo and Zimbabwe;

c. Holders of a re-entry permit issued by Ghana;

(TWOV)

d. Those who continue their journey to a third country within 24 hours, provided holding tickets with reserved seats and other documents for their onward journey. They are not allowed to leave the airport. In case they will spend the night in a hotel in town, they must be in possession of a transit visa.

3. TAX: Passenger service charge is levied on passengers embarking in Ghana on:

a. International flights: GHC 22,000;

b. Domestic flights: GHC 500.

4. Place of payment: Airport of departure in Ghana or town terminal in Ghana.

5. Exempt are:

a. Children under 2 years;

b. Transit passengers proceeding on the first connecting service or within 24 hours.

Notes 7

❶ Those who continue their journey to a third country within 24 hours, provided holding tickets with reserved seats and other documents for their onward journey.

解释：那些在24小时内继续前往第三国的人，需要提供他们继续旅行且预定好座位的机票和其他文件。

语法：who 为定语从句。

❷ They are not allowed to leave the airport. In case they will spend the night in a hotel in town, they must be in possession of a transit visa.

解释：他们不允许离开机场。如果他们要在该国家的酒店过夜,他们必须持有过境签证。

Further Reading

Transit without Visa (TWOV)

Transit without Visa (TWOV): Passing through an international transit area of the airport in order to board a connecting (or to proceed by the same) flight, without entering the country (i.e. clearing immigration). Unless stated otherwise, passengers wishing to TWOV must:

- be en-route to a third country (e.g. itinerary TYO-LON-TYO is not considered TWOV);
- prove that they will continue their journey within the prescribed period (e.g. hold on-ward tickets);

- have documents required for entry into the country of destination and for transit through countries en-route;
- remain in the transit area (airside).

TWOV is not intended for those holding stand-by tickets, e.g. airline staff or other passengers travelling on industry discount.

New Words

publication	[ˌpʌblɪˈkeɪʃən]	n. 出版;发表;出版物
manual	[ˈmænjuəl]	n. 手册;说明书;指南
currency	[ˈkʌrənsɪ]	n. 通货;货币
alien	[ˈeɪlɪən]	n. 外国人;外侨
concerned	[kənˈsɜːnd]	adj. 担心的;关注的;忧虑的
consular	[ˈkɒnsɪələ(r)]	adj. 领事的;与领事(或领事工作)有关的
exemption	[ɪgˈzempʃən]	n. 免除;豁免
competent	[ˈkɒmpɪtənt]	adj. 有能力的;称职的
vaccination	[ˌvæksɪˈneɪʃən]	n. 接种疫苗;注射疫苗
consequence	[ˈkɒnsɪkwəns]	n. 结果;后果
embarkation	[ˌɛmbɑːˈkeɪʃən]	n. 登机
prohibit	[prəˈhɪbɪt]	v. (尤指以法令)禁止;阻止
binocular	[bɪˈnɒkjələ]	adj. 双目并用的;双眼的
capital	[ˈkæpɪtl]	n. 首都;资本

Phrases & Expressions

TIM (Travel Information Manual)	旅游信息手册
health document	健康证
issuing country	签发国
travel document	旅行证
transit visa	过境签
port of entry	入境口岸
country of destination	目的地国
country of departure	始发国
country of residence	居住国
transit station	过境站
airport of embarkation	登机机场
laissez-passer	联合国护照
seaman book	海员证

Exercises

I. Translate the following terms into Chinese or English.

1. seaman book
2. carrier's tariff publication
3. airport of embarkation
4. laissez-passer
5. 健康证
6. 旅客信息手册
7. 入境口岸
8. 过境签

II. Cloze.

(health documents/airport of embarkation/issuing country/travel document)

1. taxes failed to be collected from a passenger (if applicable) at the time of ticket issue, which as a consequence thereof will be collected at the _____ (see also appropriate carrier's tariff publications).

2. Travel agents of all sizes use the tool to make sure their customers arrive at the airport with a valid passport, the correct visa and the necessary _____.

3. An official document issued by a competent public authority to nationals or to alien residents (mostly stateless persons) of the _____.

4. An entry in a passport or other _____ made by a (consular) official of a government to indicate that the bearer has been granted authority to enter or re-enter the country concerned.

III. Translate the following sentences into Chinese.

1. Every year, airline staff and ground handlers use Travel Information Manual to check over 700 million passengers.

2. Customs regulations, including information on prohibited articles, are published for import and export of:

IV. Translate the following paragraph into Chinese.

Transit without Visa (TWOV): Passing through an international transit area of the airport in order to board a connecting (or to proceed by the same) flight, without entering the country (i.e.

clearing immigration). Unless stated otherwise, passengers wishing to TWOV must:

- be en-route to a third country (e.g. itinerary TYO-LON-TYO is not considered TWOV);
- prove that they will continue their journey within the prescribed period (e.g. hold on-ward tickets);
- have documents required for entry into the country of destination and for transit through countries en-route;
- remain in the transit area (airside).

V. Answer the following questions.

1. What TIM is published for?

2. What is visa?

Section 3
Baggage

New Rules on Baggage

On March 15, 2021, the regulations on passenger service management of public air transport will be officially implemented on September 1. The regulations delete the *unified* provisions on baggage size, weight, free baggage allowance and excess baggage fee. Air carriers can formulate relevant standards and publish them according to the business characteristics of enterprises. This adjustment aims to fully release the vitality of the market and give full play to the initiative, enthusiasm and creativity of the carrier (Figure 3-9).

Figure 3-9 A passenger with baggage

Chapter 3 PASSENGER SERVICE

📢 Special Terms

1. *Baggage allowance in piece system*: The free baggage allowance of passengers is calculated according to the number of pieces.

计件制免费行李额:行李的免费额是根据行李件数来进行计算。

2. *Baggage allowance in weight system*: The free baggage allowance of passengers is calculated according to the weight of the baggage.

计重制免费行李额:行李的免费额是根据行李重量来进行计算。

📖 Text

Baggage refers to the *articles* and *personal belongings* carried by passengers for the convenience of life and work during travel. As an integral part of air transportation, baggage transportation comes into being with the *emergence* of passenger transportation. Baggage transportation plays a very important role in passenger transportation. The success of passenger travel often depends on the *integrity* and *accuracy* of the transportation of baggage and goods carried by passengers. The quality of baggage transportation directly affects flight safety, *flight regularity* and service quality. The compensation caused by baggage transportation errors will not only bring economic losses to airlines, but also damage the reputation of airlines.

According to the new passenger transport regulations of the *Civil Aviation Administration*, it will no longer make a *unified limit* on the free baggage allowance, and each airline will *determine* the *specific* free baggage allowance. (Take China Eastern Airlines as an example)

📝 Notes 1

❶ As an integral part of air transportation, baggage transportation comes into being with the emergence of passenger transportation.

解释:行李运输作为航空运输的一个组成部分,是伴随着旅客运输的出现而产生的。

❷ The quality of baggage transportation directly affects flight safety, flight regularity and service quality. The compensation caused by baggage transportation errors will not only bring economic losses to airlines, but also damage the reputation of airlines.

解释:行李运输质量直接影响飞行安全、航班正常和服务质量。行李运输差错造成的赔偿不仅会给航空公司带来经济损失,还会损害航空公司的声誉。

语法:caused 为非谓语结构,表示被动关系。

Baggage Classification

According to the transportation responsibility, baggage is divided into *checked baggage* and *unchecked baggage*.

1. *Checked baggage*: refers to the baggage handed over by the passenger to the carrier for care and transportation. Normally, the weight of each *checked baggage* shall not *exceed* 50kg (International 32kg) and the volume shall not *exceed* 40×60×100cm. If it *exceed*s the weight or volume requirements, it can be transported as cargo only with the *consent* of the airline.

2. *Unchecked baggage*: it can also be called carry-on baggage, refers to the items brought into the cabin by passengers with the *consent* of the carrier. Normally, the weight of each passenger's free *unchecked baggage* is *limit*ed to 10kg. According to the airlines regulation, passengers holding first-class tickets can carry 2 pieces per person; Passengers holding business class or economy class tickets can only carry one item per person. The volume of each carry on item shall not *exceed* 20×40×55cm. Carry on items *exceed*ing the above weight, number and volume *limit*s shall be transported as *checked baggage* (Table 3-1).

Weight, number and volume limits of checked baggage & personal article　　Table 3-1

Classification	Checked Baggage	Carry-on Baggage
Definition	It refers to the baggage that the passenger has handed over to the carrier for care and transportation	It refers to small items brought into the cabin by passengers with the consent of the carrier
Weight	≤50kg(32kg)	≤10kg
Volume	≤40cm×60cm×100cm	First class: 2pc business class, economy class: 1pc≤20cm×40cm×55cm

Notes 2

❶ If it exceeds the weight or volume requirements, it can be transported as cargo only with the consent of the airline.

解释:如果超过重量或体积要求,只有在航空公司同意的情况下才能作为货物运输。

❷ According to the airlines regulation, passengers holding first-class tickets can carry 2 pieces per person; Passengers holding business class or economy class tickets can only carry one item per person.

解释:根据航空公司规定,持头等舱机票的旅客每人可携带2件特品;持有商务舱或经济舱机票的乘客每人只能携带一件物品。

❸ Carry on items exceeding the above weight, number and volume limits shall be transported as checked baggage.

解释:超过上述重量、数量和体积限制的随身物品应作为托运行李运输。

语法:exceeding 为非谓语结构,表示主动关系。

Free Baggage Allowance

• *Free baggage allowance in weight concept* (applicable to all domestic routes and some international routes)

Chapter 3　PASSENGER SERVICE

1. First class passengers holding adult or children tickets are 40kg. Business class passengers are 30kg and economy class passengers are 20kg. The free baggage allowance of passengers holding various China Eastern Airlines membership cards can be increased accordingly (Table 3-2).

Baggage weighing system of domestic routes　　Table 3-2

Classification	Class of Service	Card Level/Baggage Allowance				Volume Limit- per Piece	Weight Limit- per Piece
Checked baggage		Card free level	Oriental Wanlixing platinum card and gold card member	Oriental Wanlixing silver card, Trina Solar alliance super elite	Trina Solar alliance elite	Not less than 5 × 15 × 20cm and not more than 40 × 60 × 100cm	<50kg
	First-class	40kg	80kg	60kg	50kg		
	Business Premier/ business class	30kg	70kg	50kg	40 kg		
	Super economy class/economy class	20kg	60kg	40kg	30kg		
Unchecked baggage	First class	Two pieces				Not more than 20 × 40 × 55cm	<10kg
	Other class	One piece					

2. Domestic passengers with baby tickets have no free baggage allowance; Some airlines can enjoy a free baggage allowance of 10kg for passengers who meet the international transportation regulations and hold a baby ticket; Each baby can check in a baby *stroller* free of charge.

3. For International transportation including domestic *leg*, the free baggage allowance for each passenger shall be calculated according to the *applicable* free baggage allowance for international routes.

Notes 3

❶ According to the new passenger transport regulations of the Civil Aviation Administration, it will no longer make a unified limit on the free baggage allowance, and each airline will determine the specific free baggage allowance.

解释:根据民航局新的客运条例,将不再对免费行李限额进行统一限制,具体免费行李限额由各航空公司确定。

❷ The free baggage allowance of passengers holding various China Eastern Airlines membership cards can be increased accordingly.

解释:持有各种东航会员卡的旅客的免费行李限额可相应增加。

语法:holding 为非谓语结构,表示主动关系。

❸ Some airlines can enjoy a free baggage allowance of 10kg for passengers who meet the international transportation regulations and hold a baby ticket.

解释:一些航空公司可以为符合国际运输规则并持有婴儿票的乘客享受10公斤的免费行李限额。

> 语法:who 为定语从句,先行词为 passenger。
>
> ❹ For International transportation including domestic leg, the free baggage allowance for each passenger shall be calculated according to the applicable free baggage allowance for international routes.
>
> 解释:对于包括国内航段在内的国际运输,每位乘客的免费行李限额应根据国际航线适用的免费行李限额计算。

- *Free baggage allowance in piece concept* (Table 3-3)

Free baggage allowance in piece concept　　　　　　　　　　Table 3-3

Classification	Class of Service	Card Level/Baggage Allowances			Volume Limit- per Piece	Weight Limit- per Piece
Checked baggage		Card free level	Oriental Wanlixing platinum card and gold card member	Oriental wanlixing silver card, Trina Solar alliance super elite	Sum of three sides ≤158cm and sum of two bags ≤273cm	≤32kg
	First-class/ Business Premier/business class	2	3	3		
	Super economy class/economy class	2	Additional 1 Pieces (weight not exceeding 32kg)	3		≤23kg
Unchecked baggage	Class of service	2			Not more than 25 × 45 × 56cm and the sum of three sides ≤115cm	≤10kg
	Other class	1				

1. On Sino-USA, Sino-Canada and some international routes, the free baggage allowance of passengers is calculated according to the number of pieces. For each passenger holding an adult or child ticket, the free baggage allowance is 2 pieces (2pc) or 1 piece (1pc), and the weight of each piece of baggage shall not *exceed* 32kg (first class or business class) or 23kg (economy class). The *specific* number of pieces will be described in the free baggage allowance column (allow) of the ticket.

2. For passengers holding first-class or business class tickets, the sum of length, width and height of each baggage shall not *exceed* 158cm.

3. For passengers holding economy class tickets, the sum of length, width and height of each piece of baggage shall not *exceed* 158cm, but the sum of two pieces shall not *exceed* 273cm.

Notes 4

> ❶ For each passenger holding an adult or child ticket, the free baggage allowance is 2 pieces (2pc) or 1 piece (1pc), and the weight of each piece of baggage shall not exceed 32kg (first class or business class) or 23kg (economy class).

解释：持有成人票或儿童票的每位旅客，免费行李限额为2件（2件）或1件（1件），每件行李的重量不得超过32kg（头等舱或商务舱）或23kg（经济舱）。

❷ For passengers holding economy class tickets, the sum of length, width and height of each piece of baggage shall not exceed 158cm, but the sum of two pieces shall not exceed 273cm.

解释：持经济舱客票的旅客，每件行李的长、宽、高之和不得超过158cm，但两件行李之和不得超过273cm。

Charges for Excess Baggage

1. Definition: baggage *exceed*ing the free baggage allowance is excess baggage.
2. *Charges for excess baggage*:

a. Excess baggage for free baggage allowance under the weight system: the *rate* (1.5% of the published full fare of *one-way* adult *economy class* used on the date of filling in the excess baggage ticket) × the number of excess kilograms.

b. Excess baggage for free baggage allowance under the piece system: charge according to the *specific* regulations of each airline.

Notes 5

❶ The rate (1.5% of the published full fare of one-way adult economy class used on the date of filling in the excess baggage ticket) × the number of excess kilograms.

解释：超重行李额费率（填写超重行李票之日起使用的单程成人经济舱公布全额票价的1.5%）×超重公斤数。

❷ Excess baggage for free baggage allowance under the piece system: charge according to the specific regulations of each airline.

解释：计件制免费行李额的超重行李：根据各航空公司的具体规定收费。

Further Reading

Causes of Lost or Delayed Luggage

Although luggage may be lost for a variety of reasons, baggage-handling systems are often to blame. The recent *Civil Aviation Administration* reviewed industry statistics showing that causes of delayed baggage in 2015 were as follows:

Transfer baggage mishandling	61%
Failure to load at originating airport	15%
Ticketing error/passenger bag switch/security	9%
Loading/offloading error	4%
Space-weight restriction	5%

Arrival station mishandling	3%
Tagging errors	3%

New Words

article	[ˈɑːtɪkl]	n. 物品
emergence	[ɪˈmɜːdʒəns]	n. 出现；兴起
integrity	[ɪnˈtegrətɪ]	n. 诚实正直；完整
accuracy	[ˈækjərəsɪ]	n. 精确(程度)
consent	[kənˈsent]	n. 同意；准许
exceed	[ɪkˈsiːd]	v. 超过
unified	[ˈjuːnɪfaɪd]	v. 统一；使成一体
limit	[ˈlɪmɪt]	n./v. 限制
determine	[dɪˈtɜːmɪn]	v. 决定
stroller	[ˈstrəʊlə(r)]	n. 手推车
leg	[leg]	n. 腿, 航段
		v. 跑
applicable	[əˈplɪkəbl]	adj. 可应用的；适用
rate	[reɪt]	n. 速度；进度；比率
specific	[spəˈsɪfɪk]	adj. 具体的；特定的

Phrases & Expressions

personal belongings	个人物品
flight regularity	航班正常运营
checked baggage	托运行李
unchecked baggage	自理行李
personal article	个人物品
Civil Aviation Administration	民航局
free baggage allowance in weight concept	计重制免费行李额
charge for excess baggage	超重行李费
one-way economy class	单程经济舱

Exercises

Ⅰ. Translate the following terms into Chinese or English.

1. personal belongings
2. flight regularity
3. checked baggage
4. unchecked baggage

5. 个人物品

6. 民航局

7. 免费行李计重制

8. 超重行李收费

Ⅱ. Cloze.

(personal belongings/one-way adult economy class/Civil Aviation Administration/flight regularity)

1. Baggage refers to the articles and _____ carried by passengers for the convenience of life and work during travel.

2. The rate (1.5% of the published full fare of _____ used on the date of filling in the excess baggage ticket) × the number of excess kilograms.

3. According to the new passenger transport regulations of the _____, it will no longer make a unified limit on the free baggage allowance, and each airline will determine the specific free baggage allowance.

4. The quality of baggage transportation directly affects flight safety, _____ and service quality.

Ⅲ. Translate the following sentences into Chinese.

1. On Sino-USA, Sino-Canada and some international routes, the free baggage allowance of passengers is calculated according to the number of pieces.

2. Normally, the weight of each checked baggage shall not exceed 50kg (International 32kg) and the volume shall not exceed 40 × 60 × 100cm.

Ⅳ. Translate the following paragraph into Chinese.

Although luggage may be lost for a variety of reasons, baggage-handling systems are often to blame. The recent civil aviation administration reviewed industry statistics showing that causes of delayed baggage in 2015 were as follows:

Transfer baggage mishandling	61%
Failure to load at originating airport	15%
Ticketing error/passenger bag switch/security	9%
Loading/offloading error	4%
Space-weight restriction	5%
Arrival station mishandling	3%
Tagging errors	3%

V. Answer the following questions.

1. What's the excess baggage rate for free baggage allowance under the weight system?

2. If passengers who meet the international transportation regulations and hold a baby ticket, how much is the free baggage allowance?

Section 4
Overbooking

Denied Boardingat Xianyang Airport

On October 22, 2010, a group of seven passengers wanted to take a flight from Xi'an to Shanghai. When they checked in the boarding pass at Xianyang Airport (Figure 3-10), they were suddenly told that one of them could not board the plane because the airline tickets were overbooked. They were helpless. One of the passengers had to change to other flights. After the passenger complained, the company said that it would compensate the consumer 200 yuan, and the passenger thought that the compensation amount was too low.

Figure 3-10　Check-in at Xianyang Airport

Special Terms

1. DB(Denied Boarding): Passengers denied boarding due to overbooking.
拒绝登机:因航班超售而被拒绝登机的旅客。
2. SP(Spoilage): It refers to the empty seat that cannot be sold again due to temporary change of itinerary or refund.
虚耗座位:是指旅客因临时更改行程或退票而导致航班座位无法再次销售,进而出现的空载闲置座位。

Text

The objective of the flight overbooking *component* of airline *revenue* management is to determine the maximum number of bookings to accept for a future flight departure with a given physical capacity (in seats). Because the no-show behavior of passengers on future flights is uncertain, there is an element of risk involved in accepting more reservations than physical capacity. If too many reservations are accepted and more passengers show up at departure time than there are physical seats, the airline must deal with the costs and customer service issues of *denied boarding*s (DB) (Figure 3-11). On the other hand, if not enough reservations are accepted for the flight and the *no-show rate* of passengers is greater than that expected by the airline, there are costs associated with the lost *revenue* from empty seats that could otherwise have been occupied, known as *spoilage* (SP). The more *specific* objective of most airline

Figure 3-11　A denied passenger

overbooking models is therefore to minimize the total *combin*ed costs and risks of *denied boardings* and *spoilage* (lost *revenue*).

Why Is Overbooking Even Necessary?

The simple answer is that airlines have historically allowed their passengers to make reservations (i.e., remove seats from the airline's available *inventory*) and then to "no-show" with little or no penalty. In very few other service or manufacturing industries can the consumer "promise" to buy a product or service and then change his or her mind at the last minute with little or no penalty. The economic *motivation* for airline overbooking is *substantial*. Although there are differences by region and airline, no-show rates can average 10% of final pre-departure bookings and can exceed 20% during *peak* holiday periods. Given that most airlines struggle to achieve operating profit *margin*s of 5%, the loss of 10% ~ 15% of potential *revenue*s on fully booked flights (which would occur without overbooking) can *represent* a major financial impact (Figure 3-12).

Figure 3-12　Overbooking is a common practice

Notes 1

❶ The objective of the flight overbooking component of airline revenue management is to determine the maximum number of bookings to accept for a future flight departure with a given physical capacity (in seats).

解释:航空公司收入中,航班超售部分的目标是,确定在给定实际载客量(座位)的情况下,决定即将起飞的航班可接受的最大预订数量。

❷ Because the no-show behavior of passengers on future flights is uncertain, there is an element of risk involved in accepting more reservations than physical capacity.

解释:由于乘客在即将乘坐的航班上的不乘机行为是不确定的,因此接受比实际载客量更多的预订会带来一定的风险。

语法:involved 为非谓语结构,表示被动关系。

❸ On the other hand, if not enough reservations are accepted for the flight and the noshow rate of passengers is greater than that expected by the airline, there are costs associated with the lost revenue from empty seats that could otherwise have been occupied, known as spoilage (SP).

解释:另一方面,如果航班没有足够的预订,且旅客的未登机率高于航空公司的预期,则会产生与空位收入损失相关的成本,称为座位虚耗(SP)。

语法:associated 为非谓语结构,表示被动关系;that 为定语从句,先行词为 seats。

❹ Although there are differences by region and airline, no-show rates can average 10% of final pre-departure bookings and can exceed 20% during peak holiday periods.

解释:尽管不同地区和航空公司之间存在差异,但误机旅客的平均数量可能占最终出发前预订的 10%,在节假日高峰期可能超过 20%。

Safeguard Measures for Flight Overbooking

1. Establish Aviation *Volunteer* Passenger System

For aviation *volunteer* passengers, each company shall establish "*aviation volunteer files*".

After the flight is overloaded, first check whether there are aviation *volunteers* on the flight, and first pull down these *volunteer* passengers; At the same time, establish an aviation *volunteer* reward system to enable aviation *volunteers* to enjoy certain flight *preferential* rewards in a certain period of time.

2. Passenger Arrangement Measures shall Be Taken after the Flight Ticket Is Sold

After the flight is sold, the ground service personnel shall *formulate corresponding* passenger arrangement measures for the flights that are expected to be overloaded according to the flight sales.

3. Establish *Standard Compensation Regulation*

After the *domestic flight*s are actually overloaded, the passenger compensation standards will vary due to different airlines, and the compensation standards are not clearly specified, which is easy to cause passenger complaints due to inconsistent compensation standards after the flights are actually overloaded. Therefore, each airline shall *formulate corresponding* passenger compensation system. No matter whether passengers voluntarily give up boarding or involuntarily refused boarding, they shall provide compensation to passengers when the overbooking compensation conditions are met.

4. *Flight Data Feedback* Analysis

After the flight overbooking, conduct *corresponding* data analysis on whether the flight is actually overbooked and whether the actual *overbooked passenger*s are traveling, *follow-up service tracking* and return visit the actual *overbooked passengers*, establish the *overbooked passenger* data analysis process, and feed back the analysis results to relevant departments, so as to provide convenience for further overbooking.

Notes 2

❶ After the flight is overloaded, first check whether there are aviation volunteers on the flight, and first pull down these volunteer passengers; At the same time, establish an aviation volunteer reward system to enable aviation volunteers to enjoy certain flight preferential rewards in a certain period of time.

解释:航班超载后,首先检查航班上是否有航空志愿者,并先将这些志愿者乘客拉下;同时,建立航空志愿者奖励制度,使航空志愿者在一定时间内享受一定的飞行优惠奖励。

❷ After the domestic flights are actually overloaded, the passenger compensation standards will vary due to different airlines, and the compensation standards are not clearly specified, which is easy to cause passenger complaints due to inconsistent compensation standards after the flights are actually overloaded.

解释:国内航班实际超负荷后,旅客赔偿标准会因航空公司不同而有所不同,赔偿标准没有明确规定,很容易因航班实际超负荷后赔偿标准不一致而引起旅客投诉。

语法:which 为非限制性定语从句。

❸ No matter whether passengers voluntarily give up boarding or are involuntarily refused boarding, they shall provide compensation to passengers when the overbooking compensation conditions are met.

解释：无论旅客是自愿放弃登机还是非自愿拒绝登机，均应在满足超售赔偿条件时，向旅客提供赔偿。

语法：when 为时间状语从句。

The New Regulation of *Denied Boarding*

On March 15, 2021, the day of consumer rights and interests, the regulations on the administration of passenger services in public air transport were officially promulgated and will be implemented from September 1, 2021. This revision focuses on the protection of passengers' rights and interests, puts forward clear requirements for key links prone to disputes such as ticket sales, refund and modification, baggage transportation, and standardizes new civil aviation business forms such as online ticket sales, electronic boarding vouchers, connecting flights and overbooking.

The regulations added a chapter on overbooking, requiring the carrier to fully consider the route, flight frequency, time, model and connecting flights before overbooking, so as to avoid passengers being refused boarding due to overbooking to the greatest extent. At the same time, the regulations give clear guidance on the advance notification of overbooking information and the solicitation of *volunteers*.

New Words

component	[kəmˈpəʊnənt]	n. 组成部分；成分
revenue	[ˈrevənjuː]	n. 收入；收益
inventory	[ˈɪnvəntri]	n. 库存；(建筑物里的物品、家具等的)清单
motivation	[ˌməʊtɪˈveɪʃn]	n. 动机；动力；诱因
substantial	[səbˈstænʃl]	adj. 大量的
volunteer	[ˌvɒlənˈtɪə(r)]	n. 义务工作者；志愿者
formulate	[ˈfɔːmjuleɪt]	v. 制定；制订
corresponding	[ˌkɒrəˈspɒndɪŋ]	adj. 符合的；相应的
specific	[spəˈsɪfɪk]	adj. 具体的；特定的
combine	[kəmˈbaɪn]	v. (使)结合；联合
spoilage	[ˈspɔɪlɪdʒ]	n. (食物的)变质，腐败
margin	[ˈmɑːdʒɪn]	n. 边缘；页边空白
peak	[piːk]	n. 峰；高峰；顶峰

| represent | [ˌrepriˈzent] | v. 代表 |
| preferential | [ˌprefəˈrenʃl] | adj. 优先的；优惠的 |

Phrases & Expressions

denied boarding	未接受登机
no-show rate	误机者的比例
aviation volunteer file	航空志愿者档案
standard compensation regulation	标准补偿条例
domestic flight	国内航班
flight data feedback	航班数据反馈
overbooked passenger	超售旅客
follow-up service tracking	后续服务跟踪

Exercises

Ⅰ. Translate the following terms into Chinese or English.

1. denied boarding
2. no-show rate
3. aviation volunteer file
4. standard compensation regulation
5. 国内航班
6. 航班数据反馈
7. 超售旅客
8. 后续服务跟踪

Ⅱ. Cloze.

(denied boarding/domestic flight/overbooked passenger/no-show rate)

1. The more specific objective of most airline overbooking models is therefore to minimize the total combined costs and risks of _____ and spoilage (*lost revenue*).

2. After the _____ are actually overloaded, the passenger compensation standards will vary due to different airlines, and the compensation standards are not clearly specified, which is easy to cause passenger complaints due to inconsistent compensation standards after the flights are actually overloaded.

3. After the flight overbooking, conduct corresponding data analysis on whether the flight is actually overbooked and whether the actual _____ are traveling.

4. On the other hand, if not enough reservations are accepted for the flight and the _____ of passengers is greater than that expected by the airline, there are costs associated with the lost *revenue* from empty seats that could otherwise have been occupied, known as spoilage (SP).

Ⅲ. Translate the following sentences into Chinese.

1. After the flight is sold, the ground service personnel shall formulate corresponding passenger arrangement measures for the flights that are expected to be overloaded according to the flight sales.

2. Therefore, each airline shall formulate corresponding passenger compensation system.

Ⅳ. Translate the following paragraph into Chinese.

On March 15, 2021, the day of consumer rights and interests, the regulations on the administration of passenger services in public air transport were officially promulgated and will be implemented from September 1, 2021. This revision focuses on the protection of passengers' rights and interests, puts forward clear requirements for key links prone to disputes such as ticket sales, refund and modification, baggage transportation, and standardizes new civil aviation business forms such as online ticket sales, electronic boarding vouchers, connecting flights and overbooking.

Ⅴ. Answer the following questions.

1. Why is overbooking even necessary?

2. What are the safeguard measures for flight overbooking?

Section 5
Flight Delay

Lead in

The Delay Conflict Event of Spring Airlines

In July 2007, the delay *conflict* incident involving Spring Airlines caused an *uproar*. Due to the bad weather, Spring Airlines' round-trip flight between Shanghai and Dalian was delayed, leaving dozens of passengers stranded at the airport. And then the *strand*ed passengers disturbed the airport order, resulting in the *follow-up* flights taking off or landing abnormally, and more than 2000 passengers were affected. In addition, due to flight delays, some passengers *block*ed security checkpoints and boarding gates, *smash*ed *ferry bus*es, and pulled banners in protest, which have seriously affected the normal operation of flights (Figure 3-13).

Figure 3-13　Spring Airlines

Special Terms

1. The right to know: The right to know the cause of a flight delay.
知情权是指有权利知道航班延误造成的原因。

2. The option: If the delay is caused by the airline, passengers can choose to change the flight, refund the ticket or give financial compensation and accommodation arrangements.
自主选择权是指如果是由于航空原因造成的延误,可以选择改签、退票或者给予经济补偿和住宿的安排的选择。

3. The right of claim: Passengers can demand compensation from airlines for their flight delay. Airlines generally have a time limit for cash compensation, and cash compensation is available only if the flight is delayed more than four hours.
索赔权是指旅客可以针对其航班延误的情况要求航空公司给予相关的赔偿,对于现金的赔偿航空公司一般都有相应的时间的限制要求,只有航班延误在四个小时以上才会有现金补偿。

Text

China's civil aviation has maintained a rapid growth rate in the past 20 years. In 2019, the passenger traffic exceeded 660 million passengers, an increase of 7.9% over the *previous* year. However, as the number of flights and passenger trips increases each year, so does the number of flight delays. The definition of flight delay in China is that the flight landing time (*Actual Time of Arrival*) is more than 15 minutes later than the planned landing time (scheduled time of arrival) or the flight is canceled (Figure 3-14).

Based on the average on-schedule flight rate and passenger transport volume in 2019, about 120 million passengers are affected by flight delays every year. In recent years, the Civil Aviation Administration of China (CAAC) accepted passenger complaints, in which the *proportion* involving flight delays ranked first. How to improve the service quality and management level of flight delay has become a problem that the industry pays close attention to and makes effort to solve.

Figure 3-14　Flight delays

Notes 1

❶ The definition of flight delay in China is that the flight landing time (Actual Time of Arrival) is more than 15 minutes later than the planned landing time (Scheduled Time of Arrival) or the flight is canceled.

解释:我国对航班延误的定义是:航班降落时间(航班实际到港时间)比计划降落时间(航班时刻表上的时间)延迟15分钟以上或航班取消的情况。

❷ In recent years, the Civil Aviation Administration of China (CAAC) accepted passenger complaints, in which the proportion involving flight delays ranked first.

解释:近年来,民航局受理旅客投诉中,涉及航班延误的比例居首位。

语法:which引导的定语从句中包含固定搭配involve in,因此介词in提前。

❸ How to improve the service quality and management level of flight delay has become a problem that the industry pays close attention to and makes effort to solve.

解释:如何改进航班延误服务质量和管理水平,已成为行业高度关注和努力解决的问题。

Service Status of Flight Delays

Flight delay information *notification* is not in place. The most *intolerable* thing for passengers is not the delay itself, but not knowing what happened, how long to wait, or what caused it. Therefore, information *transmission* is particularly important when flight delays occur (Figure 3-15).

The compensation standards of flight delay are not uniform. At present, there is no unified processing procedures and compensation standards for flight delay in China (The CAAC has only issued guidelines on compensation after flight delays). Thus, there are great differences between airlines in practice, which also leads to the dissatisfaction of many passengers.

Figure 3-15　The delay passengers

The *expertise* of the delayed service personnel needs to be improved. When Passengers *encounter* flight delays, they generally will be more *irritable*, or even have some extreme behavior. At this time, the staff needs to deal with it flexibly, but if the way is not good, it is easy to cause more serious *consequences*.

Notes 2

❶ The most intolerable thing for passengers is not the delay itself, but not knowing what happened, how long to wait, or what caused it.

解释：旅客最无法忍受的不是延误本身，而是不知道发生了什么事，不知道还要等多久，也不知道是何种原因引起的。

语法：not…but…意为"不是……而是……"，but 表示转折。

❷ At present, there is no unified processing procedures and compensation standards for flight delay in China (The CAAC has only issued guidelines on compensation after flight delays). Thus, there are great differences between airlines in practice, which also leads to the dissatisfaction of many passengers.

解释：目前，我国还没有统一的航班延误处理程序和赔偿标准（民航局只发布了航班延误赔偿指南）。因此，实际操作中航空公司之间存在着很大的差异，这也导致了很多乘客的不满。in practice 意为"在实践中；实际上，事实上"。

❸ At this time, the staff needs to deal with it flexibly, but if the way is not good, it is easy to cause more serious consequences.

解释：此时需要工作人员灵活处理，但如果方式欠佳，极易造成更严重的后果。

Solutions

1. Ensure delayed passengers "right to know".
- The release of flight information shall ensure uniqueness, timeliness and accuracy;
- Keep a positive communication with the passengers and have full communication;
- Establish an official and authoritative public inquiry system for flight delays.

2. Provide fast change service to protect delayed passengers' "options".

Making passengers travel as quickly as possible is the greatest compensation for a delayed flight. If the delay cannot be resolved within a short time, offering a change service is also a solution.

3. Improve the standard of economic compensation for flight delays.

On the basis of learning from the advantages of the *compensation schemes* of various airlines, the actual problems are analyzed and a clear compensation standard is formulated, so as to reduce the conflicts and the occurrence of the phenomenon of "occupation, strike".

4. Enhance the skills and *service awareness* of the *service personnel*.

On the one hand, the service personnel should adhere to the service concept of "*sincere service*", and improve service awareness; on the other hand, quickly respond to the needs of passengers. Rapid response to passengers' needs after flight delays is an important embodiment of efficient and quality service.

5. Strengthen the operation management of flight and reduces flight delays.

• Coordinate with all the departments of the airlines to address flight delays caused by internal causes. Meanwhile, formulate and improve flight plans to reduce the proportion of delays due to flight plans.

• Stop the illegal behavior of passengers and prevent artificial delay. The airport should stop the *irrational behavior* of some passengers based on the principle of protecting the interests of most passengers.

• Further improve flight ground support. Airports should establish flight operation supervision and accountability *mechanisms* to further strengthen *supervision* and avoid flight delays caused by *inadequate* ground support.

Notes 3

❶ Making passengers travel as quickly as possible is the greatest compensation for a delayed flight.

解释:航班延误后能使乘客尽快成行是对其最大的补偿。

❷ On the basis of learning from the advantages of the compensation schemes of various airlines, the actual problems are analyzed and a clear compensation standard is formulated, so as to reduce the conflicts and the occurrence of the phenomenon of "occupation, strike".

解释:在借鉴各家航空公司补偿方案优势点的基础上,分析现实问题,制定明确的补偿标准,从而降低矛盾减少"占机、罢乘"等现象的发生。

语法:on the basis of 根据;基于……;so as to 表示目的,意为以便;以致。

❸ Rapid response to passengers' needs after flight delays is an important embodiment of efficient and quality service.

解释:航班延误后快速响应乘客需求是高效优质服务补救的重要体现。

❹ The airport should stop the irrational behavior of some passengers based on the principle of protecting the interests of most passengers.

解释:机场应该基于保障大多数乘客利益的原则,制止部分乘客的不理智行为。

> ❺ Coordinate with all the departments of the airlines to address flight delays caused by internal causes. Meanwhile, formulate and improve flight plans to reduce the proportion of delays due to flight plans.
>
> 解释：与航空公司各部门协调，解决因内部原因造成的航班延误问题。同时，制定和完善飞行计划，减少因飞行计划造成的延误比例。
>
> 语法：address, vt. 设法解决。

Flight delay is always an *inevitable occurrence*, so people need to constantly discuss and improve related services, not only to reduce the occurrence of flight delay as much as possible, but also to maximize the satisfaction of customers after the delay.

Further Reading

The Blacklist of Spring Airlines

In April 2012, Ms. Liu from Harbin took Spring Airlines Flight 9C8511 from Shanghai Pudong to Harbin. At that time, due to more than eight hours, some passengers took *excessive actions* such as "*denied deplaning*", which seriously affected the normal operation of subsequent flights. In order to *appease* the *disgruntled* passengers, the airline offered them 200 yuan in economic compensation on the spot. However, when Ms. Liu ordered Spring Airlines tickets again on June 28, she found that she had been included in Spring Airlines's "*incompetent passenger list*", commonly known as the "blacklist", unable to buy Spring Airlines tickets.

The "*blacklist*" system is an independent operation and management system formulated by Spring Airlines. It is to bring individual passengers who take excessive rights protection behaviors such as plane *bullying*, occupying, and attacking counters into the "blacklist", indicating that Spring Airlines is "temporarily unable" to serve these passengers (Figure 3-16).

Figure 3-16　The "blacklist"

New Words

conflict	[ˈkɒnflɪkt]	n. 冲突，矛盾
		vi. 冲突，抵触
uproar	[ˈʌprɔː(r)]	n. 骚动；喧嚣
strand	[strænd]	vt. 使搁浅；使陷于困境
		vi. 搁浅

follow-up	[ˈfɒləʊ ʌp]	adj.	后续的
		n.	后续行动
block	[blɒk]	vt.	阻止；阻塞；限制
		adj.	交通堵塞的
smash	[smæʃ]	vt.	粉碎；撞击
		vi.	粉碎；打碎
ferry	[ˈferɪ]	n.	摆渡
		vt.	空运
		vi.	摆渡
previous	[ˈpriːvɪəs]	adj.	以前的
		adv.	在先；在……以前
proportion	[prəˈpɔːʃən]	n.	比例
		vt.	使成比例
notification	[ˌnəʊtɪfɪˈkeɪʃən]	n.	通知；通告；[法] 告示
intolerable	[ɪnˈtɒlərəbl]	adj.	无法忍受的；难耐的
transmission	[trænzˈmɪʃən]	n.	传动装置，传送
expertise	[ˌekspɜːˈtiːz]	n.	专门知识；专门技术
encounter	[ɪnˈkaʊntə(r)]	vt.	遭遇；遇到
		n.	遭遇；偶然碰见
irritable	[ˈɪrɪtəbl]	adj.	过敏的；急躁的；易怒的
consequence	[ˈkɒnsɪkwəns]	n.	结果；重要性；推论
mechanism	[ˈmekənɪzəm]	n.	机制；途径
supervision	[ˌsjuːpəˈvɪʒn]	n.	监督，管理
inadequate	[ɪnˈædɪkwət]	adj.	不充分的，不适当的
inevitable	[ɪnˈevɪtəbl]	adj.	必然的，不可避免的
occurrence	[əˈkʌrəns]	n.	发生；出现；事件；发现
blacklist	[ˈblæklɪst]	n.	黑名单
		vt.	将……列入黑名单
appease	[əˈpiːz]	vt.	安抚；抚慰；平息
disgruntle	[dɪsˈɡrʌnt(ə)l]	vt.	使……不高兴，使愠怒
bullying	[ˈbʊlɪɪŋ]	n.	恃强欺弱的行为

Phrases & Expressions

Actual Time of Arrival (ATA)	实际到达时间
Scheduled Time of Arrival (STA)	计划到达时间
ferry bus	摆渡车
service awareness	服务意识

service personnel	服务人员
sincere service	真情服务
irrational behavior	冲动行为
compensation schemes	赔偿方案
excessive actions	过激行为
denied deplaning	霸机
incompetent passenger list	暂无能力服务旅客名单

Exercises

I. Translate the following terms into Chinese or English.

1. Scheduled Time of Arrival (STA)
2. sincere service
3. irrational behavior
4. compensation schemes
5. service personnel
6. 过激行为
7. 摆渡车
8. 服务意识
9. 暂无能力服务旅客名单
10. 实际到达时间

II. Cloze.

(embodiment/irritable/intolerable/flexibly/flight delay)

1. When Passengers encounter flight delays, they generally will be more _____, or even have some extreme behavior.

2. The definition of _____ in China is that the flight landing time (Actual Time of Arrival) is more than 15 minutes later than the planned landing time (scheduled time of arrival) or the flight is canceled.

3. The most _____ thing for passengers is not the delay itself, but not knowing what happened, how long to wait, or what caused it.

4. At this time, the staff needs to deal with it _____, but if the way is not good, it is easy to cause more serious consequences.

5. Rapid response to passengers' needs after flight delays is an important _____ of efficient and quality service.

III. Translate the following sentences into Chinese.

1. On the basis of learning from the advantages of the compensation schemes of various airlines, the actual problems are analyzed and a clear compensation standard is formulated, so as

to reduce the conflicts and the occurrence of the phenomenon of "occupation, strike".

2. And then the stranded passengers dominated the aircraft for 15 hours, resulting ineight follow-up flights from Shanghai to Guilin, Sanya and Shenyang were not allowed to take off or land normally, and more than 2,000 passengers were affected.

3. In order to appease the disgruntled passengers, the airline offered them 200 yuan in economic compensation on the spot.

IV. Translate the following paragraph into Chinese.

Based on the average on-schedule flight rate and passenger transport volume in 2019, about 120 million passengers are affected by flight delays every year. In recent years, the Civil Aviation Administration of China (CAAC) accepted passenger complaints, in which the proportion involving flight delays ranked first. How to improve the service quality and management level of flight delay has become a problem that the industry pays close attention to and makes effort to solve.

V. Answer the following questions.

1. What is the status of flight delay service in China?

2. How to improve domestic flight delay service?

Chapter 4

AIR CARGO

Section 1
Air Cargo Market Characteristics

Lead in

JD Layout Air Logistics

On December 20, 2018, JD and Nantong *Municipal* Government signed a strategic cooperation *framework agreement*. The two sides will build Nantong Airport into a global air *freight hub* of JD *Logistics* and jointly strive to build Nantong Airport into a hub of JD Logistics air freight (Figure 4-1). As one of the logistics giants, JD wants to build a series of aviation hubs and *strive* to seize more market share.

Figure 4-1 JD Logistics

Special Terms

1. *Freight hub*: Storage and transfer center of the goods.
货运枢纽:货物的仓储、转运中心。
2. *Air freight rate*: Price of air cargo transport per weight or unit volume.
航空货物运费:单位重量或单位体积的航空货物运输价格。

Text

Cargo transportation is an intermediate service, which adds value to some other product without generally being a *standalone* purchase. The demand for air freight services therefore depends on the underlying demand for goods requiring rapid transportation as well as on the cost and benefits of air cargo compared to alternative modes of transport. While road or rail services compete with air cargo on short to medium sectors, sea freight is usually the only *viable* alternative mode on *intercontinental route*s.

Notes 1

Cargo transportation is an intermediate service, which adds value to some other product without generally being a standalone purchase.

解释:货物运输是一种中间服务,它增加了其他产品的价值,而通常不是独立购买。

语法:which 引导定语从句,修饰 intermediate service。

High Added Value of Are Freight

Around 35% of world trade value is carried by air, which, however, only represents around 1% of global *tonnage*. This indicates that the *unit value per kg* of commodities carried by air freight tends to be significantly higher than that of surfaces modes. Global value chains, enabling economies to specialize in defined tasks within a *supply chain*, like the production of computer components or their assembly, play an increasing role for air freight: the *World Trade Organization* estimates that almost half of global trade now takes place within such value chains, up from 36% in 1995, thus growing more rapidly than other types of trade since the 1990s. International movements *of-often* small and highly valuable-component parts are a key element of this business model, making it particularly attractive for air cargo.

Figure 4-2 illustrates the individual shares of different commodity groups carried by air and surface transportation modes. While world trade is dominated by *bulk* cargo with very little *propensity* to be carried by air, there is some *overlap* between commodities normally carried by container ships and those that are typically carried by air freight.

*Air freight rate*s often exceed competing surface rates by a factor of 10 to 15. As air cargo is generally charged based on shipment weight, the final market price of commodities with a high value in relation to their weight is less impacted by transportation costs. The authors of the *Boeing World Air Cargo Forecast* have identified a strong tendency for products carried by air to be valued at more than $16 per kg.

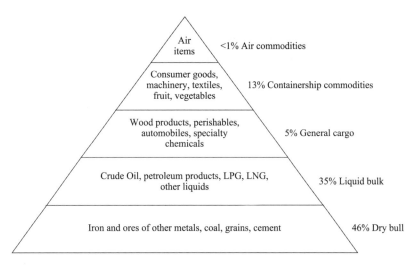

Figure 4-2 Individual shares of different commodity groups carried by transportation modes

Notes 2

❶ Global value chains, enabling economies to specialize in defined tasks within a supply chain, like the production of computer components or their assembly, play an increasing role for air freight.

解释：全球价值链，使各经济体能够专门从事供应链内的明确任务，如计算机部件的生产或组装，在空运中发挥着越来越大的作用。

play…role：起到……作用。

语法：同位语对其同位成分只作补充解释时，可用逗号隔开。

❷ International movements of- often small and highly valuable? component parts are a key element of this business model, making it particularly attractive for air cargo.

解释：通常小的和高价值的零部件的国际运输是这种商业模式的一个关键因素，这对航空货物特别有吸引力。

international movements：国际位移，国际运输。

❸ While world trade is dominated by bulk cargo with very little propensity to be carried by air, there is some overlap between commodities normally carried by container ships and those that are typically carried by air freight.

解释：虽然世界贸易以散装货物为主，而用空运运输的倾向很小，但通常由集装箱船运输的商品与通常由空运运输的商品有一些重叠。

语法：While 意为"当……时候，和……同时"，引导时间状语从句。

while 意为"虽然，尽管"，引导让步状语从句。

while 连接两个并列句子，表示"对比"关系。

Changes in the Air Freight Market

The majority of air cargo shipments are transported within the Northern *hemisphere*. While the

North Atlantic market dominated the air freight industry until the 1970s, the centre of gravity has shifted to the Asia/Pacific region during the past three decades. Nowadays, more than 50% of global cargo (measured in *tonne-kms*) is either carried from, to or within this region, with significant directional imbalances. The cargo tends to move from manufacturing to distribution centers, or from production to consumption centers, driven by the economic activity in the *importing* region.

Driven by the global sourcing of products and components, the emerging economies in Asia, especially China, have strongly developed their *manufacturing industries* over the past decades. Countries producing consumer goods with relatively high value-to-weight ratio such as high-tech are the largest exporters of air freight. Most industry *analysts* expect these imbalances to persist, although *mitigate*d by the increasing purchasing power of a growing middle class in emerging economies like China and India.

Notes 3

❶ The cargo tends to move from manufacturing to distribution centers, or from production to consumption centers, driven by the economic activity in the importing region.

解释：受进口区域的经济活动的驱动，货物倾向于从制造业转移到配送中心，或从生产中心转移到消费中心。

driven by：受……驱动。

语法：or 为并列连词，含有选择意义，连接同等成分的词、短语或句子，并使用同一种形式。

❷ Driven by the global sourcing of products and components, the emerging economies in Asia, especially China, have strongly developed their manufacturing industries over the past decade.

解释：在全球产品和零部件采购的推动下，亚洲的新兴经济体，特别是中国，在过去十年中大力发展了其制造业。

语法：especially 在句中可修饰名词、动词、形容词、介词短语等。一般说来，especially 放在它所修饰的那个词的前面；但是如果放在句首，句子就要倒装。

❸ Most industry analysts expect these imbalances to persist, although mitigated by the increasing purchasing power of a growing middle class in emerging economies like China and India.

解释：大多数行业分析师预计，这些失衡将持续下去，尽管受到中国和印度等新兴经济体中产阶级购买力的不断增长影响而有所缓解。

语法：although 作连词，意思是虽然；尽管；即使；不过；然而。although 引导的从句放在主句前后均可，有时还可放在句中。请注意，although 引导的从句不能与 but、however 连用，但可与 yet、still 连用。

The Diversity of Air Cargo Types

Compared to the passenger business, the demand for air freight is much more *heterogeneous*

(Figure 4-3). Air cargo shipments can be of any size and weight, ranging from document envelopes to heavy and bulky shipments weighing several tonnes. Various approaches for a *categorisation* can be applied, mainly distinguishing between commodity types, shipment weight and size or by transportation urgency.

Figure 4-3　Diversified types of goods

About one-third of the worldwide air cargo tonnage consists of manufactured goods such as office equipment, computers and other electronic goods. Machinery and transport equipment including *capital equipment*, automotive parts and tools account for another third. The remaining third consists of a variety of different commodities among which fresh foodstuffs, medical and *pharmaceutical* goods as well as chemicals are of particular importance.

Notes 4

❶ Various approaches for a categorization can be applied, mainly distinguishing between commodity types, shipment weight and size or by transportation urgency.

解释：可以采用各种分类方法，主要通过商品类型、托运重量和大小或运输的紧迫性来区分。

❷ About one-third of the worldwide air cargo tonnage consists of manufactured goods such as office equipment, computers and other electronic goods.

解释：全世界航空货运吨位的大约三分之一由办公设备、计算机和其他电子产品等制成品组成。

语法：分数的表示方法为"基数词(分子)+序数词(分母)"。

Further Reading

China's Air Cargo Market Is Developing Strong

Global passenger air travel demand remained *sluggish* in 2021, but air freight demand recovered quickly. According to regular global air cargo data in April 2021, air freight demand continued to exceed pre-COVID-19 levels, with air cargo increasing 12% from April 2019. According to IATA data, the overall scale of China's air cargo market has been about 85 *billion* to 90 billion yuan in recent years, ranking it as the second largest air cargo market in the world after the United State.

New Words

municipal	[mjuːˈnɪsɪpl]	adj. 市政的；地方政府的
logistics	[ləˈdʒɪstɪks]	n. 后勤；物流；组织工作
strive	[straɪv]	vi. 努力；奋斗；力争；力求
standalone	[ˌstændəˈləʊn]	n. 脱机 adj. 单独的；独立的
viable	[ˈvaɪəbl]	adj. 可行的；可实施的
tonnage	[ˈtʌnɪdʒ]	n.（表示船舶大小或载重量的）吨位；（某物的）总重量
bulk	[bʌlk]	n. 主体；大宗
overlap	[ˌəʊvəˈlæp , ˈəʊvəlæp]	v. 重叠；（物体或时间上）部分重叠；交叠
hemisphere	[ˈhemɪsfɪə(r)]	n.（球体的、地球的、大脑的）半球
propensity	[prəˈpensəti]	n. 倾向性；习性；（行为方面的）倾向
forecast	[ˈfɔːkɑːst]	n. 预测；预报
import	[ˈɪmpɔːt , ɪmˈpɔːt]	n. 进口；输入的产品（或劳务）
analyst	[ˈænəlɪst]	n. 分析师；分析者；化验员
mitigate	[ˈmɪtɪɡeɪt]	vt. 减轻；缓和
heterogeneous	[ˌhetərəˈdʒiːniəs]	adj. 由很多种类组成的；各种各样的
categorisation	[ˌkætəɡəraɪˈzeɪʃn]	n. 分类
pharmaceutical	[ˌfɑːməˈsuːtɪkl]	adj. 制药的；配药的；卖药的
sluggish	[ˈslʌɡɪʃ]	adj. 行动迟缓的；缓慢的；迟缓的；懒洋洋的
billion	[ˈbɪljən]	num. 十亿；数以十亿计；大量

Phrases & Expressions

freight hub	货运枢纽
framework agreement	框架协议
unit value per kg	每公斤单位价值
intercontinental route	洲际航线
supply chain	供应链
World Trade Organization	世界贸易组织
of-often	通常
air freight rate	航空货运费率
tonne-kms	吨公里
manufacturing industry	制造业
capital equipment	固定设备

Ⅰ. Translate the following terms into Chinese or English.

1. manufacturing industry
2. unit value per kg
3. air freight rate
4. intercontinental route
5. 散装货物
6. 货运枢纽
7. 世界贸易组织
8. 北半球

Ⅱ. Cloze.

(India/air/China/logistics/intercontinental/rates/hub)

1. While road or rail services compete with air cargo on short to medium sectors, sea freight is usually the only viable alternative mode on _____ routes.

2. Around 35% of world trade value is carried by _____, which, however, only represents around 1% of global tonnage.

3. Air freight _____ often exceed competing surface rates by a factor of 10 to 15.

4. Driven by the global sourcing of products and components, the emerging economies in Asia, especially _____, have strongly developed their manufacturing industries over the past decades.

Ⅲ. Translate the following sentences into Chinese.

1. While the North Atlantic market dominated the air freight industry until the 1970s, the centre of gravity has shifted to the Asia/Pacific region during the past three decades.

2. Machinery and transport equipment including capital equipment, automotive parts and tools account for another third.

Ⅳ. Translate the following paragraph into Chinese.

Global passenger air travel demand remained sluggish in 2021, but air freight demand recovered quickly. According to regular global air cargo data in April 2021, air freight demand continued to exceed pre-COVID-19 levels, with air cargo increasing 12% from April 2019. According to IATA data, the overall scale of China's air cargo market has been about 85 billion-90 billion yuan in recent years, ranking it as the second largest air cargo market in the world after the United State.

V. Answer the following questions.

1. How much does air cargo account for the global cargo trade value?

2. How much does air cargo account for global freight transport tonnage?

Section 2
Air Cargo Facilities

Current Status of All-Cargo Aircraft in China

At present, there are 173 *all-cargo aircraft* in China, accounting for only 4.5% of China's civil aviation transport aircraft fleet, while there are more than 550 all-cargo aircraft in the United States (Figure 4-4). There are 10 airlines of all-cargo aircraft, compared with 55 airlines, the share is very small. The number of all-cargo aircraft grew slowly, with a total of 49 increasing in the previous years of the 13*th Five-Year Plan*, accounting for 40% of the original forecast of the 13th Five-Year Plan. The *belly hold of passenger aircraft* accounted for two thirds of the air cargo volume and only one third of the all-cargo aircraft. There are great differences in international and domestic routes, in international routes, Chinese bell hold of passenger aircraft capacity is 49%, in domestic routes, the bell hold of passenger aircraft accounted for 82%, the amount of air all-cargo aircraft in the market is small.

Figure 4-4 All-cargo aircraft

Special Terms

1. Bulk cargo: Loose cargo, not unitized, not loaded in containers or on pallets.
散货:松散的货物,未成组,未装入集装箱或集装板上。
2. Unit Load Device (ULD): Term commonly used when referring to containers, pallets and pallet nets.
集装设备:指集装箱、集装板和集装板网罩的术语。
3. Combi aircraft: An airplane configured to carry both passengers and unitized cargo on the main deck.
康比型飞机:可在飞机主舱上同时运载乘客和成组货物的飞机。

Text

Modern Airport Cargo Terminal

Airport cargo terminals are similar to post office sorting offices. They are automated with a minimum of *supervision* and organized to process freight by computer. The *facilities* are capable of sorting materials that require special treatment. Live animals are kept in cages and *perishable* goods in cold or *refrigerated* stores. Dangerous goods such as explosives, corrosives, flammable and toxic materials are carried regularly but are subject to *rigorous* controls.

Full automation in the huge cargo center operated by Lufthansa at Frankfurt Airport means that over 4,500 items can be handled per hour by only 24 men. Goods and mail in a steady stream pass through import and export sections, each *oversee*n by a separate customs department. The processes, including receiving, routing, *stack*ing while awaiting shipment, recalling and dispatching for loading, are controlled with minimum supervision by electronics. Computers keep automatic track of every packet that enters the terminal complex.

A terminal for temporary storage and customs examination will be provided by airport controlling authorities. A cargo terminal has a *landside* where exporters/importers or their agents deliver or collect consignments, and an *airside* where an airline or an authorized aircraft handling company delivers loads to or collects loads from the aircraft (Figure 4-5).

Figure 4-5 Airside

Notes 1

❶ Airport cargo terminals are similar to post office sorting offices. They are automated with a minimum of supervision and organized to process freight by computer.

解释:机场货站类似邮局分拣。它们是自动化的,需要最少的监督,并通过计算机处理货物。

语法:be similar to…与……相似。

❷ The processes, including receiving, routing, stacking while awaiting shipment, recalling and dispatching for loading, are controlled with minimum supervision by electronics.

解释:这些过程,包括接收、按路线发送、堆码等待托运、召回及派送装载,都由电子设备在最低限度的监督下进行控制。

语法:在 while 引导的时间状语从句中,其谓语动词只能是延续性的,而且也只能与主句中的谓语动词同时发生或存在。

❸ A cargo terminal has a landside where exporters/importers or their agents deliver or collect consignments, and an airside where an airline or an authorized aircraft handling company delivers loads to or collects loads from the aircraft.

解释:货站有一个陆侧,出口商/进口商或其代理人在陆侧交付或收取货物;还有一个空侧,航空公司或经授权的飞机装卸公司在空侧向飞机交付货物或从飞机收取货物。

an authorized aircraft handling company 可以理解为航空公司的地面操作代理人。

语法:where 引导定语从句时,其作为关系副词,在定语从句中作地点状语,且其前有一个表示地点的先行词"an airside"。此时,where 也可以转换成"介词 + which"的结构。请注意,where 引导的定语从句只能位于主句之后或句中,不能位于句首。

Aircraft and ULDs

Conventional aircraft operating passenger service can carry several tons of cargo in holds under the floor of the passenger cabin. Packages are individually loaded and secured in the holds. The various shapes and sizes require a team of men to work often in very *confined* areas.

The new generation of *wide-bodied aircraft* is designed to carry large loads of passengers, mail and cargo. One feature is a change in the concept of the aircraft's loading facilities to avoid long periods of loading and unloading on the ground. This change is commonly referred to as using *Unit Load Device*s or ULDs, which form parts of the aircraft's standard operating equipment and are sized to fit the aircraft (Figure 4-6). They are filled in a cargo terminal by airlines or an authorized agent and then positioned and secured in the *aircraft's hold*.

Cargo *consignments* are assembled on large *pallets*. The whole assembly is bound by *stoutnetting* to prevent internal movement in transit. Bulky consignments are loaded in large containers. *Mechanized rollers* carry the containers into the aircraft via a truck with a *mechanized roller* platform.

Air freight is carried on board all-cargo aircraft as well as in the lower deck compartments (also referred to as "belly hold") of passenger services. All-cargo aircraft are aircraft that have been converted to use the main cabin for the carriage of cargo. This is done almost exclusively by replacing the seats, and with equipment. Even though all-cargo aircraft only comprise around 8% of the global commercial jet fleet, they carry more than 50% of all cargo(Table 4-1). All-cargo aircraft are produced in many different *configurations*, and payload penalties may be experienced using converted aircraft or those with different engines. Weights may vary due to varying equipment or cargo doors.

Figure 4-6   ULDs

Top 10 most popular all-cargo aircraft   Table 4-1

Aircraft Type	In Service	On Order	Stored	Stored(%)
Boeing 757F	284	—	8	3
Boeing 767F	245	63	6	2
Boeing 737-300/400F	230	—	23	9
Boeing 747-400F	190	—	32	14
Airbus A300F	183	—	11	6
Boeing 777F	130	30	1	1
McDonnell Douglas MD-11F	120	—	21	15
Hyushin ll-76	104	6	30	22
Boeing 747-8F	74	14	1	1
Boeing 727F	48	—	36	43
Total above	1,608	113	169	10
Total jet fleet	1,945	127	252	11

The interchangeable passenger/freight aircraft, sometimes called a "combi", is designed so that whole blocks of seats *mount*ed on pallets, plus *galleys* can be re moved, and roller-equipped freight floors fitted in less than an hour(Figure 4-7).

Figure 4-7　Combi aircraft

Notes 2

❶ One feature is a change in the concept of the aircraft's loading facilities to avoid long periods of loading and unloading on the ground.

解释:其中一个特点是改变了飞机装载设施的概念,以避免在地面上进行长时间的装卸。

语法:动词不定式。

❷ Freighter aircraft are produced in many different configurations, and payload penalties may be experienced using converted aircraft or those with different engines. Weights may vary due to varying equipment or cargo doors.

解释:生产出的货机有许多不同的布局,使用改装飞机或使用不同发动机的飞机可能会导致业务载量的损失。飞机重量可能因设备或货舱门的不同而有所不同。Penalty:本意是惩罚,在这可以理解为损失或消耗。

语法:被动语态。

may 的用法:解释为"可以"时,表示许可;解释为"或许""也许"时,表示可能性,用于目的从句、用于让步从句。

❸ The interchangeable passenger/freight aircraft, sometimes called a "combi", is designed so that whole blocks of seats mounted on pallets, plus galleys can be removed, and roller-equipped freight floors fitted in less than an hour.

解释:这种可互换的客货两用飞机,有时被称为"组合型",其设计目的是在不到一小时的时间内拆除安装在托盘上的整座座椅和厨房,并安装有滚轴的货运地板。

语法:同位语。

Further Reading

Ranking of the World's Top 20 Freight Airports in 2018

International Airport Association (Airports Council International) reported that the top five global freight turn volume rankings were unchanged in 2018, with Hong Kong International Airport, Memphis International Airport, Shanghai Pudong Airport, Incheon Airport and Anchorage

Airport being all the top five cargo hub ports last year (Figure 4-8).

Rank 2018	Rank 2017	Airport City / Country or Area / Code	Cargo (Metric tonnes) (Loaded and unloaded)	% Change
1	1	Hong Kong, CN (HKG)	5,121,029	1.5
2	2	Memphis TN, US (MEM)	4,470,196	3.1
3	3	Shanghai, CN (PVG)	3,768,573	−1.5
4	4	Incheon, KR (ICN)	2,952,123	1.0
5	5	Anchorage AK, US (ANC)	2,806,743	3.5
6	6	Dubai, AE (DXB)	2,641,383	−0.5
7	7	Louisville KY, US (SDF)	2,623,019	0.8
8	9	Taipei, CN (TPE)	2,322,823	2.4
9	8	Tokyo, JP (NRT)	2,261,008	−3.2
10	13	Los Angeles CA, US (LAX)	2,209,850	2.4
11	16	Doha, QA (DOH)	2,198,308	8.8
12	12	Singapore, SG (SIN)	2,195,000	1.4
13	11	Frankfurt, DE (FRA)	2,176,387	−0.8
14	10	Paris, FR (CDG)	2,156,327	−1.8
15	14	Miami FL, US (MIA)	2,129,658	2.8
16	15	Beijing, CN (PEK)	2,074,005	2.2
17	18	Guangzhou, CN (CAN)	1,890,816	6.2
18	20	Chicago IL, US (ORD)	1,807,091	5.0
19	17	London, GB (LHR)	1,771,342	−1.3
20	19	Amsterdam, NL (AMS)	1,737,984	−2.7
		TOTAL	51,313,665	1.4

Figure 4-8　Ranking of the world's top 20 freight airports in 2018

In 2018, the turn volume of Rockford airport in the United States exceeded 250,000 tons, making it the fastest growing airport. This is due to the airport's e-commerce business for online retail giant Amazon (Figure 4-9).

Fastest-growing airports (handling orer 250,000 metric tonnes of air cargo)			
Rank	Airport	Cargo	% Change
1	Rockford Airport, USA	306,332	56.6
2	Nairobi Airport, Kenya	342,579	25.2
3	Liege Airport, Belgium	871,596	21.6
4	Xi'An Airport, China	312,639	20.3
5	Philadelphia Airport, USA	503,766	20.0

Figure 4-9　The five fastest-growing airports

New Words

supervision	[ˌsuːpəˈvɪʒn]	n. 监督；管理
facility	[fəˈsɪləti]	n. 设施；设备
perishable	[ˈperɪʃəbl]	adj. 易逝的；易腐烂的；易变质的

refrigerate	[rɪˈfrɪdʒəreɪt]	vt.使冷却；使变冷；冷藏
rigorous	[ˈrɪɡərəs]	adj.严格缜密的；严格的
oversee	[ˌəʊvəˈsiː]	vt.监督；监视
stack	[stæk]	n.堆栈；(通常指码放整齐的)一叠，一摞，一堆
conventional	[kənˈvenʃənl]	adj.依照惯例的；遵循习俗的
confined	[kənˈfaɪnd]	adj.受限制的；狭窄而围起来的
landside	[ˈlændsaɪd]	n.陆侧
airside	[ˈeəsaɪd]	n.空侧
consignment	[kənˈsaɪnmənt]	n.批；装运的货物；运送物
pallet	[ˈpælət]	n.托盘；平台；运货板
configuration	[kənˌfɪɡəˈreɪʃn]	n.(计算机的)配置；结构
mount	[maʊnt]	v.攀登；登上；准备；安排
galley	[ˈɡælɪ]	n.(船或飞机上的)厨房

Phrases & Expressions

all-cargo aircraft	全货机
13th Five-Year Plan	"十三五"规划
belly hold	腹舱
airport cargo terminal	机场货站
wide-bodied aircraft	宽体飞机
Unit Load Devices (ULDs)	集装器
aircraft's hold	飞机货舱
stoutnetting	粗网
mechanized rollers	机械滚轴

Exercises

Ⅰ. Translate the following terms into Chinese or English.

1. airside
2. belly hold
3. airport cargo terminal
4. aircraft's hold
5. 陆侧
6. 全货机
7. 宽体飞机
8. 集装器

II. Cloze.

(all-cargo/airside/landside/logistics/Unit Load Devices/perishable/combi)

1. Live animals are kept in cages and _____ goods in cold or refrigerated stores.

2. A cargo terminal has a _____ where exporters/importers or their agents deliver or collect consignments.

3. This change is commonly referred to as using _____, which form parts of the aircraft's standard operating equipment and are sized to fit the aircraft.

4. Even though _____ aircraft only comprise around 8% of the global commercial jet fleet, they carry more than 50% of all cargo.

5. The interchangeable passenger/freight aircraft, sometimes called a "_____".

III. Translate the following sentences into Chinese.

1. Full automation in the huge cargo center operated by Lufthansa at Frankfurt Airport means that over 4,500 items can be handled per hour by only 24 men.

2. Freighters are aircraft that have been converted to use the main cabin for the carriage of cargo. This is done almost exclusively by replacing the seats, and with equipment.

IV. Translate the following paragraph into Chinese.

The International Airport Association (Airports Council International) reported that the top five global freight volume rankings were unchanged in 2018, with Hong Kong International Airport, Memphis International Airport, Shanghai Pudong Airport, Incheon Airport and Anchorage Airport being all the top five cargo hub ports last year. In 2018, the throughput of Rockford airport in the United States exceeded 250,000 tons, making it the fastest growing airport. This is due to the airport's e-commerce business for online retail giant Amazon.

V. Answer the following questions.

1. What type of aircraft is capable of carrying cargo in the main cabin?

2. What are the several common forms of ULDs?

Section 3
Air Cargo Rates and Charges

Lead in

Freight Rates Rose During the Epidemic

Since 2020, COVID-19 has hit the global aviation market hard. Many countries and regions even have the *phenomenon* of "one hold is difficult to find". Air cargo volume and *freight rates* rose sharply, the air freight rates probably doubled compared to before the epidemic (Figure 4-10).

Figure 4-10 Air freight rates rose

Special Terms

1. Dimensional weight: It also knows as volume weight, which is a method to calculate the weight of light bubble goods in the transportation industry. Volume weight is the weight of the goods to be obtained by using the conversion formula.

尺寸重量:也称为体积重量,是运输行业内的一种计算轻泡货物重量的方法。体积重量是利用换算公式得出的货物重量。

2. Gross weight: It is the weight of the commodity itself plus the weight of the package.
毛重:是指商品本身的重量加包装物的重量。

3. Tare weight: It is the weight of the commodity packaging material (i.e. the weight of the transportation package), excluding the weight of the internal packaging material.
皮重:是指商品外包装材料的重量(即运输包装的重量),不包括内包装材料和衬垫物的重量。

Text

Deciding on a pricing policy for air freight presents airlines with many difficulties, because freight *consignments* vary greatly in shape, size and weight, and this must be taken into account in the price structure. Costs of documentation fixed for almost any size of consignments are generally much lower for large consignment than for small ones. Costs will also vary according to commodity type. Some items such as hazardous goods and valuable cargoes need special handling, which incurs extra costs. These costs must be recovered as far as possible from the shippers of this type of cargo. Freight consignments vary in *density*, so airlines must decide whether charging should be based on weight, on volume or on a mixture of two, with high-density cargoes charged on weight, and low-density ones on volume. The types of published rate available in most regulated air freight markets can be divided into the following categories.

Notes 1

❶ Costs of documentation fixed for almost any size of consignments are generally much lower for large consignment than for small ones.

解释:对于几乎任何规模的托运货物的固定文件成本,大型托运货物通常比小型托运货物低得多。

语法:比较级。than 用作连词的意思是"比",可指两个不同的人或物在同一方面进行比较,也可指同一个人或物在两个不同方面进行比较。

❷ Freight consignments vary in density, so airlines must decide whether charging should be based on weight, on volume or on a mixture of two, with high-density cargoes charged on weight, and low-density ones on volume.

解释:货物的密度不同,因此航空公司必须决定是根据重量、体积收费,还是按两种方式混合收费,即高密度货物按重量收费,低密度货物按体积收费。

low-density cargo:低密度货物,行业也称为"轻泡货物",它的收费一般按其体积重量来计算。

语法:with 引导的独立主格结构。在句子中做状语,表伴随、方式、原因、结果等。

General Cargo Rates(GCR)

The air freight rate structure is similar to the passenger fare structure in that there is a normal or basic price applicable to all commodities in all markets. This is called the general commodity rate. General commodity shipments are rated by weight. *Dimensional weight* is used if the shipment is of very low density. As the weight of a shipment increases, the per-pound rate decreases.

Notes 2

As the weight of a shipment increases, the per-pound rate decreases.

解释:随着托运货物重量的增加,每磅货物的费率就会下降。

per-pound rate:理解为每磅货物的费用,也称之为费率。

语法:as 引导时间状语从句,强调"同一时间"或"一先一后"。

Specific Commodity Rates(SCR)

Specific commodity rates are established for unusually *high-volume shipping* of certain products between certain cities, such as fish from *Alaska* to certain points in the continental United States. Specific commodity rates are offered for a vast number of commodities.

In most cases, specific commodity rates are lower than general commodity rates. They are subject to a minimum weight and may implement special conditions relating to minimum charges and density requirements.

> **Notes 3**
>
> They are subject to a minimum weight and may implement special conditions relating to minimum charges and density requirements.
> 解释：它们受到最低重量及可实施的与最低收费和密度要求相关的特殊条件的限制。
> 语法：subject to 作形容词用，是"受限于……""服从于……"的意思。
> subject to 作副词用，是"在……条件下""依照……"的意思。
> relating 是分词形式，可以作后置定语。说明 sth 和主语的主动关系。

Commodity Classification Rates/Class Rates (CCR)

Commodity classification rates, known as class rates, apply to particular commodities within or between certain *designated* areas. They are usually shown in terms of a percentage increase or reduction in the normal general cargo rates. Class rates are applicable to carriage of the following commodities:

1. live animals;
2. charges for animal stalls or container;
3. *valuable cargo*;
4. newspapers, magazines, *periodicals*, books, talking books for the blind;
5. baggage shipped as cargo;
6. human remains;
7. *automotive vehicles*.

Under class rates certain commodities are offered a discount (Table 4-2). For example, for baggage shipped as cargo, 50% of normal GCR will apply, and such baggage is subject to a minimum charge for 10kg.

CCR example   Table 4-2

Type of Goods	IATA Area (see Rule 1.2.2. "Definitions of Areas")					
	Within 1	Within 2	Within 3	Between 1&2	Between 2&3	Between 3&1
All live animals except Baby poultry less than 72 hours old	175% of normal GCR	175% of normal GCR	150% of normal GCR	175% of normal GCR	150% of normal GCR	150% of normal GCR
Baby poultry less than 72 hours old	Normal GCR	Normal GCR	Normal GCR	Normal GCR	Normal GCR	Normal GCR

However, surcharged rates are applicable for many more commodities, such as live animals, human remains, valuable cargoes and etc (Figure 4-11).

Figure 4-11 Live animals

Notes 4

They are usually shown in terms of a percentage increase or reduction in the normal general cargo rates.

解释：它们通常根据普通货物运价附加或附减后的百分比来显示。

Bulk Unitization Rates(BUR)

BUR is the rate charged by carrier to shipper or freight forwarder on the basis of container or pallet (Figure 4-12). There are many types of containers designed for air freight, suitable for shipping quantities from 400 pounds to 5 tons. Some types are owned by the airline and made available to the shipper on request. Other types are purchased by shippers for regular use or rented from various sources. The charges for the consignments will consist of the minimum charge for the sector carried and the unit load device used. Airline-owned ULDs will be charged at the actual *gross weight* excluding the *tare weight* of the ULDs.

Figure 4-12 Container cargo

Notes 5

The charges for the consignments will consist of the minimum charge for the sector carried and the unit load device used.

解释：货物的费用包括运输航段的最低费用和集装器设备的使用费。

语法：consist of 意为"由……组成，构成"。

the sector carried 过去分词作定语，放在名词之后。

Minmum Charges

General cargo rates are usually *supplemented* by provisions for a minimum charge. This means that in most cases a shipper cannot be charged less than the appropriate rate of 4kg, even though his particular consignment may weigh less than this. On some routes minimum charges apply at higher weight of up to 8kg. There is considerable justification for the minimum charge principle, because the costs of documentation and customs clearance are fixed irrespective of consignment size.

Notes 6

There is considerable justification for the minimum charge principle, because the costs of documentation and customs clearance are fixed irrespective of consignment size.

解释：最低收费原则是有充分理由的，因为文件和清关的费用是固定的，与托运货物的规模大小无关。

语法：There be …句型表示的是"某处有(存在)某人或某物"，其结构为 There be (is, are, was, were) + 名词 + 地点状语。

Further Reading

Light Bubble Goods

Light bubble goods are also known as "light goods", "bubble" goods. In air transport, it refers to goods weighing less than 167kg per cubic meter. When the means of transportation loads light bubble goods, although its volume makes full use, the load capacity is wasted. Therefore, the freight charged for light bubble goods cannot be calculated according to its actual weight, and the volume is generally converted into weight according to a certain standard.

New Words

phenomenon	[fəˈnɒmɪnən]	n. 现象；杰出的人
consignments	[kənˈsaɪnmənts]	n. 装运的货物；运送物
density	[ˈdensəti]	n. 密集；稠密；密度；浓度
Alaska	[əˈlæskə]	n. 阿拉斯加州

Chapter 4　AIR CARGO

designate	[ˈdezɪgneɪt]	vt. 命名；指定；选定，指派，委任
periodical	[ˌpɪərɪˈɒdɪkl]	n. (学术)期刊
unitization	[juːnɪtaɪˈzeɪʃən]	n. 配套；使成套
supplement	[ˈsʌplɪmənt]	vt. 补充；增补
bubble	[ˈbʌbl]	n. 泡；气泡；肥皂泡
cubic	[ˈkjuːbɪk]	adj. 立方体的；立方的

Phrases & Expressions

one hold is difficult to find	一舱难求
freight rate	货物运价
cargo rate	货物运价
General Cargo Rates (GCR)	普通货物运价
dimensional weight	尺寸重量、体积重量
Specific Commodity Rates (SCR)	指定商品运价
high-volume shipping	大宗运输
Commodity Classification Rates / Class Rates (CCR)	等级商品运价
valuable cargo	贵重货物
automotive vehicle	车辆
Bulk Unitization Rates (BUR)	集装货物运价
gross weight	毛重
tare weight	皮重
light bubble goods	轻泡货物

Exercises

Ⅰ. Translate the following terms into Chinese or English.

1. light bubble goods
2. General Cargo Rates (GCR)
3. Class Rates (CCR)
4. freight rate
5. 毛重
6. 贵重货物
7. 指定商品运价
8. 体积重量

Ⅱ. Cloze.

(GCR/CCR/SCR/BUR/logistics/rates/weight)

1. With high-density cargoes charged on _____, and low-density ones on volume.

2. The _____ similar to the passenger fare structure in that there is a normal or basic price applicable to all commodities in all markets.

3. _____ are established for unusually high-volume shipping of certain products between certain cities.

4. _____ apply to particular commodities within or between certain designated areas. They are usually shown in terms of a percentage increase or reduction in the normal general cargo rates.

Ⅲ. Translate the following sentences into Chinese.

1. General cargo rates are usually supplemented by provisions for a minimum charge. This means that in most cases a shipper cannot be charged less than the appropriate rate of 4kg, even though his particular consignment may weigh less than this.

2. Under Class Rates certain commodities are offered a discount. For example, for baggage shipped as cargo, 50% of normal GCR will apply, and such baggage is subject to a minimum charge for 10kg.

Ⅳ. Translate the following paragraph into Chinese.

Light bubble goods are also known as "light goods", "bubble" goods. In air transport, it refers to goods weighing less than 167kg per cubic meter. When the means of transportation loads light bubble goods, although its volume makes full use, the load capacity is wasted. Therefore, the freight charged for light bubble goods cannot be calculated according to its actual weight, and the volume is generally converted into weight according to a certain standard.

Ⅴ. Answer the following questions.

1. Which types of cargo rates are generally composed of air published cargo rates?

2. How is CCR constituted?

Section 4
The Air Waybill

Lead in

Sichuan Logistics Open the Era of Electronic Freight

On September 17, 2020, Sichuan Airlines Logistics Cargonest 2.0 online freight platform was put into *trial* operation in Chengdu-Guangzhou/Beijing routes, simultaneously implementing the electronic waybill business (Figure 4-13). On September 16, with the online booking, electronic consignment declaration, electronic inspection, electronic security declaration and mobile assembly 5 steps complete electronic delivery process, 2 pieces/10kg, Chengdu to Guangzhou goods, complete the collection and *verification* of all electronic data. Sichuan logistics first *e-AWB*, marks Sichuan logistics open the era of electronic freight.

Figure 4-13 Online freight platform

Special Terms

1. Master air waybill: It is a transportation contract between the airline and the shipper or agent, and each air shipment has its own corresponding master air waybill.

航空主运单:是航空公司和托运人或代理人订立的运输合同,每一批航空运输的货物都有自己相对应的航空主运单。

2. House Air Waybill: It is the cargo receipt and delivery document signed by the consolidator and issued to each shipper.

航空分运单:是集运商签发给各托运人的货物收据及提货凭证。

3. Neutral Air Waybill: A standard air waybill without identification of issuing carrier.

航空中性运单:没有签发承运人识别标志的标准航空运单。

Text

The most important document in air cargo transportation is the *Air Waybill* (*AWB*). It is both a contract for transportation between a carrier and a shipper (or an agent for a shipper) and a receipt and delivery of the shipments. A cargo agent or airline *draws up* the contract by issuing an Air Waybill, the form of which is approved by the International Air Transport Association (IATA).

Notes 1

A cargo agent or airline draws up the contract by issuing an Air Waybill, the form of which is approved by the International Air Transport Association (IATA).

解释：货运代理或航空公司通过签发航空货运单来起草合同,其形式得到了国际航空运输协会(IATA)的批准。

The Functions of the AWB

- It confirms the transportation contract between the shipper and the agent, and between the agent and the airline.
- It confirms that goods have been accepted as an air cargo shipment. It is an important document for *customs clearance*.
- It is a receipt for payment of air cargo and insurance charges.
- It serves as the shipper's proof of ownership under Article 12 of the *Warsaw Convention*.
- In air freight, the air waybill also serves as *the bill of landing*.
- It defines the limits of the carrier's liability.

Notes 2

It confirms that goods have been accepted as an air cargo shipment. It is an important document for customs clearance.

解释：它确认货物已被接受为航空货物来进行运输。这是一个重要的通关文件。

The AWB Number

The AWB number is the identification of each *consignment*. It comprises three parts: a three-digit *prefix* identifying the carrier, the main portion identifying the consignment, and the last check digit for accounting and security purposes.

Some Rules About the AWB

Usually, an air waybill is *non-negotiable*, that is, the goods must be sent to the *consignee* titled in the air waybill.

Each shipment has an air waybill. For consolidated shipments, individual air waybills, called the *house air waybills* (*HAMB*), are also combined into a *master air waybill* (*MAWB*).

Each air waybill may have over ten copies (Figure 4-14). They are sent to the shipper, the *consignees*, and various departments (e.g., cargo section, accounting section, warehouse, etc.) of the carrier of goods. The first three copies are classified as originals. The copy marked "Original 3" is given to the shipper and serves as proof of receipt of the goods and documentary evidence of carrier's and shipper's signature to the contract of carriage. "Original 1" is retained by the carrier issuing the AWB for accounting purposes and "Original 2" is to accompany consignment to the final destination and delivered to the consignee as the basis for the receipt.

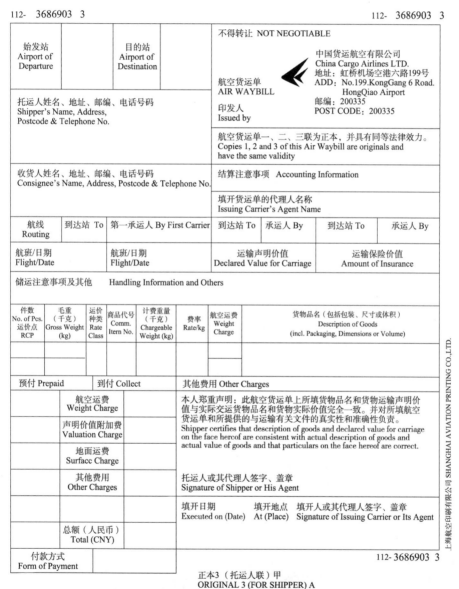

Figure 4-14 AWB blank specimen

The *consignor* is responsible for the accuracy of the contents of the Air Waybill and is liable to any person for any loss or damage caused by its *irregularity*, incorrectness or incompleteness.

An AWB is called a *neutral* AWB if the air carrier is not specified in the air waybill.

Notes 3

❶ For consolidated shipments, individual air waybills, called the house air waybills, are also combined into a master air waybill.

解释：对于集运运输，单独的航空货运单（称为航空分运单），也要被合并到航空主运单中。

❷ The copy marked "Original 3" is given to the shipper and serves as proof of receipt of the goods and documentary evidence of carrier's and shipper's signature to the contract of carriage.

解释：标有"正本3"的复印本交给托运人，作为收到货物的证明，以及承运人和托运人签署运输合同的书面证明。

House Air Wawbill (HAWB)

The House Air Waybill (HAWB) is an air waybill issued by a *centralized* shipper (*Consolidators*) for a centralized consignment business (Figure 4-15). In the case of centralized shipping, in addition to the airline issuing of the MAWB, the consolidator will also issue the HAWB. The HAWB acts as the transportation contract between the shipper A, B, C and the consolidator; While the MAWB acts as a cargo transportation contract between the airline and the consolidator, the parties are the consolidator and the airline, and the shippers have no direct contractual relationship with the airline. In addition, since a large number of *bulk cargoes* at the origin are delivered to the airline after being combined or integrated by the consolidator, and the consolidator or its agent picks up the cargoes from the airline or airport cargo office at the destination, and then transfers them to the consignee, there is no direct cargo *hand-over* relationship between the consignee and the airline.

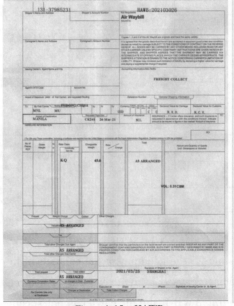

Figure 4-15 HAWB

Notes 4

❶ The HAWB acts as the transportation contract between the shipper A, B, C and the consolidator; While the MAWB acts as a cargo transportation contract between the airline and the consolidator, the parties are the consolidator and the airline, and the shippers have no direct contractual relationship with the airline.

解释：航空分运单作为集运商与托运人之间的货物运输合同,合同双方分别为托运人 A、B、C 和集运商;而航空主运单作为航空公司与集运商之间的货物运输合同,当事人则为集运商和航空公司,托运人与航空公司没有直接的契约关系。

shipper A, B, C:托运人 A、B、C,也可以理解为货主 A、B、C。

❷ In addition, since a large number of bulk cargoes at the origin are delivered to the airline after being combined or integrated by the consolidator, and the consolidator or its agent picks up the cargoes from the airline or airport cargo office at the destination, and then transfers them to the consignee, there is no direct cargo handover relationship between the consignee and the airline.

解释：除此之外,由于在始发地大量散货由集运商拼单或整合后交付给航空公司,在目的地由集运商或其代理从航空公司或机场货运处提取货物,再转交至收货人,因而收货人与航空公司也没有直接的货物交接关系。

Further Reading

e-AWB

Electronic freight transportation is one of the specific measures of IATA to *simplify business*, and it is also the mainstream development trend of air freight at home and abroad. e-AWB is the most core and fundamental application form of e-commerce in the field of air freight (Figure 4-16). Compared with the traditional paper waybill, electronic waybill can not only save paper waybill in manufacturing, transportation, storage and management, can also provide more accurate and timely waybill data, avoid key information is malicious tampering, reduce data *redundancy*, to improve the efficiency of freight business and speed up the internationalization of enterprise process.

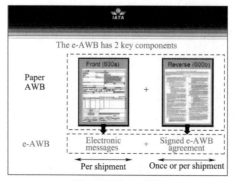

Figure 4-16　e-AWB

New Words

trial	[ˈtraɪəl]	v. 试验；试用
verification	[ˌvɛrɪfɪˈkeɪʃən]	n. 检验，检查，审核；验收
consignment	[kənˈsaɪnmənt]	n. 批；装运的货物
prefix	[ˈpriːfɪks]	n. 前缀
negotiable	[nɪˈɡəʊʃɪəbl]	adj. 可商议的；流通的；可转让的
consignee	[ˌkɒnsaɪˈniː]	n. 收货人；受托人；承销人；代售人
consignor	[kənˈsaɪnə]	n. 发货人，委托人，寄售人，托运人
irregularity	[ɪˌreɡjəˈlærəti]	n. 不合乎常规的行为；不正常的做法
neutral	[ˈnjuːtrəl]	adj. 中立的；中性的
centralized	[ˈsentrəlaɪzd]	v. 集权控制；实行集中
consolidator	[kənˈsɒlɪdeɪtə]	n. 集运人；集装箱集装承运商
hand-over	[ˈhændˈəʊvə(r)]	n.（权力、责任等的）移交，移交期
redundancy	[rɪˈdʌndənsɪ]	n. 冗余；多余

Phrases & Expressions

e-AWB	电子航空货运单
Air Waybill (AWB)	航空货运单
draws up	起草
customs clearance	通关
Warsaw Convention	华沙公约
the bill of landing	提单
house air waybill (HAWB)	航空分运单
master air waybill (MAWB)	航空主运单
bulk cargo	散装货
simplify business	商务简化

Exercises

Ⅰ. Translate the following terms into Chinese or English.

1. consignee
2. consignor
3. Air Waybill (AWB)
4. HAWB
5. 散装货
6. 航空主运单
7. 电子航空货运单

8. 集运商

II. Cloze.

(Master Air Waybill/House Air Waybill/landing/platform/Air Waybill/non-negotiable)

1. The most important document in air cargo transportation is the _____. It is both a contract for transportation between a carrier and a shipper (or an agent for a shipper) and a receipt and delivery of the shipments.

2. In air freight, the air waybill also serves as the bill of _____.

3. Usually, an air waybill is _____, that is, the goods must be sent to the consignee titled in the air waybill.

4. The _____ is an air waybill issued by a centralized shipper (consolidators) for a centralized consignment business.

III. Translate the following sentences into Chinese.

1. "Original 1" is retained by the carrier issuing the AWB for accounting purposes and "Original 2" is to accompany consignment to the final destination and delivered to the consignee as the basis for the receipt.

2. In the case of centralized shipping, in addition to the airline issuing of the MAWB, the consolidator will also issue the HAWB.

IV. Translate the following paragraph into Chinese.

Electronic freight transportation is one of the specific measures of IATA to simplify business, and it is also the mainstream development trend of air freight at home and abroad. E-AWB is the most core and fundamental application form of e-commerce in the field of air freight. Compared with the traditional paper waybill, electronic waybill can not only save paper waybill in manufacturing, transportation, storage and management, can also provide more accurate and timely waybill data, avoid key information is malicious tampering, reduce data redundancy, to improve the efficiency of freight business and speed up the internationalization of enterprise process.

V. Answer the following questions.

1. How many "originals" does the AWB have?

2. Who issued the transport document of the HAWB?

Chapter 5
AIRPORT

Section 1
Hub Airport

Lead in

Logistics Hub Takes Off at Qingdao New Airport

The newly opened Qingdao Jiaodong International Airport has *injected tremendous vitality* into the logistics industry in surrounding areas, local media reported. Construction of the Jiaodong Airport Economic Demonstration Zone, which will become a new development engine in the Jiaodong Economic Circle area, is being accelerated.

The zone, which aims to become a world-class intelligent aviation hub, will foster a diversified and integrated airport economy featuring industries for modern logistics, aviation, high-tech manufacturing and others.

The airport will also help Qingdao play a bigger role in the Belt and Road Initiative and give full play to the China-Shanghai Cooperation Organization Demonstration Zone for Local Economic and Trade Cooperation in Jiaozhou (Figure 5-1).

Figure 5-1　Qingdao Jiaodong International Airport

Special Terms

1. Scale economy effect: The increase of economic benefit caused by the change of economic scale.

规模经济效益:是指由于经济规模的变动所引起的经济效益的提高。

2. Traffic rights: The power of transnational air transport, known by international practice as "air freedom". The concept of "Traffic rights" originated in the *Chicago Convention* in 1944. It is also known as the "freedom of the air" right. The essence of the opening of traffic rights is the liberalization of air transport.

航权:是指跨国航空运输的权力,按国际惯例被称为"空中自由"。"航权"的概念起源于1944年签订的《芝加哥公约》,亦称之为"空中自由"权。航权开放的实质就是航空运输自由化。

3. Economic demonstration zone: The zone taking the airport as the geographical center, taking the development of aviation industry as the core includes leading industries and related industries. Leading industry are: transportation industry, civil aviation comprehensive service industry; Related industries consists of supporting services, traditional manufacturing, logistics, business catering, residential development and high-tech industries.

临空经济区:是以机场为地理中心,以发展临空产业(包括先导产业和相关产业)为核心的区域。先导产业有:运输业(客运、货运)、民航综合服务业;相关产业包括配套服务、传统的制造业、物流配送、商务餐饮、住宅开发和高新技术产业等。

4. China's Belt and Road Initiative (BRI): The strategy initiated by the People's Republic of China that seeks to connect Asia with Africa and Europe via land and maritime networks with the aim of improving regional integration, increasing trade and stimulating economic growth.

中国的"一带一路"倡议(BRI):是由中华人民共和国发起的一项倡议,通过陆地和海洋构筑亚洲与非洲、欧洲的联系网,旨在促进区域一体化、增加贸易和推动经济增长。

Text

Hub airport refers to a civil airport with a relatively large international and domestic flight *density*, where passengers and cargo can easily transfer in this airport.

The hub airport is able to provides an efficient, convenient and inexpensive service, so airlines and passengers tend to choose it as route destination or transit port. Hub airport is able to promote the development of not only national economic, but also civil aviation industry.

Notes 1

The hub airport is able to provides an efficient, convenient and inexpensive service, so airlines and passengers tend to choose it as route destination or transit port.

枢纽机场能够提供高效、便捷、廉价的服务,因此航空公司和旅客更倾向于选择该类机场作为航线目的地或中转港。

Classification of Hub Airports

In terms of function, the hub airport can be divided into three *categories*: ① the regional hub airport, is the *intersection* center of various domestic airlines; ② the international hub airport, is the *intersection* center of domestic and foreign airlines; ③ the *complex* hub airport, combined with the *characteristics* of the regional hub airport and the international hub airport, serves as a regional portal and an international hub. China's current hub airport system can be summarized as follow (Table 5-1).

China's hub airport system Table 5-1

Type	The Airport	Function
International hub airport	Beijing Capital Airport, Shanghai Pudong Airport, Guangzhou Baiyun Airport	To enhance the competitiveness of international hubs
Complex hub airport	Urumqi Diwopu Airport, KunMing Changshui Airport, Harbin Taiping Airport, Shanghai Hongqiao Airport, Chengdu Shuangliu Airport, Xi'an Xianyang Airport, Shenzhen Bao'an Airport, Chongqing Jiangbei Airport	To strengthen the link in international and regional carriage
Regional hub airport	Tianjin Binhai Airport, Hangzhou Xiaoshan Airport, Wuhan Tianhe Airport, Changsha Huanghua Airport, Dalian Zhoushuizi Airport, Hohhot Baita Airport, Shenyang Taoxian Airport, Changchun Longjia Airport, Xiamen Gaoqi Airport, Nanjing Lukou Airport, Qingdao Liuting Airport (closed in 2021), Fuzhou Changle Airport, Jinan Yaoqiang Airport, Sanya Phoenix Airport, Nanchang Changbei Airport, Wenzhou Yongqiang Airport, Xining Caojiapu Airport, Ningbo Lishe Airport, Lanzhou Zhongchuan Airport, Hefei Xinqiao Airport, Nanning Caojiabao Airport, Guilin Liangjiang Airport, Haikou Meilan Airport, Zhengzhou Xinzheng Airport, Guiyang Longdongbao Airport, Lasa Gonggar Airport, Yinchuan Hedong Airport, Taiyuan Wusu Airport, Shijiazhuang Zhengding Airport	To play the role of the core hub of a specific region

Role of the Hub Airport

1. Adapt to air transportation demand. The hub airport *undertakes* most of the aviation transportation, making the air route network between cities more smooth. The convenient transport mode further *stimulates* the market demand.

Notes 2

① The complex hub airport, combined with the characteristics of the regional hub airport and the international hub airport, serves as a regional portal and an international hub.

解释：结合区域枢纽机场和国际枢纽机场二者的特性，兼具地区门户作用及国际枢纽作用。

combine with：与……结合；serve as：担任……，充当……；起……的作用。

❷ Adapt to air transportation demand. The hub airport undertakes most of the aviation transportation, making the air route network between cities more smooth. The convenient transport mode further stimulates the market demand.

解释：能够适应运输市场需求。枢纽机场承担了大部分的航空需求，使城市间的空中航线网络变得更加通畅，便利的运输模式又进一步刺激了市场需求。

adapt to：适应。

2. Improve the efficiency of airport operation. The broad market *coverage* can better play the *scale economy effect* and density effect of the hub airport, and thus greatly increase the airport's business volume, improve the *utilization* rate of the airport, reduce the unit cost, and increase the income.

Notes 3

The broad market coverage can better play the scale economy effect and density effect of the hub airport, and thus greatly increase the airport's business volume, improve the utilization rate of the airport, reduce the unit cost, and increase the income.

解释：广阔的市场覆盖率可以更好地发挥枢纽机场的规模经济效益和密度效益，从而大大增加机场的业务量，提高机场的利用率，降低单位成本，增加收入。

语法：play 意为"发挥作用"，等同于"play a role in / play a part in"。

3. Promote cooperation between airlines. Since the hub airport flight transfer is generally operated by two airlines, the two sides can form into *strategic alliances* and represent each other for local sales and services, which improves the *operation efficiency* of the airport, attracts more passengers and obtains higher benefits.

4. Provide convenient travel for passengers. For passengers who stop or transfer, after completing the check-in at the departure airport, there is no need to check-in again during the stop or transit at the hub airport, which is more time-saving and efficient.

Notes 4

❶ Since the hub airport flight transfer is generally operated by two airlines, the two sides can form into strategic alliances and represent each other for local sales and services, which improves the operation efficiency of the airport, attracts more passengers and obtains higher benefits.

解释：由于枢纽机场中转一般是由两个航空公司运营，双方可以结为战略联盟，互相代理在当地的销售和服务，从而提高机场的运营效率，吸引更多旅客，获取更高的效益。

since：由于，因为。

❷ For passengers who stop or transfer, after completing the check-in at the departure airport, there is no need to check-in again during the stop or transit at the hub airport, which is more time-saving and efficient.

解释：对于经停或中转的旅客，其在始发机场办理完登机手续之后，在枢纽机场经停或中转时，无须重新办理登机手续，出行更加省时、高效。

语法：(1) there is no need to do sth 没有必要去做……

(2) which 引导非限制性定语从句，前句 "there is no need to check-in again during the stop or transit at the hub airport" 做补充说明。

Construction Conditions of the Hub Airport

1. Strategic location. The location of the airport should *facilitate* the *air route network*. It should take into account *the economy of the voyage*, the *potential* development market, and the future development strategy.

2. Enormous demand for air transportation. The location of the hub airport should meet the demand of airline passenger and cargo transportation.

3. Complete airport Infrastructures. Hub airport facilities need to include multiple runways flight areas, reasonable transfer facilities, advanced flight information systems, and related supporting services, etc.

4. Strong airlines. The main performance is *sufficient capacity*, *reasonable fleet structure*, dense route network, with strong domestic and foreign airlines partners.

5. Cooperation and coordination among related departments. It includes the close cooperation between the hub airport, base airline, air traffic control, customs, border *inspection* and other departments.

Notes 5

❶ It should take into account the economy of the voyage, the potential development market, and the future development strategy.

解释：既要考虑航程的经济性，又要考虑到潜在的发展市场，还要与未来的发展战略相联系。

take into account：考虑；重视；体谅。

❷ The location of the airport should facilitate the air route network. It should take into account the economy of the voyage, the potential development market, and the future development strategy.

解释：机场的位置应当有利于航路网络的建设。它既要考虑航程的经济性，又要考虑到潜在的发展市场，还要与未来的发展战略相联系。

❸ The main performance is sufficient capacity, reasonable fleet structure, dense route network, with strong domestic and foreign airlines partners.

解释：主要表现在运力充足，机队结构合理，航线网络密集，拥有实力雄厚的国内外航空公司合作伙伴。

In the 21st century, the air transportation industry in the United States, Europe, Asia and other countries has developed rapidly, and each has its own characteristics and advantages in the planning and operation of hub airports. From the *perspective* of *passenger throughput*, the scale of China's hub airports have a certain *competitiveness*. However, China's hub airports still need to be improved in terms of route network richness, route competitiveness and shortest transit time.

Notes 6

❶ From the perspective of passenger throughput, the scale of China's hub airports have a certain competitiveness.

解释:从旅客吞吐量来看,我国枢纽机场的规模具有一定的竞争力。

from the perspective of:从……的角度。

❷ However, China's hub airports still need to be improved in terms of route network richness, route competitiveness and shortest transit time.

解释:我国枢纽机场在航线网络丰富性、航线竞争力、最短中转时间等方面仍需改进。

in terms of:在……方面。

Further Reading

The Opening of Air Freedoms is the Premise of the Hub Airport

Under the background of globalization and liberalization, air transportation deregulation has become an irreversible trend. Air freedoms opening is the premise and necessary condition of the construction of hub airport, especially the fifth and sixth traffic rights opening. It is mainly because the fifth traffic rights "extension right" and the sixth traffic rights "bridge right" can bring more transit opportunities for passengers and cargo, can construct more complete international route network for airlines, especially base airlines. The opening of traffic rights is conducive to the introduction of foreign airlines, increasing aviation business and expand airport capacity. At the same time, the capacity of air traffic control will be enhanced, and the related aviation information, jet fuel supply and aircraft maintenance industry will also be developed in a coordinated manner. The number and extent of the navigation rights will ultimately determine the scale and nature of the hub airport (Figure 5-2).

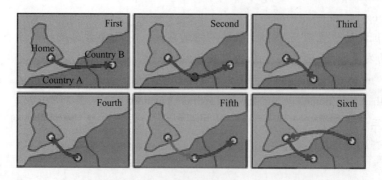

Figure 5-2

Chapter 5　AIRPORT

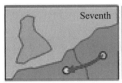 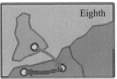 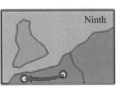

Figure 5-2　The classification of air freedoms

New Words

inject	[ɪnˈdʒekt]	vt.	注入；注射
tremendous	[trəˈmendəs]	adj.	极大的，巨大的；惊人的；极好的
vitality	[vaɪˈtæləti]	n.	活力，生气；生命力，生动性
density	[ˈdensəti]	n.	密度
category	[ˈkætəɡɔːri]	n.	种类，分类
intersection	[ˌɪntərˈsekʃən]	n.	交叉；十字路口；交集；交叉点
complex	[kəmˈpleks]	adj.	复杂的
		n.	复合体；综合设施
characteristic	[ˌkærəktəˈrɪstɪk]	n.	特性，特征；特色
undertake	[ˌʌndərˈteɪk]	vt.	承担，保证；从事；同意；试图
stimulate	[ˈstɪmjʊleɪt]	vt.	刺激，激励
		vi.	起促进作用
coverage	[ˈkʌvərɪdʒ]	n.	覆盖，覆盖范围；新闻报道
utilization	[ˌjuːtɪlaɪˈzeɪʃən]	n.	利用，使用
facilitate	[fəˈsɪlɪteɪt]	vt.	促进；帮助；使容易
voyage	[ˈvɔɪɪdʒ]	n.	航行
		vi.	航行
		vt.	飞过；渡过
potential	[pəˈtenʃl]	adj.	潜在的，可能的
		n.	潜能，可能性
sufficient	[səˈfɪʃnt]	adj.	足够的；充分的
fleet	[fliːt]	n.	舰队，车队
inspection	[ɪnˈspekʃən]	n.	视察，检查
perspective	[pərˈspektɪv]	n.	观点；远景；透视图
		adj.	透视的
throughput	[ˈθruːpʊt]	n.	（某一时期内的）生产量，吞吐量
competitiveness	[kəmˈpetətɪvnəs]	n.	竞争力，好竞争
mismatch	[ˌmɪsˈmætʃ]	vt.	使混搭
		n.	错配；不匹配，不协调
orientation	[ˌɔːriənˈteɪʃnl]	n.	方向；定向；适应；情况介绍

Phrases & Expressions

scale economy effect	规模经济效益
operation efficiency	运行效率
strategic alliances	战略联盟
air route network	航线网络
the economy of the voyage	航程经济性
sufficient capacity	运力充足
reasonable fleet structure	机队结构合理
passenger throughput	客运吞吐量

Exercises

Ⅰ. Translate the following terms into Chinese or English.

1. scale economy effect
2. operation efficiency
3. reasonable fleet structure
4. continuous development
5. transit port
6. 民航业
7. 广阔的市场覆盖
8. 战略联盟
9. 运力充足
10. 客运吞吐量

Ⅱ. Cloze.

(stimulates/combined with/mismatch/tend to/undertakes)

1. The key to solve the problem of demand and capacity _____ lies in defining the function orientation of hub airports.

2. The hub airport is able to provides an efficient, convenient and inexpensive service, so airlines and passengers _____ choose it as route destination or transit port.

3. The hub airport _____ most of the aviation transportation, making the air route network between cities more smooth.

4. The convenient transport mode further _____ the market demand.

5. The complex hub airport, _____ the characteristics of the regional hub airport and the international hub airport, serves as a regional portal and an international hub.

Ⅲ. Translate the following sentences into Chinese.

1. The broad market coverage can better play the scale economy effect and density effect of the hub airport, and thus greatly increase the airport's business volume, improve the utilization rate of the airport, reduce the unit cost, and increase the income.

2. The location of the airport should facilitate the air route network. It should take into account the economy of the voyage, the potential development market, and the future development strategy.

3. The main performance is sufficient capacity, reasonable fleet structure, dense route network, with strong domestic and foreign airlines partners.

IV. Translate the following paragraph into Chinese.

In the 21st century, the air transportation industry in the United States, Europe, Asia and other countries has developed rapidly, and each has its own characteristics and advantages in the planning and operation of hub airports. From the perspective of passenger throughput, the scale of China's hub airports have a certain competitiveness. However, China's hub airports still need to be improved in terms of route network richness, route competitiveness and shortest transit time.

V. Answer the following questions.
1. What is hub airport?

2. Please state the role of hub airport.

3. What is construction conditions of the hub airport?

Section 2
Regional Airport

Lead in

The Development of Regional Airport in China

On March 15, the Civil Aviation Administration of China (CAAC) held a press conference. A reporter mentioned the support measures that the CAAC proposed to develop regional aviation in third and fourth tier cities. The regional aviation is an important part of the civil aviation transport service network. During the 13th Five-Year Plan period, regional aviation has achieved good development. In the 14th Five-Year Plan period, Civil Aviation Administration of China will pay more attention to the development of regional aviation. Through the construction the air transport network, expand network coverage, meet the air travel needs of the people in the area where small and medium-sized airports are located, and serve the local economic and social development (Figure 5-3).

Figure 5-3   Regional airport I

Special Terms

1. The Civil Aviation Administration of China (CAAC): A national bureau under The State Council of the People's Republic of China, which is in charge of civil aviation.

中国民用航空局(简称中国民航局或民航局,英文缩写CAAC):中华人民共和国国务院主管民用航空事业的且由部委管理的国家局(归交通运输部管理)。

2. The Five-Year Plan: The Outline of the Five-Year Plan for National Economic and Social Development of China, is an important part of China's national economic plan and also a long-term plan. Currently, China is implementing its 14th Five-Year Plan (2021-2025).

五年规划:全称为中华人民共和国国民经济和社会发展五年计划纲要,是中国国民经济计划的重要部分,属长期计划。中国正在实施第十四个五年计划(2021—2025年)。

Text

Regional airport is not only an important part of the transportation airport, but also an important basic platform to realize the regional aviation transportation. Strengthening the construction of regional machinery can not only improve China's transportation network, but also be *consistent* with the growing demand for *passenger flow* and *cargo flow*. It is also an important way to achieve a civil aviation power.

Notes 1

❶ Strengthening the construction of regional machinery can not only improve China's transportation network, but also be consistent with the growing demand for passenger flow and cargo flow.

解释:强化支线机物的建设不仅能够完善我国交通运输网络,而且可以满足日益增长的客流和物流需求。

语法:Not only...but also...用于连接两个表示并列关系的成分,意思是"不仅……而且……";be consistent with 与……一致,符合。

❷ It is also an important way to achieve a civil aviation power.

解释:这也是实现民航强国的重要途径。

In China, the regional airport is defined from three aspects: *annual passenger throughput*, *take-off and landing aircraft type* and *range of direct flight*, that is, annual passenger throughput is not higher than 2 million, short-range takeoff and landing aircraft and direct flight range of 800~1500km.

Notes 2

In China, the regional airport is defined from three aspects: annual passenger throughput, take-off and landing aircraft type and range of direct flight, that is, annual passenger throughput is not higher than 2 million, short-range takeoff and landing aircraft and direct flight range of 800~1500km.

解释:在我国,支线机场是从年旅客吞吐量、起降飞机类型和直达航班航程范围3个方面来进行定义的,即:年旅客吞吐量不高于200万人次、起降短程飞机、直达航班在800~1500km范围内。

that is:即;就是说;换言之。

Function

1. Improve the overall transportation network. The construction of regional airports means that the *connectivity* between different regions is improved. By opening a certain number of routes, we can make up for the shortage of ground transportation. In addition, the ground transportation cannot provide remote and rapid services of the fresh and agricultural products, while regional airport can achieve it.

2. Gather regional high-quality resources. As the *distribution center* of regional passengers and cargo, the regional airport can concentrate and transport a large number of people and goods

to other regions. It also can gather a large number of high-quality resources, such as talents, resources, information and technology, which is helpful to strengthen regional *competitiveness*.

3. Increase employment opportunities. The construction of the regional airport has increased the demand for labor in the surrounding industry, commerce and service industry. *In the meantime*, it has promoted the transfer of farmers to industries, services and other industries.

Notes 3

❶ In addition, the ground transportation cannot provide remote and rapid services of the fresh and agricultural products, while regional airport can achieve it.

解释：此外，地面交通无法提供远距离快速服务的生鲜、农产品市场得以开拓。

❷ As the distribution center of regional passengers and cargo, the regional airport can concentrate and transport a large number of people and goods to other regions.

解释：支线机场作为区域旅客以及货物的集散中心，能把大量人和货物集中并分运到其他地区。

❸ The construction of the regional airport has increased the demand for labor in the surrounding industry, commerce and service industry.

解释：支线机场配套设施建设和服务供给，能够创造更多的就业机会。

Current Situation

By the end of 2019, there were 238 *certified* transport airports in China and 165 regional airports with an annual passenger *throughput* of less than 2 million. According to the statistics of the *first navigation time* of regional airports (Table 5-2), 64 new regional airports have been added since *the 12th Five-Year Plan*, and the number of construction airports has increased rapidly. In 2019, the annual passenger throughput of Chinese airports exceeded 1.3 billion, but the regional airport passenger throughput only accounted for 13.21% of the total passenger throughput.

Number and proportion of new regional airports in China   Table 5-2

Term Time	before 1990	1991—2000	2001—2010	2011—2019
The Number of Additional Regional Airport	37	20	44	64
The Proportion of New Additions to the Total Number	22.6%	12.2%	26.8%	38.8%

Notes 4

❶ According to the statistics of the first navigation time of regional airports, 64 new regional airports have been added since the 12th Five-Year Plan, and the number of construction airports has increased rapidly.

解释：通过对支线机场首次通航时间统计，"十二五"以来新增通航支线机场64个，建设数量快速增长。

❷ In 2019, the annual passenger throughput of Chinese airports exceeded 1.3 billion, but the regional airport passenger throughput only accounted for 13.21% of the total passenger throughput.

解释:2019年我国机场全年旅客吞吐量超过13亿人次,但支线机场旅客吞吐量只占总旅客吞吐量的13.21%。

account for:占有,占……的百分比。

From 2011-2019, the *average annual growth rate* of regional airport passenger volume has been more than 10%, faster than the national average level, and *maintained a good growth trend*. However, one of the reasons for the rapid growth is the small original base, and the rapid overall growth does not *mask* the huge differences in individual development. Some cities have developed regional airports rapidly due to their unique resource conditions, or their relatively good economic level.

Notes 5

❶ However, one of the reasons for the rapid growth is the small original base, and the rapid overall growth does not mask the huge differences in individual development.

解释:然而,快速增长的原因之一是原有基数小,且总体增长快并不能掩盖个体发展的巨大差异。

❷ Some cities have developed regional airports rapidly due to their unique resource conditions, or their relatively good economic level.

解释:部分城市由于其资源条件得天独厚或经济水平相对较好,支线航空得以快速发展。

due to:由于;应归于。economic level:经济水平。

Since COVID-19 in 2020, regional airport has been affected much more than hub airport, mainly because the *epidemic* leads to serious excess capacity in the transportation field. For the eastern regions with developed transportation, the market of regional airport has been strongly impacted by *high-speed rail*. At the same time, for the western regions with rich tourism resources and relatively inconvenient ground transportation, *the depression of tourism* has made the local air transportation *lose the stable customers*. For example, Zhangjiajie Hehua Airport saw a 55.5% year-on-year drop in passenger capacity in 2020.

Notes 6

❶ Since COVID-19 in 2020, regional airport has been affected much more than hub airport, mainly because the epidemic leads to serious excess capacity in the transportation field.

解释:自2020年新型冠状病毒肺炎疫情以来,支线航空受到的影响比干线航班受到的影响大得多,主要原因是疫情导致交通领域的运力严重过剩。

❷ For the western regions with rich tourism resources and relatively inconvenient ground transportation, the depression of tourism has made the local air transportation lose the stable customers.

解释:对于旅游资源丰富且地面交通较为不便的西部地区而言,旅游业的萧条使得当地航运失去了稳定的客源。

Existing Problems

1. Uneven Distribution. Due to regional economy, natural environment and population distribution, the number of regional airports in eastern, central and northeast China is relatively high, while the western region is lower than the national level (Figure 5-4).

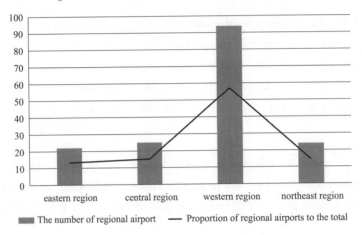

Figure 5-4　The coverage of China's regional airports in 2019

2. Poor Operating Conditions. In terms of total aviation business, the annual passenger throughput of 165 regional airports in 2019 reached 92.495 million, accounting for 6.8% of the national total. The annual cargo throughput was 17,5000 tons, accounting for 1% of the national total. The regional airports are far from enough to play a role in air passenger and cargo transportation.

A widely recognized standard in international civil aviation is introduced to determine the operating status of regional airports: whether the annual passenger throughput reaches 500,000, and if more than 500,000 it is considered to be *profitable*, otherwise it will be a loss. According to the above judgment method, in 2019, there were 95 regional airports below 500,000 person-times, accounting for 57.5% of the total regional airports in China. Due to the small business volume and low *revenue capacity*, together with high investment and cost of construction, operation and maintenance, the regional airports are facing great operating pressure (Figure 5-5).

Figure 5-5　Regional airport Ⅱ

Notes 7

❶ Due to regional economy, natural environment and population distribution, the number of regional airports in eastern, central and northeast China is relatively high, while the western region is lower than the national level.

解释：受区域经济、自然环境和人口分布影响，东部、中部和东北地区分布的支线机场数量较高，相反地，西部地区较低，并低于全国水平。

❷ The regional airports are far from enough to play a role in air passenger and cargo transportation.

解释：支线机场在航空客货运输方面发挥的效用还远远不够。

语法：far from 意为"远非，决不"，其后可接名词、动名词、形容词等。

❸ A widely recognized standard in international civil aviation is introduced to determine the operating status of regional airports: whether the annual passenger throughput reaches 500,000, and if more than 500,000 it is considered to be profitable, otherwise it will be a loss.

解释：引入国际民航中一个被广泛认同的标准来判断支线机场的运营状态：年旅客吞吐量是否达到 50 万人次，若超过 50 万人次即认为处于盈利状态，否则为亏损状态。

Further Reading

The Regional Airports in Yunnan

As a large tourism province, Yunnan enjoys a good reputation at home and abroad for its rich tourism resources, which also brings great opportunities for the development of air transport industry. In addition to Kunming Changshui International Airport, serving as a regional hub, there are 14 regional airports, including Xishuangbanna, Lijiang and Tengchong. Although these regional airports are still operating at a loss, they have achieved a full aviation coverage of Yunnan.

Local residents are more convenient to travel, and the tourists brought by flights also make a significant contribution to the local economic development, bringing the local *revenue* far more than the loss of airport operation.

Now, Yunnan Province has formed a relatively complete *axis-amplitude* route network. Fourteen regional airports provide passenger flow to Changshui Airport. On the one hand, it *revitalize* the circular tourism resources with Kunming as the center, on the other hand, it also relies on the hub status of Changshui airport to connect the rest of the country with the cities of Yunnan.

At present, the annual passenger flow of Kunming Changshui International Airport has exceeded 47 million, continuing to compete with Shenzhen Bao'an International Airport for the position of the fifth largest airport in China (Figure 5-6).

Figure 5-6 The regional airports in Yunnan

New Words

consistent	[kənˈsɪstənt]	adj.	始终如一的,一致的;坚持的
connectivity	[kəˌnekˈtɪvətɪ]	n.	连通(性),联结(度)
competitiveness	[kəmˈpetətɪvnəs]	n.	竞争力,好竞争
certify	[ˈsɜːtɪfaɪ]	vt.	证明;证实
		vi.	证明;宣告
throughput	[ˈθruːpʊt]	n.	(某一时期内的)生产量,吞吐量
navigation	[ˌnævɪˈgeɪʃən]	n.	航行;航海
mask	[mɑːsk]	n.	面具;掩饰
		vi.	掩饰
		vt.	掩饰;使模糊
epidemic	[ˌepɪˈdemɪk]	n.	传染病
		adj.	流行的;传染性的
depression	[dɪˈpreʃən]	n.	沮丧;不景气
profitable	[ˈprɒfɪtəbl]	adj.	有利可图的;赚钱的;有益的
revenue	[ˈrevənjuː]	n.	税收收入;财政收入;收益
axis	[ˈæksɪs]	n.	轴;轴线;轴心国
amplitude	[ˈæmplɪtjuːd]	n.	振幅;丰富,充足;广阔
revitalize	[riːˈvaɪtəlaɪz]	vt.	使……复活;使……复兴;使……恢复生气

Phrases & Expressions

passenger flow	客流量
cargo flow	物流量
annual passenger throughput	年旅客吞吐量
take-off and landing aircraft type	起降飞机类型
range of direct flight	直达航班范围
distribution center	集散中心;物流中心
in the meantime	在此期间;与此同时
first navigation time	首次通航时间
the 12th Five-Year Plan	"十二五"规划
average annual growth rate	平均年增长率
maintain a good growth trend	保持良好的增长趋势
high-speed rail	高速铁路
the depression of tourism	旅游业的萧条
lose the stable customers	丧失稳定客源
revenue capacity	收益能力

Ⅰ. Translate the following terms into Chinese or English.

1. passenger flow
2. annual passenger throughput
3. direct range
4. distribution center
5. first navigation time
6. 平均年增长率
7. 保持良好的增长趋势
8. 高速铁路
9. 丧失稳定客源
10. 收益能力

Ⅱ. Cloze.

(regional airport/play a role in/axis-amplitude/distribution/surrounding)

1. In addition, the ground transportation cannot provide remote and rapid services of the fresh and agricultural products, while _____ can achieve it.

2. As the _____ center of regional passengers and cargo, the regional airport can concentrate and transport a large number of people and goods to other regions.

3. The construction of the regional airport has increased the demand for labor in the _____ industry, commerce and service industry.

4. The regional airports are far from enough to _____ air passenger and cargo transportation.

5. Now, Yunnan Province has formed a relatively complete _____ route network.

Ⅲ. Translate the following sentences into Chinese.

1. Strengthening the construction of regional machinery can not only improve China's transportation network, but also be consistent with the growing demand for passenger flow and material flow.

2. Since COVID-19 in 2020, regional airport has been affected much more than hub airport, mainly because the epidemic leads to serious excess capacity in the transportation field.

3. For the western regions with rich tourism resources and relatively inconvenient ground transportation, the depression of tourism has made the local air transportation lose the stable customers.

IV. Translate the following paragraph into Chinese.

As a large tourism province, Yunnan enjoys a good reputation at home and abroad for its rich tourism resources, which also brings great opportunities for the development of air transport industry. In addition to Kunming Changshui International Airport, serving as a regional hub, there are 14 regional airports, including Xishuangbanna, Lijiang and Tengchong.

V. Answer the following questions.

1. What is the definition of regional airport?

2. What is the current situation of regional airport in china?

Section 3
Beijing Daxing International Airport

Beijing Daxing International Airport is Finally Open

President Xi Jinping announced the official opening of the Beijing Daxing International Airport on September 25, 2019. The new airport complex, consisting of a main terminal, a supporting service building and a parking lot, covers an area of about 1.4 million square meters. On the southern border of Beijing is a *gigantic* field occupied by a massive "starfish", a structure with six arms. That's equivalent to 63 Tian'anmen Squares, according to Beijing Review (Figue 5-7).

Chapter 5　**AIRPORT**

Figue 5-7　Beijing Daxing International Airport

Special Terms

1. Beijing Daxing International Airport (IATA: PKX): Designed by legendary IraqiBritish architect Zaha Hadid, was listed as the first of the "seven wonders of the modern world near completion" by the *Guardian* in 2015. It is expected to ease pressure on the Beijing Capital International Airport.

北京大兴国际机场(国际航协代码:PKX):由伊拉克裔英国籍传奇建筑师扎哈·哈迪德设计,2015年被《卫报》列为"即将竣工的新世界七大奇迹"榜首。新机场的建成将缓解北京首都国际机场的运行压力。

2. Beijing Capital International Airport (IATA: PEK): The main international airport serving the city of Beijing in People's Republic of China. It is the world's busiest airport and the largest Chinese airport, which handled more than 100 million passengers in 2018, which is close to its capacity.

北京首都国际机场(国际航协代码:PEK):是中华人民共和国北京市的主要国际机场,是世界上最繁忙的机场,也是中国最大的机场。首都机场在2018年旅客吞吐量已突破1亿人次,处于超饱和的运行状态。

Text

Beijing Daxing International Airport (PKX), also known as Beijing New Airport, is the biggest airport in the world. It is also the second international airport of Beijing along with Beijing Capital International airport. The airport's design is *pioneering* while its location on Daxing District (the southern *suburbs* of Beijing) is ideal in order to serve the Chinese capital and the neighboring areas of Hebei and Tianjin. The new *mega-airport hub* is expected to handle up to 45 million passengers per year by 2021 and reach an outstanding 100 million in the future.

Daxing airport is located at the frontier between Beijing and Langfang, Hebei Province and is expected to serve the needs of Beijing, Tianjin and Hebei areas. Its location was selected after *thorough analysis*. With a 46km-distance from Tiananmen Square, a 67km-distance from Beijing

International Airport and a 26km-distance from Langfang City Center, Daxing airport aims to become the main airport hub of the region.

Notes 1

❶ The airport's design is pioneering while its location on Daxing District (the southern suburbs of Beijing) is ideal in order to serve the Chinese capital and the neighboring areas of Hebei and Tianjin.

解释:机场设计独具创新,坐落于大兴地区(北京南郊),位置得天独厚,未来将助力京津冀一体化建设发展。

❷ Daxing airport is located at the frontier between Beijing and Langfang, Hebei Province and is expected to serve the needs of Beijing, Tianjin and Hebei areas.

解释:大兴机场位于北京和河北廊坊的交界处,旨在满足京津冀地区的航空运输需求。

be expected to:有望做某事,旨在做。

❸ With a 46km-distance from Tiananmen Square, a 67km-distance from Beijing International Airport and a 26km-distance from Langfang City Center, Daxing airport aims to become the main airport hub of the region.

解释:大兴机场距离天安门广场46公里,距北京国际机场67公里,距廊坊市中心26公里,大兴机场将打造成为该地区的主要枢纽机场。

aim to:计划,打算;目标在于……;以……为目标。

General Airport Information

The glorious Daxing airport is the second biggest world's *aerodrome* and the second Beijing aviation hub along with Beijing Capital Airport (PEK). The giant "starfish" is *innovatively* designed in order to be completely functional (the walking distance to each gate is no more than 600 meters), *ecologically* friendly and *luxuriously stunning* at the same time. Located in Daxing District, in a 46km distance from Beijing city center, the US $17.47 billion Chinese *colossal* master plan is here to *decongest* the *overcrowded* old Beijing airport and is expected to eventually serve 100 million passengers annually.

Notes 2

The giant "starfish" is innovatively designed in order to be completely functional (the walking distance to each gate is no more than 600 meters), ecologically friendly and luxuriously stunning at the same time.

解释:气势恢宏的"海星"形状设计独具匠心,充分体现其功能性(从航站楼中心到每个指廊最远端登机口步行距离不超过600米),同时尽显华贵、生态友好。

walking distance:步行距离。

Terminals

The airport with the second biggest terminal building in the world has five *corridors* and a large central area where all the airport's facilities are located. The airport's design is so *groundbreaking* that despite the building's size, the passengers don't need more than an 8-minute walk to reach their gate. The arrivals are separated from the departures occupying 2 floors each. In the future, a second terminal building—the South Terminal—is planned to be added to Daxing airport complex(Figue 5-8).

Figue 5-8　The lounge of Beijing Daxing International Airport

Notes 3

❶ The airport with the second biggest terminal building in the world has five corridors and a large central area where all the airport's facilities are located.

解释:这个拥有世界上第二大航站楼的机场有五条指廊和一个很大的中心区域,机场的所有设施都位于这里。

❷ The arrivals are separated from the departures occupying 2 floors each. In the future, a second terminal building—the South Terminal—is planned to be added to Daxing airport complex.

解释:机场首次采用双层出发双层到达设计。未来,大兴机场还计划增建第二座航站楼——南航站楼。

Hotels

The hotel options near the new airport are varied. According to the *disposable budget*, the *personal preferences* and the journey purpose, you can find luxurious 5-star hotels, cosy motels, low-cost hostels and comfy B&B choices. However, you should always *keep in mind* that some accommodations don't accept reservations from non-Chinese citizens.

Facilities and Services

Daxing airport has the second biggest terminal and is one of the most technologically advanced airports globally. Designed to *minimize* the waiting lines and all the passenger's *hassle*, the new Beijing airport has adopted *cutting-edge procedures* for traveler's and luggage checking-in while the airport is designed to operate in the most *environmental-friendly way* possible. Check out Daxing airport's facilities and services and *optimize* the time spent there.

Parking

Enjoy convenient, secure and pocket-friendly parking services at Daxing airport. More than 4,200 parking spots inside the two Parking Buildings and 4,800 ones on the outside area of the airport are available to *accommodate* your vehicle. Automatic parking robots raise the services' level while you can enjoy *amenities* such as car washing and electric charge stations.

Notes 4

❶ Designed to minimize the waiting lines and all the passenger's hassle, the new Beijing airport has adopted cutting-edge procedures for traveler's and luggage checking-in while the airport is designed to operate in the most environmental-friendly way possible.

解释:为了减少排队等候和旅客的所有麻烦,北京新机场采用了最先进的旅客和行李登记程序,与此同时机场旨在以最环保的方式运作。

语法:while引导状语从句,表示某个动作进行的同时,另一动作也在发生,意为"与……同时"。

❷ Automatic parking robots raise the services' level while you can enjoy amenities such as car washing and electric charge stations.

解释:自动泊车机器人提高了服务水平,同时您还可以享受诸如洗车和充电桩等便利设施。

Layover at the Airport

Are you stuck at Daxing airport waiting for your transit flight? Multiple-hours waiting time can be a real hassle and is certainly a waste of time. Make the most of your *layover* at Daxing airport and enjoy a "mini-vacation" between your flights. With your *Temporary Entry Card* on hand, you can explore the *popular tourist attractions* in Beijing. Diversely, if you don't have the *mood* or the money to leave the airport, at Daxing airport you will discover plenty of things to do so that you still get to enjoy your *downtime*.

Notes 5

❶ Multiple-hours waiting time can be a real hassle and is certainly a waste of time. Make the most of your layover at Daxing airport and enjoy a "mini-vacation" between your flights.

解释：几个小时的转机等待时间不仅枯燥无味且虚度时光。充分利用您在大兴机场的停留时间，享受航班间的"迷你假期"体验。

❷ With your Temporary Entry Card on hand, you can explore the popular tourist attractions in Beijing.

解释：持临时入境卡便可以领略北京热门旅游景点。

temporary Entry Card：临时入境卡。popular tourist attraction：热门旅游胜地。

Further Reading

The Type-IV Airport

With China's economic and social development entering a new era, the people have higher requirements for the airport operation and service. Under such a background, the CAAC put forward the strategy of high-quality development in the new era to build a "type-IV airport" of safe, green, intelligent and humanistic nature (Figue 5-9).

"Safe airport" is an airport with solid production foundation, complete security system, stable and controllable operation.

"Green airport" is a source-intensive, low-carbon and environment-friendly airport in the whole life cycle.

Figue 5-9 The theme of type-IV airport

"Intelligent" airport is an airport with comprehensive Internet of Things, data sharing, collaborative efficiency and intelligent operation.

"Humanistic" airport is an airport that upholds the principle of people-oriented, is rich in cultural heritage, embodies the spirit of The Times and the spirit of contemporary civil aviation, and carries forward socialist values.

New Words

gigantic	[dʒaɪˈgæntɪk]	adj.	巨大的，庞大的
pioneer	[ˌpaɪəˈnɪr]	n.	先锋；拓荒者
		vt.	开辟
		vi.	作先驱
suburb	[ˈsʌbɜːrb]	n.	郊区；边缘
mega	[ˈmegə]	adj.	巨大的；优秀的
		adv.	的确
hub	[hʌb]	n.	中心
aerodrome	[ˈerədroʊm]	n.	飞机场；航空站
innovatively	[ˈɪnəveɪtɪv]	adv.	独创性地；创新地

ecologically	[ˌiːkəˈlɑːdʒɪklɪ]	adv.	从生态学的观点看
luxuriously	[lʌgˈʒʊrɪəslɪ]	adv.	豪华地；奢侈地
stun	[stʌn]	vt.	使震惊
		n.	令人惊叹的事物
colossal	[kəˈlɑːsl]	adj.	巨大的；异常的，非常的
decongest	[ˌdiːkənˈdʒest]	vt.	缓解……的阻塞
overcrowd	[ˌoʊvərˈkraʊd]	vt.	使过度拥挤
		vi.	过度拥挤；塞得太满
corridor	[ˈkɔːrɪdɔːr]	n.	走廊
groundbreaking	[ˈgraʊndbreɪkɪŋ]	adj.	开创性的
		n.	动工
disposable	[dɪˈspoʊzəbl]	adj.	可自由支配的；一次性的
minimize	[ˈmɪnɪmaɪz]	vt.	使减到最少；小看，极度轻视
		vi.	最小化
hassle	[ˈhæsl]	n.	困难
		v.	烦扰；与……争辩
optimize	[ˈɑːptɪmaɪz]	vt.	使最优化，使完善
		vi.	优化；持乐观态度
accommodate	[əˈkɑːmədeɪt]	vt.	容纳；使适应
		vi.	适应；调解
amenity	[əˈmiːnətɪ]	n.	舒适；礼仪；愉快；便利设施
layover	[ˈleɪoʊvər]	n.	中断期间，中途短暂的停留；终点停车处
mood	[muːd]	n.	情绪，语气；心境；气氛
downtime	[ˈdaʊntaɪm]	n.	停工期；停机时间

Phrases & Expressions

airport hub	航空枢纽
thorough analysis	深入分析
disposable budget	可支配预算
personal preference	个人喜好
keep in mind	牢记，记住
cutting-edge procedure	先进流程
environmental-friendly way	环境友好的方式
Temporary Entry Card	临时入境卡
popular tourist attraction	热门旅游胜地

Exercises

I. Translate the following terms into Chinese or English.

1. 航空枢纽
2. 先进流程
3. 环境友好的方式
4. 提高服务水准
5. new airport complex
6. walking distance
7. personal preference
8. parking spot

II. Cloze.

(corridors/gigantic/pocket-friendly/hassle/equivalent)

1. On the southern border of Beijing is a _____ field occupied by a massive "starfish", a structure with six arms.

2. That's _____ to 63 Tian'anmen Squares, according to Beijing Review.

3. The airport with the second biggest terminal building in the world has five _____ and a large central area where all the airport's facilities are located.

4. Enjoy convenient, secure and _____ parking services at Daxing airport.

5. Multiple-hours waiting time can be a real _____ and is certainly a waste of time.

III. Translate the following sentences into Chinese.

1. The giant "starfish" is innovatively designed in order to be completely functional (the walking distance to each gate is no more than 600 meters), ecologically friendly and luxuriously stunning at the same time.

2. Multiple-hours waiting time can be a real hassle and is certainly a waste of time. Make the most of your layover at Daxing airport and enjoy a "mini-vacation" between your flights.

3. Humanistic airport is an airport that upholds the principle of people-oriented, is rich in cultural heritage, embodies the spirit of the times and the spirit of contemporary civil aviation, and carries forward socialist values.

Ⅳ. Translate the following paragraph into Chinese.

With China's economic and social development entering a new era, the people have higher requirements for the airport operation and service. Under such a background, the CAAC put forward the strategy of high-quality development in the new era to build a "type-Ⅳ airport" of safe, green, intelligent and humanistic nature.

Ⅴ. Answer the following questions.

1. Where is the Beijing Daxing International Airport located?

2. Why the airport was built in the shape of "starfish"?

Chapter 6

SAFETY

Section 1
Dangerous Goods Transportation

UPS Lithium Battery Accident

On September 3, 2010, UPS (United Parcel Service of America) Flight 6 operated from Dubai, United Arab Emirates to Cologne, Germany. The flight was flown by a Boeing 747-400F, which caught fire shortly after takeoff and crashed out of control (Figure 6-1). All 2 members of the crew died.

Figure 6-1 UPS Lithium battery accident

After investigation, the cause of the *accident* is the dangerous goods loaded in the cargo compartment-lithium battery fire. The cargo manifest showed UPS Air Flight 6 carrying dozens of boxes of *lithium* batteries and electronics containing lithium batteries. The lithium batteries burned over 1,100℃, burned through the liner of the cargo compartment, damaged the aircraft's control system, and the fire *extinguishing* equipment in the cargo compartment could not extinguish the intense fire, eventually leading to the *tragedy*. The accident led to new U.S. restrictions on air freight, including new requirements for lithium battery packaging and restrictions on the transport of lithium batteries and electronic products.

Special Terms

1. Not otherwise specified: A generic term for a class of substances not specifically listed.

泛指名称:不具体列明的某一类物质的统称。

2. Single packaging: are packaging which do not require any inner packaging in order to perform their containment function during transport.

单一包装:不需要内包装即能在运输中起到盛装作用的包装。

3. Packing group: An indication of relative degree of dangerous presented by various articles and substances with a class or division.

包装等级:对交运的同一类别或项别的各种物品及物质按其危险程度进行区分的一种表示方法。

Text

In 1953, the Member airlines of IATA recognized the growing need to transport by air, articles and substances having *hazardous* properties which, if uncontrolled, could adversely affect the safety of the passengers, crew and/or aircraft on which they are carried. Experience in other modes of transport had *demonstrated* that most such articles and substances could be carried safely provided that the article or substance was properly packed and the quantities in each package were properly limited. Using this experience together with the industry's knowledge of the specialized characteristics of air transport, IATA developed the first regulations for the transport of dangerous goods by air. The first edition of the IATA *Dangerous Goods Regulations* was published in 1956 as the IATA *Restricted Articles Regulations*.

Dangerous goods (Figure 6-2) are articles or substances which are capable of posing a hazard to health, safety, property or the *environment* and which are shown in the list of dangerous goods in these regulations or which are classified according to these regulations.

Figure 6-2　Dangerous goods

Dangerous goods are defined as those goods which meet the criteria of one or more of nine UN hazard classes and where applicable, to one of three UN *Packing group*. The nine classes relate to the packing groups relate to the applicable degree of danger.

Dangerous goods can be transported safely by air transport provided certain principles are strictly followed. The IATA *Dangerous Goods Regulations* is an easy-to-use manual based on the International Civil Aviation Organization (ICAO) *Technical Instructions for the Safe Transport of Dangerous Goods by Air*. It *incorporates* additional operational requirements, which provide a *harmonized* system for operators to accept and transport dangerous goods safely and efficiently.

> **Notes 1**
>
> ❶ Dangerous goods are articles or substances which are capable of posing a hazard to health, safety, property or the environment and which are shown in the list of dangerous goods in these regulations or which are classified according to these regulations.
>
> 解释：危险品是指能够对健康、安全、财产或者环境造成危害并列入《国际航空运输协会危险品条例》危险品名录或者依照《国际航空运输协会危险品条例》分类的物品或者物质。
>
> these regulations 指 IATA *Dangerous Goods Regulations*（IATA *DGR*）。
>
> 语法：which 引导两个非限制性定语从句，修饰先行词"dangerous goods"，其中第二个 which 前要加 and。
>
> ❷ It incorporates additional operational requirements, which provide a harmonized system for operators to accept and transport dangerous goods safely and efficiently.
>
> 解释：它包含了额外的操作要求，为操作员提供了一个安全和有效地接受和运输危险货物的协调系统。
>
> additional operational requirement 指的是国际航空运输协会的附加操作规定。

Dangerous Goods Regulations (Figure 6-3)

The Regulations include a detailed list of individual articles and substances specifying the United Nations classification of each article or substance and their acceptability for air transport as well as the conditions for their transport. Since no listing can be complete, the list also includes many generic or "*not otherwise specified*" entries to assist in the classification of those articles or substances not listed by name. Some dangerous goods have been identified as being too dangerous to be carried on any aircraft under any circumstances; others are forbidden under normal circumstances but may be carried with specific approvals from the States concerned; some are restricted to carriage on all cargo aircraft; most however, can be safely carried on passenger aircraft as well, provided certain requirements are met.

Figure 6-3 Dangerous goods regulations

Packaging is the essential component in the safe transport of dangerous goods by air. The IATA *Dangerous Goods Regulations* provide *packing instructions* for all dangerous goods acceptable for air transport with a wide range of options for inner, outer and *single packaging*. The packing instructions normally require the use of *UN performance-tested specification packaging*, however these are not required when dangerous goods are shipped in *Limited Quantities* under the provisions of Limited Quantity "Y" Packing Instructions. The quantity of dangerous goods permitted within these packaging is strictly limited by the Regulations so as to minimize the risk when an *incident* occur.

Notes 2

❶ The packing instructions normally require the use of UN performance-tested specification packaging, however these are not required when dangerous goods are shipped in Limited Quantities under the provisions of Limited Quantity "Y" Packing Instructions.

解释：包装说明通常要求使用联合国性能测试规范包装，但根据有限数量"Y"包装说明的规定，以有限数量运输危险货物时，不需要使用联合国性能测试规范包装。

❷ Since no listing can be complete, the list also includes many generic or "not otherwise specified" entries to assist in the classification of those articles or substances not listed by name.

解释：由于列表不可能完整化，该列表还包括许多通用的或"泛指名称"的条目，以帮助对未按名称列出的物品或物质进行分类。

语法：since 作为连词，引导原因状语从句，表示因为；既然；鉴于。

Training and Information Notification

Training is also an essential element in maintaining a safe regulatory *regime*. It is necessary for all individuals involved in the preparation or transport of dangerous goods to be properly trained to carry out their responsibilities. Depending on the job-function, this may entail only *familiarization* training or may also include more detailed training in the *intricacies* of the regulations. It is important to remember that dangerous goods are very unlikely to cause a problem when they are prepared and handled in compliance with the IATA *Dangerous Goods Regulations*.

The proper declaration of dangerous goods by the shipper ensures that all in the transportation chain know what dangerous goods they are transporting, how to properly load and handle them and what to do if an incident or accident occurs either in-flight or on the ground. The *pilot-in-command* must know what is on board the aircraft in order to properly deal with any emergencies, which may occur. The pilot must also convey this information, if possible, to air traffic services to aid in the response to any aircraft incident or accident. Information regarding "*Hidden Dangerous Goods*" must also be conveyed to passengers to assist them in recognizing dangerous goods, which they are not permitted to carry on their person or in their baggage and which may not be readily recognizable as being dangerous (Figure 6-4).

Lastly, dangerous goods accidents or incidents must be reported, so that an *investigation* by the relevant authorities can establish the cause and take corrective action. Also, if as a result of these investigations changes are required in the Regulations, appropriate regulatory action can be taken without delay.

Figure 6-4 Hidden dangerous goods

> Notes 3
>
> ❶ Training is also an essential element in maintaining a safe regulatory regime.
> 解释:培训也是维持安全监管制度的一个基本要素。
> ❷ Depending on the job-function, this may entail only familiarization training or may also include more detailed training in the intricacies of the regulations.

解释：根据工作职能的不同,这可能只需要熟悉培训,也可能包括条例复杂的更详细的培训。

❸ Information regarding "Hidden Dangerous Goods" must also be conveyed to passengers to assist them in recognizing dangerous goods, which they are not permitted to carry on their person or in their baggage and which may not be readily recognizable as being dangerous.

解释：有关"隐含危险物品"的信息也必须传达给旅客,以协助他们识别危险物品,此类"隐含危险品"不得随身携带或放入旅客行李中,因为它们可能不容易被识别出危险性。

Further Reading

Classification of Dangerous Goods

Dangerous goods are divided into 9 classes in air transportation, these 9 classes are:

Class1 - explosive;

Class2 - gases;

Class3 - flammable liquid;

Class4 - flammable solids; substances liable to *spontaneous combustion* substances which in contact with water, emit flammable gases;

Class5 - *oxidizing* substances and *organic peroxides*;

Class6 - toxic and infectious substances;

Class7 - *radioactive* material;

Class8 - corrosive;

Class9 - *miscellaneous* dangerous substances.

In recent years, with the popularization of electronic products with lithium battery as the main power source, the ninth class of lithium battery [especially lithium ion battery (Figure 6-5)] transportation volume increased year by year, its transportation volume has accounted for the first transportation quantity of dangerous goods. Dangerous goods accidents of lithium battery has brought great hidden dangers to air transportation safety, therefore, the relevant practitioners need to strictly abide by the industry regulations to ensure transportation safety.

Figure 6-5　Lithium ion battery marking and label

New Words

accident	[ˈæksɪdənt]	n.	事故；意外
lithium	[ˈlɪθɪəm]	n.	锂(符号 Li)
extinguish	[ɪkˈstɪŋgwɪʃ]	vt.	熄灭；压制；偿清
tragedy	[ˈtrædʒədɪ]	n.	悲剧；灾难；惨案
hazardous	[ˈhæzədəs]	adj.	有危险的；冒险的；碰运气的
demonstrate	[ˈdemənstreɪt]	vt.	证明；展示；论证
		vi.	示威
environment	[ɪnˈvaɪrənmənt]	n.	环境，外界
incorporate	[ɪnˈkɔːpəreɪt]	vt.	包含；把……合并
		vi.	合并
		adj.	合并的
harmonize	[ˈhɑːməˌnaɪz]	vt.	使和谐；使一致
		vi.	协调；和谐
incident	[ˈɪnsɪdənt]	n.	事件；插曲
		adj.	易发生的，伴随而来的
regime	[reɪˈʒiːm]	n.	政权，政体；社会制度；管理体制
familiarization	[fəˌmɪlɪəraɪˈzeɪʃən]	n.	熟悉，精通；亲密
intricacy	[ˈɪntrɪkəsɪ]	n.	错综，复杂；难以理解
investigation	[ɪnˌvestɪˈgeɪʃən]	n.	调查；调查研究
spontaneous	[spɒnˈteɪnɪəs]	adj.	自发的；自然的；无意识的
oxidize	[ˈɒksɪdaɪz]	vt.	使氧化；使生锈
		vi.	氧化
radioactive	[ˌreɪdɪəʊˈæktɪv]	adj.	[核] 放射性的；有辐射的
miscellaneous	[ˌmɪsəˈleɪnɪəs]	adj.	混杂的，多方面的

Phrases & Expressions

packing group	包装等级
not otherwise specified	泛指名称
packing instructions	包装说明、包装指令
single packaging	单一包装
UN performance-tested specification packaging	联合国性能测试的规格包装
limited quantities packaging	有限数量包装
pilot-in-command	机长
hidden Dangerous Goods	隐含危险品
organic peroxides	有机过氧化物

I. Translate the following terms into Chinese or English.

1. 包装等级
2. 单一包装
3. 有限数量包装
4. 隐含危险品
5. UN performance-tested specification packaging
6. organic peroxides
7. not otherwise specified
8. dangerous goods regulations

II. Cloze.

(packaging/report/packing group/environment/dangerous goods regulations/hazardous)

1. The first edition of the IATA _____ was published in 1956 as the IATA *Restricted Articles Regulations*.

2. Dangerous goods are articles or substances which are capable of posing a hazard to health, safety, property or the _____.

3. Dangerous goods are defined as those goods which meet the criteria of one or more of nine UN hazard classes and where applicable, to one of three UN _____.

4. _____ is the essential component in the safe transport of dangerous goods by air.

5. Lastly, dangerous goods accidents or incidents must be _____, so that an investigation by the relevant authorities can establish the cause and take corrective action.

III. Translate the following sentences into Chinese.

1. The IATA *Dangerous Goods Regulations* is an easy-to-use manual based on the International Civil Aviation Organization (ICAO) *Technical Instructions for the Safe Transport of Dangerous Goods by Air*.

2. Training is also an essential element in maintaining a safe regulatory *regime*. It is necessary for all individuals involved in the preparation or transport of dangerous goods to be properly trained to carry out their responsibilities.

IV. Translate the following paragraph into Chinese.

In recent years, with the popularization of electronic products with lithium battery as the main power source, the ninth class of lithium battery (especially lithium ion battery) transportation volume increased year by year, its transportation volume has accounted for the first transportation quantity of dangerous goods. Dangerous goods accidents of lithium battery has brought great hidden dangers to air transportation safety, therefore, the relevant practitioners need to strictly abide by the industry regulations to ensure transportation safety.

V. Answer the following questions.

1. What is the definition of air dangerous goods?

2. Which document was DGR made from?

Section 2
Weight and Balance of Aircraft

Qantas Plane Lost Its Balance

A Qantas plane lost its *balance* by missing 87 primary students as adults (Figure 6-6). The Australian Transportation Safety Agency mentioned the details in a report released. The flight flew from Canberra to Perth on May 9, 2014 with 150 passengers, 87 pupils who were placed in the seat behind the plane. Sales staff mistakenly classified 87 primary school students as adults. This means that each child is counted as 87kg instead of 32kg, almost 3.5 tons. This led the Boeing 737 to appear *overhead* on takeoff. Fortunately, the captain operated properly, and this saved the danger.

Figure 6-6 Qantas plane lost its balance

Special Terms

1. MTOW: Maximum Takeoff Weight, the aircraft reaches the full weight limit when taking off and lifting the front wheel speed.

最大起飞重量：飞机在起飞滑跑并达到抬起前轮速度时全部重量的限额。

2. MLDW: Maximum Landing Weight, Maximum limit of full weight upon landing.

最大落地重量：飞机着陆时全部重量的最大限额。

3. MZFW: Maximum Zero Fuel Weight, Maximum full weight when the aircraft is without fuel.

最大无油重量：飞机没有燃油时全部重量的最大限额。

Text

Aircraft *weight and balance* work is the connection link between civil aviation commercial transportation and flight, which is directly related to the flight safety and economic benefits of airlines. Safety is the *eternal* theme of civil aviation industry, and the *pursuit* of efficiency on the basis of safety is the basis of the high-quality and efficient development of civil aviation industry.

Weight and balancing work can be divided into two parts: load control and balance. Load control is to solve the problem of how much to install, and balance is to solve the problem of how to install. The essence of the load balance is to accurately report the flight loading information to the crew and relevant departments, and make the flight load meet the various restrictions of this flight, and control the *payload* weight and aircraft *center of gravity* within the prescribed scope, to achieve safe, economic and efficient purposes. Weight and balancing work is not only balance calculation, but also related work done to obtain real and reasonable data; controls to ensure correct results; reviews to ensure effective control; specifications to ensure orderly work; and *monitoring* of various factors affecting load and balance.

Duty weight and balance work is the last link of the ground work of civil aviation transportation business, which is the connection link between business activities and flight, which is directly related to the flight safety and efficiency of airlines. It has close contact with the ticket sales, check-in, passenger service, freight, *operation control* and *navigation* departments in ground business, etc (Figure 6-7).

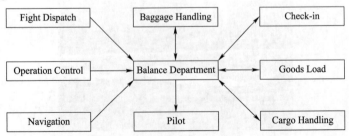

Figure 6-7　Contact with the various departments

Chapter 6 SAFETY

> 📝 **Notes 1**
>
> ❶ Aircraft weight and balance work is the connection link between civil aviation commercial transportation and flight, which is directly related to the flight safety and economic benefits of airlines.
>
> 解释:飞机载重与平衡工作是连接民航商业运输与飞行的纽带,直接关系到航空公司的飞行安全和经济效益。
>
> ❷ Weight and balancing work is not only balance calculation, but also related work done to obtain real and reasonable data; controls to ensure correct results; reviews to ensure effective control; specifications to ensure orderly work; and monitoring of various factors affecting load and balance.
>
> 解释:载重与平衡不仅是平衡计算,而且包括为获取真实、合理数据所做的相关工作,如控制结果正确、审查有效控制、规范确保工作有序以及对影响装载和平衡的各种因素的监测。
>
> 语法:not only... but also 意为"不仅……而且……",用于连接两个对等的成分。
>
> ❸ It has close contact with the ticket sales, check-in, passenger service, freight, operation control and navigation departments in ground business, etc.
>
> 解释:与地面业务中的机票销售、值机、客运服务、货运、运营控制及航行等部门有密切联系。

Control of the Aircraft Payload Weight

Payload weight means the full weight of commercial passengers, baggage, goods, mails loaded on an aircraft. The maximum available payload of an aircraft is the maximum allowable weight of passengers, baggage, goods and mails that can be loaded. It should be emphasized that the maximum available payload is not for an aircraft, but for an aircraft performing a particular flight, since the maximum available payload of the same aircraft is different for the same aircraft. Each flight must calculate the maximum available payload for the aircraft based on different *circumstances*. The available payload of every aircraft performing flight missions must be strictly controlled, and *overloading* in any case will cause serious accidents or even destruction.

Strict control of the aircraft payload is to ensure that flights can take off, fly and land safely. To ensure safe take-off, the weight of the aircraft shall not exceed the maximum takeoff weight of the aircraft (*MTOW*); to ensure safe landing, the maximum landing weight of the plane is not exceeded (*MLDW*). Also considering the abnormal landing under special circumstances, the aircraft needs no fuel so that the aircraft weight shall not exceed the maximum zero fuel weight (*MZFW*). The maximum landing weight and maximum zero fuel weight are the performance data of the aircraft, provided by the aircraft *manufacturer*.

Notes 2

❶ The maximum available payload of an aircraft is the maximum allowable weight of passengers, baggage, goods and mails that can be loaded.

解释:飞机的最大可用业务载量是指一架飞机可装载的旅客、行李、货物和邮件的最大允许重量。

Payload 指飞机的业务载量或商务载量,也称为付费载量。

❷ It should be emphasized that the maximum available payload is not for an aircraft, but for an aircraft performing a particular flight, since the maximum available payload of the same aircraft is different for the same aircraft.

解释:应当强调的是,最大可用业务载量不是指某一架飞机,而是执行特定飞行的飞机,因为同一飞机的最大可用业务载量会不同。

语法:not...but...意为"不是……而是……",but 表示转折。

❸ Also considering the abnormal landing under special circumstances, the aircraft needs no fuel so that the aircraft weight shall not exceed the maximum zero fuel weight.

解释:还要考虑到在特殊情况下飞机非正常状态降落时需要飞机上没有燃油,所以飞机的重量不能超过最大无油重量。

语法:considering 作介词,就……而论,考虑到。

Air Center of Gravity and Balance

The operation control of the aircraft is not enough to ensure that the weight does not exceed the maximum allowance, and that aircraft center of gravity does not exceed the allowable range at any time. An allowable center of gravity range should be determined according to the *operability*, stability requirements and aircraft structure restrictions, so the passengers and cargo must be properly arranged to ensure that the aircraft center of gravity does not exceed the allowable range at any time during takeoff and landing and flight (Figure 6-8). Over the weight limit or the center of gravity limit may endanger safety, for example, aircraft *tail wipe*, structural damage, aircraft instability, *pneumatic* instability, ground instability (aircraft *overturning*), passenger boarding insecurity, increased oil consumption, shortened structural fatigue life, and runway damage, etc.

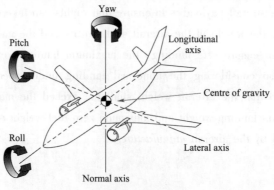

Figure 6-8　The center of gravity of the aircraft

The balance of the aircraft is closely related to the position of the aircraft center of gravity. The ultimate purpose of the load and balance work is to determine the reasonable center of gravity position of the aircraft and guide the pilot to adjust the flight parameters, so as to safely and accurately *manipulate* the aircraft and successfully complete the flight mission.

Notes 3

① An allowable center of gravity range should be determined according to the operability, stability requirements and aircraft structure restrictions, so the passengers and cargo must be properly arranged to ensure that the aircraft center of gravity does not exceed the allowable range at any time during takeoff and landing and flight.

解释:根据可操作性、稳定性要求和飞机结构限制确定允许的重心范围,必须正确安排旅客和货物,保证起降、飞行期间飞机重心不超过允许范围。

② Over the weight limit or the center of gravity limit may endanger safety, for example, aircraft tail wipe, structural damage, aircraft instability, pneumatic instability, ground instability (aircraft overturning), passenger boarding insecurity, increased oil consumption, shortened structural fatigue life, and runway damage, etc.

解释:超过重量极限或重心极限可能危及安全,例如,飞机尾翼擦拭、结构损坏、飞机不稳定、气动不稳定、地面不稳定(飞机倾覆)、旅客登机不安全、油耗增加、结构疲劳寿命缩短和跑道损坏等。

Load and Balance Chart

In practical work, the load and balance chart is designed based on the index method in the aircraft center of gravity calculation method, namely the *diagramming* of the *index method*. Using a balance chart to calculate the position of the center of gravity of the aircraft can greatly shorten the time and intensity of the balance work, and it is the main form of manual balance work now. The load and balance chart is designed according to the plane model. The load and balance chart includes: load sheet and balance diagram (Figure 6-9). There are two different design versions of linear method and index method, and the design of load sheet is in a *unified* format.

Notes 4

① In practical work, the load and balance chart is designed based on the index method in the aircraft center of gravity calculation method, namely the diagramming of the index method.

解释:在实际的工作中,载重平衡图是以飞机重心计算法中的指数法为基础设计出来的,即指数法的图解化。

② The load and balance chart includes: load sheet and balance diagram. There are two different design versions of linear method and index method, and the design of load sheet sheet is in a unified format.

解释：载重平衡图包括：装机单和平衡图。平衡图有折线法和指数法两种不同设计版本，装机单表的设计格式是统一的。

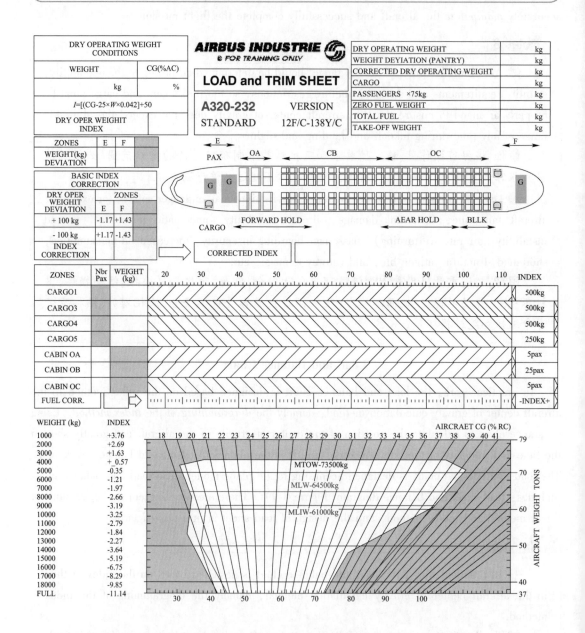

Figure 6-9 Balance diagram

Accurate and timely weight and balance work can ensure the positive point and safety; good center of gravity can also make flight more stable and *fuel efficient*, reduce flight cost and improve airline efficiency.

Further Reading

LDP

LDP means *Load Planning*, and is an application module in the CAAC *computer departure system* for airlines and airport loading staff. The traditional manual loading process is complicated, many links affect human factors, easy to produce mistakes. Computer load balancing freed employees from *cumbersome* manual methods, greatly improves load distribution efficiency and load accuracy, has been widely adopted for the world aviation community. Main realization: establish loaded flight information; determine payload distribution according to aircraft balance requirements; make *flight manifest*; and send relevant business messages.

New Words

balance	['bæləns]	n. 平衡
		vt. 使平衡
		vi. 保持平衡；相称
overhead	[ˌəʊvə'hed]	adv. 在头顶上方
		adj. 在头上方的
		n. (飞机的)顶舱
eternal	[ɪ'tɜːnl]	adj. 永恒的；不朽的
pursuit	[pə'sjuːt]	n. 追赶，追求；职业，工作
payload	['peɪləʊd]	n. 有效负荷；收费载重
monitor	['mɒnɪtə(r)]	n. 监视器
		vt. 监控
navigation	[ˌnævɪ'geɪʃən]	n. 航行；航海
circumstance	['sɜːkəmstəns]	n. 环境；境遇
		vt. 处于某种情况
overload	[ˌəʊvə'ləʊd]	v. (使)过载，超载
		n. 超载量
manufacture	[ˌmænjʊ'fæktʃə(r)]	n. 制造
		vt. 制造；加工
		vi. 制造
operability	[ˌɒpərə'bɪlɪtɪ]	n. 可操作性
pneumatic	[njuː'mætɪk]	adj. 气动的；充气的；有气胎的
		n. 气胎
overturn	[ˌəʊvə'tɜːn]	vt. 推翻；破坏
		vi. 倾覆
		n. 倾覆；破灭

manipulate	[məˈnɪpjʊleɪt]	vt. 操纵;操作
diagramming	[ˈdaɪəˌgræmɪŋ]	n. 图表,图样;图形表示
unify	[ˈjuːnɪfaɪ]	vt. 使统一
		vi. 统一;一体化
cumbersome	[ˈkʌmbəsəm]	adj. 笨重的;累赘的;难处理的

Phrases & Expressions

weight and balance	载重与平衡
center of gravity	重心
operation control	操作控制
MTOW	最大起飞重量
MLDW	最大落地重量
MZFW	最大无油重量
tail wipe	尾翼擦地
index method	指数法
fuel efficient	燃油效率
loading plan (LDP)	配载系统
computer departure system	计算机离港系统
flight manifest	航班舱单

Exercises

Ⅰ. **Translate the following terms into Chinese or English.**

1. operation control
2. index method
3. computer departure system
4. tail wipe
5. MLDW
6. 重心
7. 载重与平衡
8. 航班舱单
9. 装机单
10. 最大起飞重量

Ⅱ. **Cloze.**

(index/center of gravity/balance/payload/weight and balance/fuel/flight manifest)

1. Aircraft _____ work is the connection link between civil aviation commercial transportation and flight, which is directly related to the flight safety and economic benefits of airlines.

2. The operation control of the aircraft is not enough to ensure that the weight does not exceed the maximum allowance, and that aircraft _____ does not exceed the allowable range at any time.

3. In practical work, the load and balance chart is designed based on the _____ method in the aircraft center of gravity calculation method, namely the diagramization of the index method.

4. Load control is to solve the problem of how much to install, and _____ is to solve the problem of how to install.

5. _____ weight means the full weight of commercial passengers, baggage, goods, mails loaded on an aircraft.

III. Translate the following sentences into Chinese.

1. Strict control of the aircraft payload is to ensure that flights can take off, fly and land safely.

2. Using a balance chart to calculate the position of the center of gravity of the aircraft can greatly shorten the time and intensity of the balance work, and it is the main form of manual balance work now.

3. The maximum landing weight and maximum zero fuel weight are the performance data of the aircraft, provided by the aircraft manufacturer.

IV. Translate the following paragraph into Chinese.

LDP means Load Planning, and is an application module in the CAAC computer departure system for airlines and airport loading staff. The traditional manual loading process is complicated, many links affect human factors, easy to produce mistakes. Computer load balancing freed employees from cumbersome manual methods, greatly improves load distribution efficiency and load accuracy, has been widely adopted for the world aviation community. Main realization: establish loaded flight information; determine payload relevant business messages distribution according to aircraft balance requirements; make flight manifest; and send relevant business messages.

V. Answer the following questions.

1. What are the main two parts of the weight and balance work?

2. What does the MTOW mean?

Section 3
Positive Passenger Bag Match

"The Lockerbie" Air Crash

On December 21, 1988, Pan American Flight 103 flew a Frankfurt-London-New York-Detroit mission, a Boeing 747 passenger aircraft. Unfortunately, the plane exploded over the British town of *Lockerbie* (Figure 6-10), killing all 259 people on board, including passengers and crew.

Figure 6-10 "The Lockerbie" air crash

After the investigation, it was found that there were more than 20 pieces of luggage and passenger list on the plane, meaning that the luggage was on the plane, but the passengers did not go on, the luggage did not follow the owner, and finally found that the problem was on a *time bomb* hidden transfer luggage, someone sent the bomb hidden luggage from Malta on 103 flights. The bomb attack was seen as one of the worst *terrorist* activities before the 9.11 attacks.

Special Terms

1. No show: The antonym of go show refers to passengers who have booked tickets but have not taken them for various reasons.

Now show: go show 的反义词,是指预订了机票但因各种原因而未搭乘的旅客。

2. Checked bag: Baggage delivered to the airline for transportation in the cargo hold and issued a baggage ticket.

托运行李:交给航空公司装入货舱内运输并开具行李票的行李。

Text

Under *positive passenger bag match* (*PPBM*), no checked luggage would travel unless accompanied by a passenger who has boarded the flight. PPBM is performed on all international flights, and also most European and other domestic flights outside the United States. But it is not required on US domestic services. Checked bags on US domestic flights are physical screened for explosives, and PPBM would be *superfluous* if these screening processes were perfect. But no one has suggested that this ideal situation *prevails*. Test results about the accuracy of explosives *detection* have not been heartening: in a widely publicized test outcome, a *simulated* bomb passed through an explosives detector at Newark and made its way to Amsterdam.

Notes 1

❶ Under positive passenger bag match (PPBM), no checked luggage would travel unless accompanied by a passenger who has boarded the flight.

解释:在旅客行李相配制度(PPBM)下,托运行李除非有登上飞机的旅客陪同,否则一律不得装上飞机。

checked luggage:专业词语,托运行李,不能理解成检查过的行李。

❷ But no one has suggested that this ideal situation prevails.

解释:但没有人认为眼下到处都是这种理想的情况。

The Role of the PPBM

The argument for *restoring* PPBM within the US is that, increasingly, the physical screening of checked luggage takes place in the absence of the passenger. A terrorist could therefore check luggage containing an explosive-perhaps using a fake *identification document* and then flee the airport before his bag is examined (Figure 6-11). If the detectors failed to recognize his bomb, then—without PPBM—his luggage would travel despite his absence, and could destroy the aircraft. If the detectors did identify the explosive, the *catastrophe* would be avoided, but the terrorist and those supporting him would quite possibly *escape* capture. Without PPBM, in other words, the explosive detector could become something of a *roulette wheel*, which a terrorist could play at almost no cost.

Figure 6-11 Explosive detection

The situation changes when PPBM at the passenger's point of origin becomes part of the security policy. To have any chance of destroying a plane, the terrorist would have to go to the boarding gate. Then, if an explosives detector uncovered his device, there is a real chance that he would be *apprehended* promptly. That prospect could be *unnerving* even to a suicidal terrorist: someone who would readily die in a successful explosion might nonetheless *flinch* at *life imprisonment* for a failed attempt.

> ### Notes 2
>
> ❶ The argument for restoring PPBM within the US is that, increasingly, the physical screening of checked luggage takes place in the absence of the passenger.
>
> 解释：在美国境内恢复旅客行李相配制度的理由是，越来越多的托运行李会在旅客缺席的情况下进行物理检查。
>
> ❷ Without bag match, in other words, the explosive detector could become something of a roulette wheel, which a terrorist could play at almost no cost.
>
> 解释：换句话说，如果没有行李相配，爆炸探测器可能会变成一个轮盘赌轮，恐怖分子几乎可以免费玩。
>
> ❸ That prospect could be unnerving even to a suicidal terrorist: someone who would readily die in a successful explosion might nonetheless flinch at life imprisonment for a failed attempt.
>
> 解释：这种可能性甚至可能让自杀性恐怖分子感到不安：一个在成功爆炸时很可能会死亡的人，可能因阴谋被挫败而被判终身监禁时，会畏缩不前。

The Argument about the PPBM

Why, then, not perform PPBM as an additional security measure? The arguments relate to its costs: PPBM can cause departure delays because passenger lists must be carefully checked for "*no shows*," and because the checked luggage of missing passengers must first be located in the luggage compartment and then removed from the airplane. PPBM can cost money when a plane is delayed at the gate (e.g., because aircraft power units must run longer than usual, and cost associated with passenger delays and crew might *accumulate*). Extra expenses could grow rapidly if new employees had to be hired to perform PPBM.

But we can go beyond framing the general cost-benefit issue because, in 2002, US carriers did perform bag match. Statistics arising from that experience- modified for various changes between 2002 and 2008-imply that bag match at the passenger's point of origin could be expected to delay approximately one in 70 departures. Among the flights *held back*, the conditional mean departure delay would be about 13 minutes. There would be no need for additional employees given that none were needed in 2002; the mean dollar cost to passengers was estimated to be *roughly* 10 cents per flight.

As noted, it is not easy to estimate the economic cost of successful terrorism. But the RAND Corporation has tried, and has estimated that the cost of another successful terrorist attack against American aviation would be $15 billion. Calculations using numbers show that the annual cost of domestic PPBM would be less than $100 million, even if we assign a *monetary* cost to passenger delay of $0.63 per minute. The comparison of $100 million and $15 billion implies that US domestic PPBM might be *cost-effective* if it saved one airplane over 150 years.

Notes 3

❶ But we can go beyond framing the general cost-benefit issue because, in 2002, US carriers did perform bag match.

解释: 但我们可以跳出这个一般成本—效益问题的框架,因为在2002年,美国航空公司确实进行了行李匹配。

❷ Statistics arising from that experience—modified for various changes between 2002 and 2008—imply that bag match at the passenger's point of origin could be expected to delay approximately one in 70 departures.

解释: 由这一经验产生的统计数据(根据2002—2008年期间的各种变化进行了修改)意味着,在旅客始发地执行行李相配制度,预计会造成大约70分之一的出发航班延误。

❸ Calculations using numbers show that the annual cost of domestic PPBM would be less than $100 million, even if we assign a monetary cost to passenger delay of $0.63 per minute.

解释: 使用数字的计算表明,国内实行旅客行李相配制度的年成本将低于1亿美元,即使我们将旅客延误的货币成本分配为每分钟0.63美元。

Further Reading

The "9.11" Terrorist Attacks

On the morning of September 11, 2001, two civilian passenger planes *hijacked* by terrorists crashed into the World Trade Center in New York, two buildings collapsed after attack (Figure 6-12). The "9.11" incident was the worst terrorist attack in the United States, with 2,996 *victims*.

Statistics on the property losses in the incident, the United Nations issued a report that the terrorist attack lost ﹩200 *billion* to the US economy, equivalent to 2% of the year's GDP. The damage to the global economy has even reached around ﹩1 *trillion*. The *psychological* impact on the American people has severely weakened their economic and political security.

Figure 6-12 "9.11" Terrorist attacks

New Words

Lockerbie	[ˈlɒkəbɪ]	n.	洛克比(苏格兰西南部城镇,1988年洛克比空难发生地)
terrorist	[ˈterərɪst]	n.	恐怖主义者
		adj.	恐怖主义者的
superfluous	[sjuːˈpɜːfluəs]	adj.	多余的;不必要的;奢侈的
prevail	[prɪˈveɪl]	vi.	盛行,流行;战胜,获胜
detection	[dɪˈtekʃən]	n.	侦查,探测;发觉,发现;察觉
simulate	[ˈsɪmjuleɪt]	vt.	模仿;假装;冒充
		adj.	模仿的;假装的
restore	[rɪˈstɔː(r)]	vt.	恢复;修复;归还
		vi.	恢复;还原
flee	[fliː]	vi.	逃走;消失,消散
		vt.	逃跑,逃走;逃避
catastrophe	[kəˈtæstrəfɪ]	n.	大灾难;大祸;惨败
escape	[ɪˈskeɪp]	vt.	逃避
		vi.	逃脱
		n.	逃跑;逃亡
apprehend	[ˌæprɪˈhend]	vt.	理解;逮捕;忧虑
		vi.	理解;担心
unnerve	[ʌnˈnɜːv]	vt.	使失去勇气;使身心交病;使焦躁;使失常
flinch	[flɪntʃ]	vi.	退缩;畏惧
		n.	退缩;畏惧

accumulate	[əˈkjuːmjəleɪt]	vi.	累积;积聚
		vt.	积攒
roughly	[ˈrʌflɪ]	adv.	粗糙地;概略地
monetary	[ˈmʌnɪtrɪ]	adj.	货币的;财政的
hijack	[ˈhaɪdʒæk]	vt.	抢劫;揩油
		vi.	拦路抢劫
		n.	劫持;威逼;敲诈
victim	[ˈvɪktɪm]	n.	受害人,牺牲品
billion	[ˈbɪljən]	n.	十亿;大量
		adj.	十亿的
trillion	[ˈtrɪljən]	n.	[数] 万亿
		adj.	万亿的
psychological	[ˌsaɪkəˈlɒdʒɪkl]	adj.	心理的;心理学的;精神上的

Phrases & Expressions

time bomb	定时炸弹
positive passenger bag match (PPBM)	旅客行李相配制度
identification document	身份证件
roulette wheel	轮盘赌
life imprisonment	终身监禁
no show	预订了机票而不搭乘的人
hold back	阻碍
cost-effective	有成本效率的;划算的

Exercises

Ⅰ. **Translate the following terms into Chinese or English.**

1. cost-effective
2. suicidal terrorist
3. life imprisonment
4. 预订了机票而不搭乘的人
5. 身份证件
6. 旅客行李相配制度

Ⅱ. **Cloze.**

(terrorist/delay/unchecked/checked/no cost/cost-effective)

1. Under positive passenger bag match, no _____ luggage would travel unless accompanied by a passenger who has boarded the flight.

2. Without PPBM, in other words, the explosive detector could become something of a roulette wheel, which a terrorist could play at almost _____.

3. PPBM can cost money when a plane is _____ at the gate.

4. The comparison of $100 million and $15 billion implies that US domestic PPBM might be _____ If it saved one airplane over 150 years.

Ⅲ. Translate the following sentences into Chinese.

1. Checked bags on US domestic flights are physical screened for explosives, and PPBM would be superfluous if these screening processes were perfect.

2. The arguments relate to its costs: PPBM can cause departure delays because passenger lists must be carefully checked for "no shows", and because the checked luggage of missing passengers must first be located in the luggage compartment and then removed from the airplane.

Ⅳ. Translate the following paragraph into Chinese.

On the morning of September 11, 2001, two civilian passenger planes hijacked by terrorists crashed into the World Trade Center in New York, two buildings collapsed after attack. The "9.11" incident was the worst terrorist attack in the United States, with 2,996 victims. Statistics on the property losses in the incident, the United Nations issued a report that the terrorist attack lost $200 billion to the US economy, equivalent to 2% of the year's GDP. The damage to the global economy has even reached around $1 trillion. The psychological impact on the American people has severely weakened their economic and political security.

Ⅴ. Answer the following questions.

1. What is the system that PPBM describes?

2. How much direct economic loss that a terrorist attack may cause to civil aviation?

Chapter 7
NEW TRENDS

Section 1
IATA New Distribution Capacity

Lead in

Xiamen Airlines Built e-Commerce Capacity Platform

On May 15, 2020, according to the NDC standard put forward by IATA and based on the concept of "large and medium platform, small front desk", Xiamen Airlines has built a set of enterprise-level e-commerce capacity *platform*. It has become the first airline in China to fully independently developed and achieve NDC18.2 standards (Figure 7-1) and successfully put into production, taking the lead in supporting the combination sales of air tickets and additional services.

Figure 7-1　NDC Certification

Special Terms

1. XML: Extensible tag language, which can be used to tag data and define data types, is a tag that allows users to mark themselves source language for a defined language. It is very suitable for world wide web transmission and provides a unified method to describe and exchange structured data independent of applications or suppliers.

可扩展标记语言:可以用来标记数据、定义数据类型,是一种允许用户对自己的标记语言进行定义的源语言。它非常适合万维网传输,提供统一的方法来描述和交换独立于应用程序或供应商的结构化数据。

2. API:Application Programming Interface refer to some predefined interfaces (such as functions and HTTP interfaces), or conventions for the connection of different components of the software system. It is used to provide a set of routines that can be accessed by applications and developers based on some software or hardware without accessing the source code or understanding the details of the internal working mechanism.

应用程序接口:是一些预先定义的接口(如函数、HTTP接口),或指软件系统不同组成部分衔接的约定。用来提供应用程序与开发人员基于某软件或硬件得以访问的一组例程,而无须访问源码或理解内部工作机制的细节。

3. Marginal Cost: It refers to the increase in the total cost caused by the new produced product of each unit.

边际成本:指的是每一单位新增生产的产品带来的总成本的增量。

Text

With the advancement of the IATA new *distribution capacity* (NDC-New Distribution Capability) standards (Figure 7-2), the whole industry has undergone huge changes. The IATA launched the NDC program in 2012, a new XML-based data transfer standard that has changed the way airlines operate as a *retailer*, providing it with a better way to sell products to buyers. According to IATA, NDC overcomes the limitations of the current distribution model to help airlines differentiate their products, accelerate time-to-market, allow channel access to complete aviation product content and create a *transparent* shopping experience for customers. NDC is transforming the airline's business platform from a pure ticket distribution model to an "air *retail business model.*"

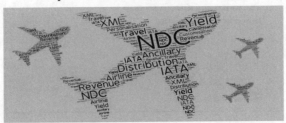

Figure 7-2　NDC

Chapter 7 NEW TRENDS

Notes 1

❶ The IATA launched the NDC program in 2012, a new XML-based data transfer standard that has changed the way airlines operate as a retailer, providing it with a better way to sell products to buyers.

解释:国际航空运输协会于2012年推出了新分销能力(NDC)计划,这是一个新的基于XML的数据传输标准,改变了航空公司作为零售商的运营方式,为其提供了向买家销售产品的更好方式。

语法:"a new XML-based data transfer standard"为同位语,对前面的"NDC program"做进一步说明。that 引导定语从句,修饰前面的"transfer standard"。

❷ According to IATA, NDC overcomes the limitations of the current distribution model to help airlines differentiate their products, accelerate time-to-market, allow channel access to complete aviation product content and create a transparent shopping experience for customers.

解释:根据国际航空运输协会的说法,NDC克服了当前分销模式的局限性,帮助航空公司实现产品差异化,加快上市时间,允许渠道访问完整的航空产品内容,并为客户创造透明的购物体验。

The Origin of the NDC

NDC starts with American direct connection mode. Because the distribution cost of GDS is high, the worse is who the product is sold to, how much to sell, when to sell, sell or do not sell is not their own final say, so airlines across GDS directly to find an agent.

This *direct connection mode* was proposed in 2008, and was immediately *besieged* by the GDS and AA's poor performance was on the *verge* of *bankruptcy*, so it quickly ended in failure. After five or six years of silence, the direct connection mode came back to the public eye with the new face of IATA NDC standard, this time the *slogan* is no longer bypass GDS, but airlines facing new challenges with GDS. The goal was to regain control of the distribution from the GDS and the coerced agents.

Notes 2

❶ This direct connection mode was proposed in 2008, and was immediately besieged by the GDS and AA's poor performance was on the verge of bankruptcy, so it quickly ended in failure.

解释:这种直接连接模式是在2008年提出的,并立即被全球分销系统(GDS)围攻,加上AA(美国航空公司)的表现不佳处于破产的边缘,因此很快以失败告终。

❷ The goal was to regain control of the distribution from the GDS and the coerced agents.

解释:其目标是从GDS和被控制的代理那里重新获得对分销的控制。

The Adcantages of the NDC

First, without a special network *backup*, a virtual private *bandwidth* still costs tens of thousands of yuan a year, and it only needs to use the Internet.

Second, without a rigid EDIFACT *protocol*, switch to flexible and *extensible* XML; NDC provides airlines with the ability to *integrate* other suppliers (including other airlines, hotels, *car rental* and other products) and be integrated by others. Positive interactions with the outside world are the basis for *cultivating* an ecosystem, when NDC becomes a new way of thinking that gives the aviation industry the basis for producing this *ecological* environment.

Third, NDC's philosophy can minimize the messaging chain between customers and suppliers, ideally completely eliminate information *asymmetry* and allow users to directly face suppliers or *vice versa*. The current air ticket sales chain is too long, with 6 or 7 links. The reasons for this are *multifaceted*, mainly driven by business development. In the past, many middlemen make money through information asymmetry, but one of the trends of the Internet is to eliminate information asymmetry, so this too long information transmission chain will eventually be eliminated.

Notes 3

❶ First, without a special network backup, a virtual private bandwidth still costs tens of thousands of yuan a year, and it only needs to use the Internet.

解释：首先，不需要一个特殊的网络备份，一条虚拟专用带宽每年仍花费数万元，而它只需要使用互联网即可。

❷ Second, without a rigid EDIFACT protocol, switch to flexible and extensible XML; NDC provides airlines with the ability to integrate other suppliers (including other airlines, hotels, car rental and other products) and be integrated by others.

解释：第二，不需要死板的 EDIFACT 协议，改用灵活可扩展的 XML 即可；NDC 为航空公司提供了集成其他供应商（包括其他航空公司、酒店、汽车租赁和其他产品）并被其他公司集成的能力。

❸ Third, NDC's philosophy can minimize the messaging chain between customers and suppliers, ideally completely eliminate information asymmetry and allow users to directly face suppliers or vice versa.

解释：第三，NDC 的理念能够将客户和供应商之间的信息传递链条缩到最短，理想情况下能够完全消除信息不对称，允许用户直接面对供应商，反之亦然。

Impact of NDC on the Air Tourism Industy

NDC gives a new idea that airlines thought their products and services could only be sold through GDS, OTA or e-commerce platforms, but now find that the products and services could not only sell but also take control back into API (Figure 7-3). These products and services have a large number of common features: high *fixed cost*, low *marginal* cost, and invalid expiration, which can be purchased in advance but delivered from person to face. The only difference is that the aviation industry started earlier and became more mature, and the adoption of NDC is the result of natural development, but this little difference is not enough to hinder the model from making a step-by-step *breakthrough* and innovation in other industries. Moreover, after the *baptism* of hotel industry and car rental industry in the years of Internet *entrepreneurship*, they have basically had this ability.

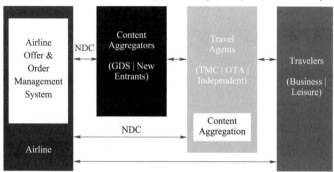

Figure 7-3　NDC Model

Notes 4

❶ NDC gives a new idea that airlines thought their products and services could only be sold through GDS, OTA or e-commerce platforms, but now find that the products and services could not only sell but also take control back into API.

解释:NDC给出了一种全新的思路,航空公司原以为自己的产品和服务只能通过GDS、线上旅行代理商(OTA)或者电商平台销售,但现在发现通过将产品和服务封装成应用程序接口(API)不仅能销售还可以将控制权完全拿回来。

❷ These products and services have a large number of common features: high fixed cost, low marginal cost, and invalid expiration, which can be purchased in advance but delivered from person to face.

解释:这些产品和服务有大量的共同特点:固定成本高、边际成本低、过期无效,可以提前购买,但要当面交付。

❸ Moreover, after the baptism of hotel industry and car rental industry in the years of Internet entrepreneurship, they have basically had this ability.

解释:而且,酒店业和租车业经过这几年互联网创业的洗礼,已经基本具备了这种能力。

Further Reading

Controversy: NDC Reduce Fare Transparency

NDC gets personal information from airline websites or travel agencies, and packaged products tailored to each consumer can actually reduce transaction transparency and bundle additional service products within the fare. For example, your fee includes several *bundled quotes*, and according to IATA, consumers can cancel bundles as long as other online shopping do if they don't need them. But even in addition to a certain service product in the packaged product, you can't know the real ticket price. Because there is no clear price list, you can see how the system calculates the total price. And each airline bundles very different from fares.

New Words

platform	[ˈplætfɔːm]	n.	平台；讲台
distribution	[ˌdɪstrɪˈbjuːʃən]	n.	分布；分配；供应
capacity	[kəˈpæsəti]	n.	能力；容量
retailer	[ˈriːteɪlə(r)]	n.	零售商；传播的人
transparent	[trænsˈpærənt]	adj.	透明的；显然的；易懂的
besiege	[bɪˈsiːdʒ]	vt.	围困；包围；烦扰
verge	[vɜːdʒ]	n.	边缘
		v.	濒临，处在边缘
bankruptcy	[ˈbæŋkrʌptsɪ]	n.	破产
slogan	[ˈsləʊɡən]	n.	标语；呐喊声
backup	[ˈbækʌp]	n.	支持；后援
		adj.	支持的；候补的
		vt.	做备份
bandwidth	[ˈbændwɪdθ]	n.	[电子][物]带宽；[通信]频带宽度
protocol	[ˈprəʊtəkɒl]	n.	协议；草案；礼仪
		vt.	拟定
		vi.	拟定
extensible	[ɪkˈstensəb(ə)l]	adj.	可延长的；可扩张的
integrate	[ˈɪntɪɡreɪt]	vt.	使……完整
		vi.	成为一体
		adj.	整合的
		n.	一体化；集成体
cultivate	[ˈkʌltɪveɪt]	vt.	培养；陶冶；耕作
ecological	[ˌiːkəˈlɒdʒɪkl]	adj.	生态的，生态学的
asymmetry	[ˌeɪˈsɪmətrɪ]	n.	不对称
multifaceted	[ˌmʌltɪˈfæsɪtɪd]	adj.	多层面的，要从多方面考虑的
marginal	[ˈmɑːdʒɪnl]	adj.	微不足道的，不重要的；边缘的
		n.	边缘席位
breakthrough	[ˈbreɪkθruː]	n.	突破；突破性进展
baptism	[ˈbæptɪzəm]	n.	洗礼；严峻考验
entrepreneurship	[ˌɒntrəprəˈnɜːʃɪp]	n.	企业家精神
controversy	[ˈkɒntrəvɜːsɪ]	n.	争论；论战；辩论
transparency	[trænsˈpærənsɪ]	n.	透明，透明度；幻灯片

Phrases & Expressions

new distribution capacity	新分销能力
retail business model	零售商业模式
direct connection mode	直连模式
car rental	汽车租赁
vice versa	反之亦然
fixed cost	固定成本
marginal cost	边际成本
bundled quote	捆绑报价

Exercises

I. Translate the following terms into Chinese or English.

1. marginal cost
2. new distribution capacity
3. direct connection mode
4. bundled quote
5. 固定成本
6. 汽车租赁
7. 零售模式
8. 分销

II. Cloze.

(direct connection/NDC/API/platform/retail/integrate)

1. The IATA launched the _____ program in 2012, a new XML-based data transfer standard that has changed the way airlines operate as a retailer, providing it with a better way to sell products to buyers.

2. NDC is transforming the airline's business platform from a pure ticket distribution model to an "air _____ business model".

3. NDC starts with American _____ mode.

4. NDC provides airlines with the ability to _____ other suppliers (including other airlines, hotels, car rental and other products) and be integrated by others.

III. Translate the following sentences into Chinese.

1. In the past, many middlemen make money through information asymmetry, but one of the trends of the Internet is to eliminate information asymmetry, so this too long information transmission chain will eventually be eliminated.

2. Because the distribution cost of GDS is high, the worse is who the product is sold to, how much to sell, when to sell, sell or do not sell is not their own final say, so airlines across GDS directly to find an agent.

3. NDC's philosophy can minimize the messaging chain between customers and suppliers, ideally completely eliminate information asymmetry and allow users to directly face suppliers or vice versa.

IV. Translate the following paragraph into Chinese.

NDC gets personal information from airline websites or travel agencies, and packaged products tailored to each consumer can actually reduce transaction transparency and bundle additional service products within the fare. For example, your fee includes several bundled quotes, and according to IATA, consumers can cancel bundles as long as other online shopping do if they don't need them. But even in addition to a certain service product in the packaged product, you can't know the real ticket price. Because there is no clear price list, you can see how the system calculates the total price. And each airline bundles very different from fares.

V. Answer the following questions.

1. What is the English full name of the NDC?

2. Who proposed the NDC?

Chapter 7 NEW TRENDS

Section 2
ONE Order Plan

Lead in

Xiamen Airlines's Digital Change

On July 8, 2021, Xiamen Airlines received its *ONE Order* certification from IATA (Figure 7-4), becoming the fourth airline to be certified worldwide. From 2019, NDC features went online and received NDC Level 4 certification, to ONE Order certification. Xiamen Airlines has accelerated the digital *empowerment*, further improved the construction of e-commerce platform and built the NDC direct connection *ecology*, and laid a good foundation for building the digital *innovation* customer-oriented ability, improving the *intelligent* business-oriented operation ability, and expanding the ecosystem connectivity capacity for the air and tourism industry.

Figure 7-4　ONE Order certification

Special Terms

1. PNR: Passenger Name Record. PNR is a database containing passenger travel information, and usually each PNR assigns an index code consisting of five or six letters.

旅客定座记录：是一个包含旅客旅行信息的数据库，通常每个旅客定座记录分配一个由5个或6个字母组成的索引代码。

2. EMD: electronic miscellaneous bill is a service and payment voucher provided by the airline when purchasing additional services such as an airport lounge or seat upgrade.

电子杂项账单:是指航空公司诸如在购买机场休息室或座位升级等额外服务时提供的服务和付款凭证。

Text

The current passenger trip booking and ticketing service operations are based on three core *components*:

• PNR: *Passenger Name Record*. PNR is a database containing passenger travel information, and usually each PNR assigns an index code consisting of five or six letters.

• *Electronic ticket* (ET): Each electronic ticket usually corresponds to a passenger, that is, a passenger's trip may be presented with multiple electronic tickets. Electronic passenger tickets are indexed by 13-digit ticket numbers.

• EMD: *Electronic miscellaneous bill* is a service and payment *voucher* provided by the airline when purchasing additional services such as an airport lounge or seat upgrade. The EMD system is independent of the PNR and electronic ticket systems and is identified by the EMD number.

These three elements are the *cornerstone* of airlines providing travelers with services such as booking, purchase, payment, electronic tickets, and additional service products. The technical challenges facing existing systems are that different systems between airlines, airports, airline partners and other service providers need to constantly exchange these passenger travel information during the marketing and service processes. One of the primary design objectives of all these systems was to achieve *mutual synchronization* between systems, but due to the complexity of background systems, sometimes (often times) information exchange has problems.

Notes 1

❶ These three elements are the cornerstone of airlines providing travelers with services such as booking, purchase, payment, electronic tickets, and additional service products.

解释:这三个要素是航空公司为旅客提供预订、购买、支付、电子客票以及附加服务产品等服务的基石。

❷ One of the primary design objectives of all these systems was to achieve mutual synchronization between systems, but due to the complexity of background systems, sometimes (often times) information exchange has problems.

解释:所有这些系统最初的主要设计目标之一就是实现系统间的互相同步,但是由于后台系统的复杂性,有时候(其实是很多时候)信息交换工作会出现问题。

Rooted in NDC

With the advancement of the IATA new distribution capacity (NDC) standards, the whole industry has undergone huge changes. NDC is transforming the airline's business platform from a ticket distribution model to an "air retail business model." ONE Order is the next step in the entire business *logic* that will further enhance airline marketing and service capabilities (Figure 7-5). At present, the system used by the industry has been running for more than 50 years, and the background situation of the system can be basically described as "*patch stack patch*". ONE Order can completely change this by providing *industry-level* XML-based data exchange standards to unlock the interaction between airline order management systems, *revenue settlement systems*, and *service delivery systems* (and business processes).

Figure 7-5　One Order age

How can we completely change this situation and eliminate the *patchwork* of information between systems? If every transaction processing in the travel experience can be found from a "single" record number, how simple the travel management becomes! "Single" orders store information about tickets, reservation, refunds, seat upgrades, lounges, and other services. What if hotel charges and ground transport services were included? The key goal of the "ONE Order" plan is to replace the three basic elements of PNR, electronic tickets and EMD with unified orders. With the use of an "order number" to obtain full travel information, the interaction complexity between all systems will disappear, making it easier, faster, and more stable and *robust* to serve customers. While detailed steps on how the plan are still planned, it is predicted that the project will revolutionize the tourism industry over the next decade. Building the business model above the plan, the total travel cost and *expenditure* will become readily available and fully *transparent*, which can greatly simplify the process of travel management, enhance the service experience of passengers, and provide more means for travel *management companies* to conduct price negotiations with airlines.

Notes 2

❶ ONE Order can completely change this by providing industry-level XML-based data exchange standards to unlock the interaction between airline order management systems, revenue settlement systems, and service delivery systems (and business processes).

解释：通过提供行业级的基于 XML 的数据交换标准来打通航空公司订单管理系统、收入结算系统以及服务交付系统(以及业务流程)之间的交互过程,"全单"能彻底改变这种情况。

❷ The key goal of the "ONE Order" plan is to replace the three basic elements of PNR, electronic tickets and EMD with unified orders.

解释:"全单"计划的关键目标是用统一的订单取代旅客定座记录、电子机票和电子杂项账单的三个基本要素。

❸ Building the business model above the plan, the total travel cost and expenditure will become readily available and fully transparent, which can greatly simplify the process of travel management, enhance the service experience of passengers, and provide more means for travel management companies to conduct price negotiations with airlines.

解释:将业务模式构建于该计划之上,差旅总花费和支出将变得随时可用并完全透明,能够极大简化差旅管理的过程,增强旅客的服务体验,并能为差旅管理公司与航空公司进行价格谈判提供更多手段。

语法:Building the business model above the plan 现在分词作条件状语,一般放句首。

An Ambitious Plan

ONE Order is an *ambitious* program that requires change, or even reform, from all *stakeholders* in air tourism. ONE Order will create a brand new air tourism data ecosystem that airlines want to achieve opening to the outside world. From an airline's perspective, it is *imperative* to narrow the gap with ordinary e-commerce, which will *prompt* a lot of innovations and things that we have never even imagined today.

Notes 3

"ONE Order" is an ambitious program that requires change, or even reform, from all stakeholders in air tourism.

解释:"全单"是一项雄心勃勃的计划,它要求航空旅游业的所有利益相关者进行改变,甚至变革。

Further Reading

Interline Transfer Between Traditional Airlines and Low-Cost Airlines

ONE Order can also be effectively integrated in the *interline transfer* business between traditional airlines and low-cost airlines. ONE Order is able to integrate segments from traditional and new low-cost carriers, such as Spirit and Ryanair, who already have the ability to create a single customer order record for each reservation. ONE Order standards make interline transfer or code-sharing business and back-office systems between traditional and new low-cost airlines simpler.

New Words

empowerment	[ɪmˈpaʊəmənt]	n. 许可,授权
ecology	[ɪˈkɒlədʒɪ]	n. 生态学;社会生态学
innovation	[ˌɪnəˈveɪʃən]	n. 创新,革新

intelligent	[ɪnˈtelɪdʒənt]	adj. 智能的;聪明的
component	[kəmˈpəʊnənt]	n. 组成部分;组件,元件
		adj. 组成的;构成的
voucher	[ˈvaʊtʃə(r)]	n. 收据;证人
		vt. 证实……的可靠性
cornerstone	[ˈkɔːnəstəʊn]	n. 基础;柱石;地基
mutual	[ˈmjuːtʃʊəl]	adj. 共同的;相互的,彼此的
synchronization	[ˌsɪŋkrənaɪˈzeɪʃən]	n. [物] 同步;同时性
root	[ruːt]	n. 根;根源
		vi. 生根
		vt. 生根;根源在于
logic	[ˈlɒdʒɪk]	n. 逻辑;逻辑学;逻辑性
patchwork	[ˈpætʃwɜːk]	adj. 拼缝的
		n. 拼缝物
robust	[rəʊˈbʌst]	adj. 强健的;粗鲁的
expenditure	[ɪkˈspendɪtʃə(r)]	n. 支出,经费
transparent	[trænsˈpærənt]	adj. 透明的;坦率的;易懂的
ambitious	[æmˈbɪʃəs]	adj. 野心勃勃的;有雄心的;热望的;炫耀的
stakeholder	[ˈsteɪkhəʊldə(r)]	n. 利益相关者;赌金保管者
imperative	[ɪmˈperətɪv]	adj. 必要的
		n. 必要的事;命令;需要
prompt	[prɒmpt]	v. 促进
		adj. 敏捷的
		n. 鼓励
		adv. 准时地

Phrases & Expressions

ONE Order	全单、单一订单
passenger Name Record	旅客定座记录
electronic ticket	电子客票
electronic miscellaneous bill	电子杂费账单
patch stack patch	补丁摞补丁
industry-level	行业标准
revenue settlement systems	收益结算系统
service delivery systems	服务交付系统
travel management company	差旅管理公司
interline transfer	联运业务

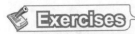

I. Translate the following terms into Chinese or English.

1. travel management company
2. revenue settlement systems
3. industry-level
4. service delivery systems
5. 全单
6. 电子杂费账单
7. 旅客定座记录
8. 电子客票

II. Cloze.

(ecosystem/NDC/PNR/platform/ONE Order/integrate)

1. _____ is a database containing passenger travel information, and usually each PNR assigns an index code consisting of five or six letters.

2. The key goal of the _____ plan is to replace the three basic elements of PNR, electronic tickets and EMD with unified orders.

3. With the advancement of the IATA _____ standards, the whole industry has undergone huge changes. It is transforming the airline's business platform from a ticket distribution model to an "air retail business model."

4. ONE Order will create a brand new air tourism data _____ that airlines want to achieve opening to the outside world.

III. Translate the following sentences into Chinese.

1. Each electronic ticket usually corresponds to a passenger, that is, a passenger's trip may be presented with multiple electronic tickets. Electronic passenger tickets are indexed by 13-digit ticket numbers.

2. ONE Order is the next step in the entire business logic that will further enhance airline marketing and service capabilities.

IV. Translate the following paragraph into Chinese.

From 2019, NDC features went online and received NDC Level 4 certification, to ONE Order certification. Xiamen Airlines has accelerated the digital empowerment, further improved the construction of e-commerce platform and built the NDC direct connection ecology, and laid a good foundation for building the digital innovation customer-oriented ability, improving the intelligent business-oriented operation ability, and expanding the ecosystem connectivity capacity for the air and tourism industry.

V. Answer the following questions.

1. What three elements can ONE Order integrate in passenger travel?

2. What does the EMD work for?

Section 3
Build Global "123" Fast Cargo Flow Circle

Convert Passenger Aircraft Into Cargo Aircraft

Aircraft Engineering (Lufthansa Technik) of Lufthansa Group is interested to convert an Airbus A380 into a cargo aircraft during COVID-19 (Figure 7-6). The customer asked the company to help *temporarily* convert a A380 aircraft into a cargo aircraft that will *implement* cabin cargo for the A380 to remove cabin seats. By May 2020, the company had received inquiries from more than 40 airlines interested in aircraft modification. Currently, about 15 projects are in progress.

Figure 7-6　Passenger plane to cargo aircraft

Special Terms

1. Supply-side structural reform: Starts from improving the quality of supply, use reform to promote structural adjustment, correct the distortion of the allocation of factors, expand effective supply, improve the adaptability and flexibility of the supply structure to demand changes, improve total factor productivity, and promote sustainable and healthy economic and social development.

供给侧结构性改革:从提高供给质量出发,用改革的办法推进结构调整,矫正要素配置扭曲,扩大有效供给,提高供给结构对需求变化的适应性和灵活性,提高全要素生产率,促进经济社会持续健康发展。

2. Belt and Road: It is called the "Silk Road Economic Belt" and the "21st Century Maritime Silk Road" for short. Relying on the existing dual-multilateral mechanism between China and relevant countries, with the help of the existing and effective regional cooperation platform, using the historical symbols of the ancient Silk Road, actively develop economic cooperation partnerships with countries along the Belt and Road, and jointly build a community of political mutual trust, economic integration and cultural inclusiveness.

一带一路:是"丝绸之路经济带"和"21世纪海上丝绸之路"的简称。依靠中国与有关国家既有的双多边机制,借助既有的、行之有效的区域合作平台,借用古代丝绸之路的历史符号,积极发展与沿线国家的经济合作伙伴关系,共同打造政治互信、经济融合、文化包容的共同体。

Text

Since the outbreak of the COVID-19 *epidemic*, China's civil aviation industry has played an important role in the prevention and control of the epidemic, continuously strengthening the transportation support, and fully ensuring the smooth flow of the international logistics *supply chain* (Figure 7-7). But at the same time, it also exposes the lack of independent and control ability of the international logistics supply chain. Strengthening air cargo capacity is a high concern and urgent problem for civil aviation.

Figure 7-7　Air freight under the epidemic

Accelerate the Development of Air Cargo

The Civil Aviation Administration of China will work hard from seven aspects to speed up the shortcomings in international air freight.

1. *Accelerate the supply-side structural reform* of air *logistics*, promote the transformation and upgrading of traditional air logistics to modern logistics, and encourage the development of *multimodal transport*, especially freight airlines to cooperate with e-commerce and express delivery enterprises, so as to achieve benefits of scale and gradually become stronger and bigger.

2. Respect the rules of the market, activate the market vitality, break the *boundary* of ownership, give policy support to the powerful air logistics enterprises, and build them into a world-class air logistics enterprises.

3. Further promote liberalization negotiations with major trading partners and national cargo rights of "*Belt and Road*" countries, better facilitate China's air cargo enterprises to set up networks overseas, build overseas transport centers, and accelerate the construction of a globally accessible and independent and controllable international logistics network.

4. Accelerate the transformation and upgrading of freight facilities at hub airports (Figure 7-8). On the basis of the existing international hubs, we will focus on building international air cargo hubs such as Zhengzhou, Tianjin, Hefei and Ezhou, and form an industrial *cluster* of air logistics distribution.

Figure 7-8 Upgrading freight facilities at hub airports

5. Further optimize the flight resource time allocation. According to the airport positioning, airports with strong cargo supply capacity will liberalize the restrictions on cargo flights during peak hours, and support airlines to build cargo flight waves.

6. Build a public information platform for air logistics, improve the digitalization and informatization of air freight, and build smart civil aviation.

7. Further *optimize* the environment of air cargo operators, strengthen cooperation with customs, and achieve "7 × 24" hour *customs clearance* in international air cargo hubs where conditions permit, to meet the needs of rapid customs clearance of air cargo.

Notes 1

❶ Respect the rules of the market, activate the market vitality, break the boundary of ownership, give policy support to the powerful air logistics enterprises, and build them into a world-class air logistics enterprises.

解释:尊重市场规律,激活市场活力,打破所有权界限,对于具有实力的航空物流企业给予政策支持,将其打造成世界级航空物流企业。

break the boundary of ownership:打破所有权界限,企业所有权可以有国有、集体、民营、中外合资等。

❷ Further optimize the flight resource time allocation. According to the airport positioning, airports with strong cargo supply capacity will liberalize the restrictions on cargo flights during peak hours, and support airlines to build cargo flight waves.

解释:进一步优化航班资源时刻配置。根据机场定位,对货物供应能力强的机场放开高峰时段对货运航班的限制,支持航空公司构建货运航班波。

❸ Further optimize the environment of air cargo operators, strengthen cooperation with customs, and achieve "7×24" hour customs clearance in international air cargo hubs where conditions permit, to meet the needs of rapid customs clearance of air cargo.

解释:进一步优化航空货运营商环境,加强与海关合作,在具备条件的国际航空货运枢纽实现"7×24"小时通关,满足航空货运快速通关需求。

Build Global "123" Fast Cargo Flow Circle (Figure 7-9)

Give full play to the *comparative* advantages of civil aviation in the long-distance transportation of high added value and high timeliness goods, and focus on promoting three aspects.

First, actively explore potential and increase efficiency, and *comprehensively* improve the service level of domestic one-day service. At present, Beijing, Shanghai, Hangzhou, Shenzhen, domestic one day service, has formed a *route network* foundation.

Figure 7-9 "123" fast cargo flow circle

Civil aviation will make comprehensive use of passenger aircraft's belly hold and all-cargo aircraft resources, further improve the flight frequency and connection efficiency, and deliver the arrival goods as soon as possible; all cargo routes between the Beijing-Tianjin-Hebei region, the Yangtze River Delta, Guangdong, Hong Kong and Macao, Chengdu-Chongqing *urban clusters*, key cities and air logistics hubs, increase flight density to Midwest transport airports, promote inter-provincial exchanges of general air logistics networks, mutual access between cities and counties, and give consideration to urban and rural areas, expand the *UAV* distribution network in areas with inconvenient transportation, expand the scope of air cargo cover; promote the "*one single system*" combined transport mode of air-railway, air-land and air-sea, accelerate the development of multimodal transport, we will build a smooth rapid, diversified and specialized freight channel for places of production, processing and consumption.

Second, strengthen regional cooperation and focus on strengthening the service capacity of two days in *neighboring countries*. At present, China and neighboring countries have exceeded 1,100 weekly cargo flights, which can basically meet the needs of the route network supporting neighboring countries in two days.

The Civil Aviation Administration will guide airlines to optimize the route and increase flight density to Southeast Asia, Russia, Japan and South Korea and other neighboring countries, further weave the express route network to the surrounding areas of Asia, and *consolidate* the network support for 2-day service from neighboring countries.

Third, optimize the network *layout*, and actively expand the route network delivered by major cities in the world for 3 days. Europe and the United States are important economic and trade partners in China, but the route network of China and its main cities needs to be further strengthened, and the flight frequency needs to be further improved. There are still gaps in the route network coverage in Africa and *Latin America*.

The Civil Aviation Administration will actively strengthen international air freedom negotiations with relevant countries, increase access to key air freedom resources, facilitate Chinese freight enterprises to set up networks overseas; speed up the layout of intercontinental remote routes, *strive* to build a safe, efficient, independent and controllable international air freight network, and strive to build a route network that supports the 3-day service by major cities around the world.

Notes 2

❶ Civil aviation will make comprehensive use of passenger aircraft's cargo hold and all-cargo aircraft resources, further improve the flight frequency and connection efficiency, and deliver the arrival goods as soon as possible.

解释:民航将综合利用客机腹舱和全货机资源,进一步提高航班频率和衔接效率,实现货物随到随走。

❷ All cargo routes between the Beijing-Tianjin-Hebei region, the Yangtze River Delta, Guangdong, Hong Kong and Macao, Chengdu-Chongqing urban clusters, key cities and air logistics hubs, increase flight density to Midwest transport airports, promote inter-provincial exchanges of general air logistics networks, mutual access between cities and counties, and give consideration to urban and rural areas, expand the UAV distribution network in areas with inconvenient transportation, Expand the scope of air cargo cover.

解释：在京津冀、长三角、粤港澳、成渝城市群和重点城市、航空物流枢纽间布局全货运航线网络，加密中西部运输机场，推进通用航空物流网络省际互通、市县互达、城乡兼顾，扩大交通不便地区无人机配送网络，扩大航空货运覆盖范围。

❸ The Civil Aviation Administration will guide airlines to optimize the route and increase flight density to Southeast Asia, Russia, Japan and South Korea and other neighboring countries, further weave the express route network to the surrounding areas of Asia, and *consolidate* the network support for 2-day service from neighboring countries.

解释：民航局将引导航空公司优化加密东南亚、俄罗斯、日韩等周边国家航线航班，进一步织密通达亚洲周边的快运航线网络，夯实周边国家2天送达的网络支撑。

neighboring countries：周边国家。

❹ The Civil Aviation Administration will actively strengthen international air freedom negotiations with relevant countries, increase access to key air freedom resources, facilitate Chinese freight enterprises to set up networks overseas.

解释：民航局将积极与有关国家加大国际航权谈判力度，增加关键航权资源的获取，便利我国货运企业在境外设点布网。

Further Reading

Air-Land Combined Transport (Figure 7-10)

Truck flights play a key role in the "*single end*" of air-land combined cargo transport. At present, China's major air cargo hubs, such as Hong Kong Airport, Beijing Capital Airport, Shanghai Pudong Airport, Guangzhou Airport, Shenzhen Airport, etc. The main way to *disperse* the surrounding goods is through truck flights. China Freight Airlines, China Eastern Airlines Logistics and other have a very mature truck flight business, support its cargo distribution at the hub airport.

Figure 7-10　Truck flight

In addition to the relatively mature international form of air-land combined cargo transport, the vast majority of air cargo requires the "*last kilometer*" distribution by land trucks. After all, air transport is airport to airport, and airport to customers depends entirely on trucks. Therefore, aviation has a strong dependence on overland trucks. In turn, the distribution of air cargo is an important service content of land trucks. The two are interdependent and promote together.

New Words

temporarily	[ˈtemprərəli]	adv.	临时地,临时
implement	[ˈɪmplɪment]	vt.	实施,使生效
		n.	工具;手段
epidemic	[ˌepɪˈdemɪk]	n.	传染病
		adj.	流行的;传染性的
accelerate	[əkˈseləreɪt]	vt.	使……加快;使……增速
		vi.	加速;促进
logistics	[ləˈdʒɪstɪks]	n.	物流;后勤工作
boundary	[ˈbaʊndri]	n.	边界;范围;分界线
cluster	[ˈklʌstə(r)]	n.	群;丛
		vi.	群聚;丛生
		vt.	使聚集
optimize	[ˈɒptɪmaɪz]	vt.	使最优化,使完善
		vi.	优化;持乐观态度
comparative	[kəmˈpærətɪv]	adj.	比较的;相当的
		n.	比较级;对手
comprehensive	[ˌkɒmprɪˈhensɪv]	adj.	综合的;有理解力的
		n.	综合学校
consolidate	[kənˈsɒlɪdeɪt]	vt.	巩固,联合
		vi.	巩固,加强
layout	[ˈleɪaʊt]	n.	布局;陈列
strive	[straɪv]	vi.	努力;奋斗
disperse	[dɪˈspɜːs]	vt.	分散;传播
		vi.	分散
		adj.	分散的

Phrases & Expressions

supply chain	供应链
supply-side structural reform	供给侧结构性改革
multimodal transport	多式联运

Belt and Road	一带一路
customs clearance	清关
route network	航线网
urban clusters	城市群
UAV	无人机
one single system	一单制
neighboring countries	周边国家
Latin America	拉丁美洲
Truck flights	卡车航班
single end	一单到底
last kilometer	最后一公里

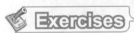

Ⅰ. Translate the following terms into Chinese or English.

1. Belt and Road
2. customs clearance
3. one single system
4. UAV
5. 航线网
6. 多式联运
7. 航空物流
8. 供应链

Ⅱ. Cloze.

(one-day/customs clearance/multimodal/logistics/two-day/hub)

1. Accelerate the transformation and upgrading of freight facilities at _____ airports.

2. Further optimize the environment of air cargo operators, strengthen cooperation with customs, and achieve "7×24" hour _____ in international air cargo hubs where conditions permit.

3. Actively explore potential and increase efficiency, and comprehensively improve the service level of domestic _____ service.

4. Promote the "one single system" combined transport mode of air-railway, air-land and air-sea, accelerate the development of _____ transport.

Ⅲ. Translate the following sentences into Chinese.

1. Encourage the development of multimodal transport, especially freight airlines to cooperate with e-commerce and express delivery enterprises, so as to achieve benefits of scale and gradually become stronger and bigger.

2. Speed up the layout of intercontinental remote routes, strive to build a safe, efficient, independent and controllable international air freight network, and strive to build a route network that supports the 3-day service by major cities around the world.

IV. Translate the following paragraph into Chinese.

In addition to the relatively mature international form of air-land combined cargo transport, the vast majority of air cargo requires the "last kilometer" distribution by land trucks. After all, air transport is airport to airport, and airport to customers depends entirely on trucks. Therefore, aviation has a strong dependence on overland trucks. In turn, the distribution of air cargo is an important service content of land trucks. The two are interdependent and promote together.

V. Answer the following questions.

According to the goal of building a fast cargo flow circle, how many days are the goods required to arrive to major cities in the world?

Appendix 1

Extract from airline two character code and ticket settlement code

两字代码	票证代号	航空公司名称	两字代码	票证代号	航空公司名称
AA	001	美国航空公司	LO	080	波兰航空公司
AB	745	柏林航空公司	LY	114	以色列航空公司
AC	014	加拿大国际航空公司	MH	232	马来西亚航空公司
AE	803	华信航空有限公司	MI	629	新加坡胜安航空公司
AF	057	法国航空公司	MS	077	埃及航空公司
AI	098	印度航空公司	MU	781	中国东方航空公司
AM	139	墨西哥航空公司	NH	205	全日本航空公司
AY	105	芬兰航空公司	NX	675	澳门航空公司
AZ	055	意大利航空公司	NZ	086	新西兰航空公司
BA	125	英国航空公司	OM	289	蒙古航空公司
BI	672	文莱皇家航空公司	OS	257	奥地利航空公司
BR	695	台湾长荣航空股份有限公司	OZ	988	韩亚航空公司
CA	999	中国国际航空公司	PG	829	曼谷航空有限公司
CI	297	台湾中华航空股份有限公司	PK	214	巴基斯坦航空公司
CX	160	国泰航空公司	PR	079	菲律宾航空公司
CZ	784	中国南方航空公司	QF	081	澳洲航空公司
DL	006	美国达美航空公司	QR	157	卡塔尔航空公司
EK	176	阿联酋航空公司	RA	285	尼泊尔皇家航空公司
ET	071	埃塞俄比亚航空公司	SK	117	北欧航空公司
EY	607	阿联酋阿提哈德航空公司	SQ	618	新加坡航空公司
FV	195	俄罗斯国家航空公司	SU	555	俄罗斯航空公司
GA	126	印度尼西亚鹰航空公司	S7	421	西伯利亚航空公司
GF	072	海湾航空公司	TG	217	泰国航空公司
HX	851	香港航空有限公司	TK	235	土耳其航空公司
HY	250	乌兹别克斯坦航空公司	UA	016	美国联合航空公司
JL	131	日本航空公司	UL	603	斯里兰卡航空公司
KE	180	大韩航空公司	UO	128	香港快运航空有限公司
KQ	706	肯尼亚航空公司	VN	738	越南航空公司
LH	220	德国汉莎航空公司	VS	932	维珍航空公司

Appendix 2

Airport code of major cities in China

机场名称	机场代码	机场名称	机场代码	机场名称	机场代码	机场名称	机场代码
北京首都	PEK	上海虹桥	SHA	香港赤鱲角	HKG	广州白云	CAN
北京大兴	PKX	上海浦东	PVG	澳门	MFM	台北桃园	TPE
福州长乐	FOC	厦门高崎	XMN	沈阳桃仙	SHE	哈尔滨太平	HRB
长春龙嘉	CGQ	大连周水子	DLC	青岛胶东	TAO	西安咸阳	XIY
武汉天河	WUH	重庆江北	CKG	合肥新桥	HFE	黄山屯溪	TXN
济南遥墙	TNA	烟台蓬莱	YNT	天津滨海	TSN	石家庄正定	SJW
太原武宿	TYN	郑州新郑	CGO	兰州中川	LHW	乌鲁木齐地窝堡	URC
长沙黄花	CSX	贵州龙洞堡	KWE	成都天府	CTU	昆明长水	KMG
桂林两江	KWL	南昌昌北	KHN	海口美兰	HAK	汕头外砂	SWA
南京禄口	NKG	连云港花果山	LYG	沙市荆州	SHS	温州永强	WNZ
襄樊刘集	XFN	宁波栎社	NGB	义乌	YIW	秦皇岛北戴河	SHP
宜昌三峡	YIH	洛阳北郊	LYA	呼和浩特白塔	HET	杭州萧山	HGH
九江庐山	JIU	黄岩路桥	HYN	深圳宝安	SZX	南宁吴圩	NNG
丹东浪头	DDG	齐齐哈尔三家子	NDG	珠海金湾	ZUH	湛江吴川	ZHA

Appendix 3

Code of major international cities

城　　市	代码	城　　市	代码	城　　市	代码
亚的斯亚贝巴	ADD	安克雷奇	ANC	亚特兰大	ATL
巴林	BAH	曼谷	BKK	柏林	BER
波士顿	BOS	布鲁塞尔	BRU	布加勒斯特	BUH
开罗	CAI	芝加哥	CHI	达拉斯	DFW
迪拜	DXB	法兰克福	FRA	河内	HAN
汉堡	HAM	伊斯坦布尔	IST	雅加达	JKT
卡拉奇	KHI	吉隆坡	KUL	科威特	KWI
伦敦	LON	洛杉矶	LAX	马德里	MAD
马尼拉	MNL	墨尔本	MEL	莫斯科	MOW
长崎	NGS	纽约	NYC	大阪	OSA
奥斯陆	OSL	巴黎	PAR	平壤	FNJ
仰光	RGN	罗马	ROM	旧金山	SFO
西雅图	SEA	首尔	SEL	沙迦	SHJ
新加坡	SIN	斯德哥尔摩	STO	悉尼	SYD
东京	TYO	多伦多	YYZ	温哥华	YVR
维也纳	VIE	万象	VTE	华盛顿	WAS
苏黎斯	ZRH				

Appendix 4

Extract from international special fare restrictions

```
FSN 033/20SEP21            CECN/CA /004/IPREUAS/ATP/8
20SEP21*20SEP21/CA   SHALON/EH/ADT   /TPM 5715/MPM  8169/CNY
33 EKWNCCBB /ADVP   7D/    7500/E/  6D.12M/21AUG 26SEP/CECNR
    D 567
00.TITLE/APPLICATION         02.DAY/TIME
03.SEASONALITY               04.FLIGHT APPLICATION
05.ADVANCE RES/TICKETING     06.MINIMUM STAY
07.MAXIMUM STAY              08.STOPOVERS
09.TRANSFERS                 10.PERMITTED COMBINATIONS
11.BLACKOUT DATES            14.TRAVEL RESTRICTIONS
15.SALES RESTRICTIONS        16.PENALTIES-CHANGES/CANCEL
17.HIP/MILEAGE EXCEPTIONS    18.TICKET ENDORSEMENT
19.CHILDREN/INFANT DISCOUNTS 31.VOLUNTARY CHANGES
```

通过 XS FSN//I 指令查询上海—伦敦运价代号为 EKWNCCBB 的成人来回程特殊运价的限制条件目录：

　　ADVP　7D（提前 7 天购票）　　票价 7500CNY　6D．12M（最小停留天数和最大停留天数分别为 6 天和 12 个月）

　　D 567（周 5、周 6、周 7 为周末，其他为工作日）

00．标题\适用范围	02．周中及周末
03．淡旺季	04．适用航班范围
05．提前定座及出票	06．最小停留天数
07．最长停留天数	08．中途分程点
09．中间点	10．运价组合
11．忌行日	14．旅行限制
15．销售限制	16．变更及取消的罚金
17．中间较高点例外情况	18．客票签转
19．儿童及婴儿折扣	31．自愿变更

Appendix 5

Extract from Singapore TIM

```
TIMATIC-3 / 18AUG21 / 0533 UTC
ALL SECTIONS FULL TEXT FOR: SINGAPORE (SG)

 GEOGRAPHICAL INFORMATION ********

CAPITAL - SINGAPORE (SIN).

 PASSPORT ********

PASSPORT REQUIRED.

 PASSPORT EXEMPTIONS:
- NATIONALS OF SINGAPORE WITH A DOCUMENT OF IDENTITY ISSUED BY
  SINGAPORE.
- NATIONALS OF SINGAPORE WITH A TEMPORARY TRAVEL DOCUMENT
  ISSUED BY SINGAPORE.
- PASSENGERS WITH A HONG KONG (SAR CHINA) "DOCUMENT OF
  IDENTITY FOR VISA PURPOSES".
- NATIONALS OF CHINA (PEOPLE'S REP.) WITH A MACAO (SAR CHINA)
  TRAVEL PERMIT.
- PASSENGERS WITH A LAISSEZ-PASSER ISSUED BY THE UNITED
  NATIONS TRAVELING ON DUTY.
▶TIPN
```

```
- PASSENGERS WITH A SEAMAN BOOK.
- PASSENGERS WITH A TRAVEL DOCUMENT ISSUED TO REFUGEES OR
  STATELESS PERSONS.
- PASSENGERS WITH AN ALIEN'S PASSPORT.
- NATIONALS OF ALGERIA, ARGENTINA, AUSTRALIA, AUSTRIA,
  BAHAMAS, BELGIUM, BRAZIL, BRUNEI DARUSSALAM, COLOMBIA,
  CZECHIA, DENMARK, DJIBOUTI, FINLAND, FRANCE, GUINEA,
  HUNGARY, ICELAND, KOREA (DEM. PEOPLE'S REP.), LIECHTENSTEIN,
  MADAGASCAR, NETHERLANDS, NORWAY, PALAU, PARAGUAY,
  PHILIPPINES, SEYCHELLES, SRI LANKA, SUDAN, SWEDEN, TRINIDAD
  AND TOBAGO AND USA WITH AN EMERGENCY PASSPORT.
- NATIONALS OF ARGENTINA, BELIZE, BULGARIA, CANADA, ECUADOR,
  FINLAND, GERMANY, HUNGARY, ITALY, JORDAN, KENYA, LITHUANIA,
  LUXEMBOURG, MADAGASCAR, MALAWI, MALDIVES, NAMIBIA, NORWAY,
  POLAND, PORTUGAL, ROMANIA, SAO TOME AND PRINCIPE, SURINAME,
  SWITZERLAND, THAILAND, TURKEY, UNITED ARAB EMIRATES,
  VENEZUELA AND ZAMBIA WITH A TEMPORARY PASSPORT.
- PASSENGERS WITH A BRITISH EMERGENCY OR TEMPORARY PASSPORT.

DOCUMENT VALIDITY:
- PASSPORTS AND OTHER DOCUMENTS ACCEPTED FOR ENTRY MUST BE
  VALID FOR A MINIMUM OF 6 MONTHS FROM THE ARRIVAL DATE.
▶TIPN
```

Appendix 5 Extract from Singapore TIM

```
- PASSPORTS AND OTHER DOCUMENTS ACCEPTED FOR ENTRY ISSUED TO
  NATIONALS OF SINGAPORE MUST BE VALID ON ARRIVAL.
- PASSPORTS AND OTHER DOCUMENTS ACCEPTED FOR ENTRY ISSUED TO
  RESIDENTS OF SINGAPORE MUST BE VALID ON ARRIVAL.
- THE GOVERNMENT OF SINGAPORE ONLY RECOGNIZES CHINESE TAIPEI
  (ON THE COVER: REPUBLIC OF CHINA TAIWAN) PASSPORTS WITH A
  PERSONAL ID NUMBER SHOWN ON THE BIO-DATA PAGE OF THE
  PASSPORT. PASSPORTS WITHOUT A PERSONAL ID NUMBER MUST BE
  ACCOMPANIED BY AN ENTRY PERMIT TO ENTER CHINESE TAIPEI.

ADMISSION AND TRANSIT RESTRICTIONS:
- PASSENGERS ARE NOT ALLOWED TO ENTER.
  - THIS DOES NOT APPLY TO NATIONALS OF SINGAPORE.
  - THIS DOES NOT APPLY TO PERMANENT RESIDENTS OF SINGAPORE.
  - THIS DOES NOT APPLY TO PASSENGERS (EXCEPT THOSE WITH TRAVEL
    HISTORY TO BANGLADESH, INDIA, MYANMAR, NEPAL, PAKISTAN OR
    SRI LANKA WITHIN THE PAST 21 DAYS PRIOR TO DEPARTURE FOR
    SINGAPORE) WITH A LONG-TERM VISIT PASS (LTVP) OR A
    LONG-TERM VISIT PASS IN-PRINCIPLE APPROVAL (LTVP IPA). THEY
    MUST HAVE AN APPROVAL LETTER FOR ENTRY (ALE) ISSUED BY THE
    SAFE TRAVEL OFFICE (STO) OR THE IMMIGRATION & CHECKPOINTS
    AUTHORITY (ICA).
▶TIPN
```

```
  PAST 21 DAYS ARE ALSO SUBJECT TO A COVID-19 RAPID ANTIGEN
  TEST UPON ARRIVAL.
- NATIONALS OF KOREA (DEM. PEOPLE'S REP.) MUST BE ESCORTED TO
  THE IMMIGRATION & CHECKPOINTS AUTHORITY.

VISA ********

VISA REQUIRED.

VISA EXEMPTIONS:
- NATIONALS OF SINGAPORE.
- NATIONALS OF ARGENTINA, AUSTRALIA, AUSTRIA, BELGIUM,
  BULGARIA, CROATIA, CYPRUS, CZECHIA, DENMARK, ESTONIA,
  FINLAND, FRANCE, GERMANY, GREECE, HUNGARY, IRELAND (REP.),
  ITALY, KOREA (REP.), LATVIA, LITHUANIA, LUXEMBOURG, MALTA,
  NETHERLANDS, NORWAY, POLAND, PORTUGAL, ROMANIA, SLOVAKIA,
  SLOVENIA, SPAIN, SWEDEN, SWITZERLAND AND USA FOR A MAXIMUM
  STAY OF 90 DAYS.
- PASSENGERS WITH A BRITISH PASSPORT WITH NATIONALITY "BRITISH
  CITIZEN" FOR A MAXIMUM STAY OF 90 DAYS.
- PASSENGERS WITH A BRITISH PASSPORT WITH NATIONALITY "BRITISH
  OVERSEAS TERRITORIES CITIZEN" WITH A CERTIFICATE OF
▶TIPN
```

```
CREW MEMBERS:
- VISA NOT REQUIRED, EXCEPT FOR NATIONALS OF BANGLADESH.
- DURATION OF STAY IS BASED ON FLIGHT SCHEDULE.

MILITARY:
- VISA NOT REQUIRED, IF HOLDING MILITARY ID CARD WITH MOVEMENT
  ORDER ISSED TO:
  - MEMBERS OF "HER MAJESTY'S FORCES"; OR
  - US MILITARY PERSONNEL (MOVEMENT ORDER MUST BE AUTHORIZED
    BY THE COMMANDER OF THE UNIT).

VISA ISSUANCE:
- E-VISAS CAN BE OBTAINED BY AUTHORIZED VISA AGENTS/PARTNERS
  OR LOCAL CONTACTS BEFORE DEPARTURE AT
  HTTP://WWW.ICA.GOV.SG/. PASSENGERS MUST HAVE A PRINTED
▶TIPN
```

```
E-VISA CONFIRMATION.

ADDITIONAL INFORMATION:
- EXTENSION OF STAY POSSIBLE.
- THIS FACILITY IS NOT APPLICABLE TO NATIONALS OF
  AFGHANISTAN, ALGERIA, BANGLADESH, EGYPT, IRAN, IRAQ,
  JORDAN, KOREA (DEM. PEOPLE'S REP.), LEBANON, LIBYA,
  MOROCCO, PAKISTAN, SAUDI ARABIA, SOMALIA, SUDAN, SYRIA,
  TUNISIA AND YEMEN.
- EXPECTANT MOTHERS VISITING SINGAPORE FOR THE PURPOSE OF
  DELIVERING THEIR CHILD IN SINGAPORE MUST APPLY FOR A VISIT
  PASS PRIOR TO THEIR VISIT. THE VISIT PASS CAN BE APPLIED FOR
  AT WWW.ICA.GOV.SG (APPLY FOR VISIT PASS). APPLICATIONS TAKE
  4 TO 6 WEEKS TO PROCESS. A VISIT PASS IS NOT REQUIRED FOR
  NATIONALS OF SINGAPORE OR RESIDENTS OF SINGAPORE HOLDING A
  RE-ENTRY PERMIT ISSUED BY SINGAPORE.

WARNING:
- VISITORS NOT HOLDING RETURN/ONWARD TICKETS COULD BE REFUSED
  ENTRY.

HEALTH ********
▶TIPN
```

```
PASSENGERS ARRIVING WITHIN 6 DAYS AFTER LEAVING OR TRANSITING
COUNTRIES WITH RISK OF YELLOW FEVER TRANSMISSION ▶TIRGL/YFIN◆
MUST HOLD A VALID YELLOW FEVER VACCINATION CERTIFICATE.
PASSENGERS NOT HOLDING ONE ARE SUBJECT TO MEDICAL SCREENING
UPON ARRIVAL AND COULD BE REFUSED ENTRY.

EXEMPT FROM YELLOW FEVER VACCINATION:
- CHILDREN UNDER 1 YEAR OF AGE.

- PASSENGERS TRANSITING SINGAPORE IF NOT LEAVING THE TRANSIT
  AREA.
- PASSENGERS TRANSITING COUNTRIES WITH RISK OF YELLOW FEVER
  TRANSMISSION WITHIN 12 HOURS IF NOT LEAVING THE TRANSIT
  AREAS.

COVID-19 REQUIREMENTS ********

AIRPORT TAX ********

NO AIRPORT TAX IS LEVIED ON PASSENGERS UPON EMBARKATION AT THE
▶TIPN
```

Appendix 5 Extract from Singapore TIM

```
AIRPORT.

CUSTOMS ********

IMPORT:
- PASSENGERS OF 18 YEARS OF AGE OR OLDER, HAVING BEEN OUTSIDE
  SINGAPORE FOR AT LEAST 48 HOURS PRIOR TO ARRIVAL: FREE
  IMPORT OF: SPIRITS, WINE AND BEER NOT EXCEEDING 1 LITER
  EACH; OR 2 LITERS OF WINE AND 1 LITER OF BEER; OR 1 LITER OF
  WINE AND 2 LITERS OF BEER.
- FREE IMPORT OF OTHER GOODS, GIFTS, SOUVENIRS AND FOODS FOR
  STAYS OUTSIDE SINGAPORE OF LESS THAN 48 HOURS: SGD 100.-; OR
  FOR STAYS OUTSIDE OF SINGAPORE OF 48 HOURS OR MORE: SGD
  500.-.
- FOOD ITEMS FOR PERSONAL CONSUMPTION ARE PERMITTED. HOWEVER,
  CERTAIN FOODS ARE PROHIBITED OR CONTROLLED DEPENDING ON
  COUNTY OF ORIGIN AND MAY BE LIMITED TO A MAXIMUM AMOUNT OR
  WEIGHT. DETAILED INFORMATION CAN BE FOUND AT
  WWW.SFA.GOV.SG/FOOD-IMPORT-EXPORT/BRINGING-FOOD-FOR-PERSONAL
  -USE .
- FREE IMPORT OF LIQUOR PRODUCTS IS NOT ALLOWED IF ARRIVING
  FROM MALAYSIA. EXEMPT ARE PASSENGERS COMING FROM A THIRD
▶TIPN
```

```
  COUNTRY TRANSITING IN MALAYSIA, WHO DID NOT ENTER MALAYSIA.
- PROHIBITED: CHEWING GUM (EXCEPT ORAL DENTAL AND MEDICATED
  GUM APPROVED BY HEALTH SCIENCES AUTHORITY (HSA)); CHEWING
  TOBACCO AND IMITATION TOBACCO PRODUCTS (INCLUDING ELECTRONIC
  CIGARETTES); CONTROLLED DRUGS AND PSYCHOTROPIC SUBSTANCES;
  ENDANGERED ANIMALS AND THEIR BY-PRODUCTS; FIRECRACKERS;
  OBSCENE ARTICLES AND MATERIALS; REPRODUCED MATERIALS
  INFRINGING COPYRIGHT.
- ALL TOBACCO PRODUCTS MUST BE DECLARED ON ARRIVAL AS THEY ARE
  SUBJECT TO TAX AND DUTY. ANY CHEWING GUM MUST ALSO BE
  DECLARED TO ENSURE THAT IT IS HSA APPROVED. FAILURE TO
  DECLARE MAY RESULT IN FINE OR IMPRISONMENT.
- WARNING: TRAFFICKING OF ILLEGAL DRUGS IS PUNISHABLE BY
  DEATH.

ARMS AND AMMUNITION:
- IMPORT OF FIREARMS OR EXPLOSIVES IS PROHIBITED, UNLESS
  CARRIER HOLDS A PERMIT FROM THE DIRECTOR GENERAL OF CIVIL
  AVIATION AUTHORITY, SINGAPORE:
  - WHEN ENTERING A POLICE PERMIT MUST BE OBTAINED 2 WEEKS
    PRIOR TO ENTRY. FEE OF SGD 45.-, FOR TRANSSHIPMENT APPLIES
    PER PASSENGER. FEE IS IMPOSED BY CAAS AUTHORITIES (CIVIL
▶TIPN
```

AVIATION AUTHORITY OF SINGAPORE). THE AIRLINE IS REQUIRED
TO SEEK APPROVAL FROM DIRECTOR GENERAL OF CAAS FOR CARRIAGE
OF FIREARMS ON BOARD THE AIRCRAFT. VIOLATION MAY RESULT IN
PROSECUTION OF PASSENGER AND CARRIER;
- WHEN TRANSITING A POLICE PERMIT FROM THE DIRECTOR GENERAL
  OF CIVIL AVIATION IS NOT REQUIRED. HOWEVER, THE AIRLINE IS
  REQUIRED TO SEEK APPROVAL FROM THE DIRECTOR GENERAL OF CAAS
  FOR CARRIAGE OF FIREARMS ON BOARD THE AIRCRAFT. FEE OF SGD
  45.-, FOR TRANSSHIPMENT APPLIES PER PASSENGER. FEE IS
  IMPOSED BY CAAS AUTHORITIES AND APPLICATION MUST BE MADE 2
  WEEKS IN ADVANCE;
- NOTE: ON SQ FLIGHTS APPLICATION MUST BE SENT TO TELEX
  SINKESQ, ATTN: DUTY OFFICER 2 WEEKS PRIOR TO TRAVEL.
  VIOLATION MAY RESULT IN PROSECUTION OF PASSENGER AND
  CARRIER.
- IMPORT OF TOY GUNS REQUIRES APPROVAL. ANY TOY GUN RESEMBLING
  REAL GUNS WILL NOT BE APPROVED.

EXPORT:
- FREE EXPORT OF REASONABLE QUANTITIES OF TOBACCO PRODUCTS AND
  ALCOHOLIC BEVERAGES.

▸TIPN

CREW MEMBERS:
- 0.25 LITER OF SPIRITS AND 1 LITER OF WINE OR 1 LITER OF
  BEER.

PETS:
1. PASSENGERS ARRIVING WITH PETS MUST OBTAIN PRIOR TO
   ARRIVAL:
   - AN IMPORT LICENSE (VALID FOR 30 DAYS) FROM THE ANIMAL AND
     VETERINARY SERVICE(AVSA) AND A VETERINARY CERTIFICATE IN
     ACCORDANCE WITH THE AVSA'S IMPORT REQUIREMENTS. FOR DETAILED
     INFORMATION, REFER TO: WWW.NPARKS.GOV.SG/AVS ; AND
   - ACCEPTANCE FOR QUARANTINE SPACE IN SEMBAWANG ANIMAL
     QUARANTINE STATION (SAQS) FOR CATS/DOGS FROM COUNTRIES OTHER
     THAN AUSTRALIA, BERMUDA, CAYMAN ISL., DENMARK, GERMANY, HONG
     KONG (SAR CHINA), ICELAND, IRELAND (REP.), JAPAN, JERSEY,
     LIECHTENSTEIN, LUXEMBOURG, NEW ZEALAND, NORWAY, PORTUGAL,
     SWEDEN, SWITZERLAND, USA (HAWAII AND GUAM ONLY) AND UNITED
     KINGDOM. THIS LIST MAY CHANGE WITHOUT NOTICE, PLEASE REFER
     TO WWW.NPARKS.GOV.SG/AVS .
   PASSENGERS MUST ALSO NOTIFY THE CHANGI ANIMAL AND PLANT
   QUARANTINE (CAPQ) OF THE AVSA OF THE FOLLOWING DETAILS, AT
   LEAST 5 WORKING DAY BEFORE ARRIVAL AT CHANGI INTERNATIONAL
▸TIPN

Appendix 5 Extract from Singapore TIM

```
  AIRPORT: PASSENGERS NAME AND LOCAL CONTACT NUMBER; DATE AND
  TIME OF ARRIVAL; IMPORT PERMIT NUMBER; WHETHER PET IS
  TRAVELING AS ACCOMPANIED BAGGAGE OR MANIFESTED CARGO.
  2. CATS/DOGS DIRECTLY IMPORTED FROM AUSTRALIA, BERMUDA,
  CAYMAN ISL., DENMARK, GERMANY, HONG KONG (SAR CHINA),
  ICELAND, IRELAND (REP.), JAPAN, JERSEY, LIECHTENSTEIN,
  LUXEMBOURG, NEW ZEALAND, NORWAY, PORTUGAL, SWEDEN,
  SWITZERLAND, USA (HAWAII AND GUAM ONLY) AND UNITED KINGDOM
  REQUIRE AN AIRLINE DECLARATION, A COPY OF WHICH MUST BE
  ATTACHED TO THE CONTAINER. PAGE 2 OF THE DECLARATION MUST BE
  COMPLETED IF THE SEAL OF THE CONTAINER HAS BEEN BROKEN.
  3. A TRANSHIPMENT LICENSE FROM AVSA MUST BE OBTAINED WHEN
  TRANSITING PETS VIA SINGAPORE.

  BAGGAGE CLEARANCE:
  - BAGGAGE IS CLEARED AT THE FIRST AIRPORT OF ENTRY IN
    SINGAPORE.
  - EXEMPT: BAGGAGE OF TRANSIT PASSENGERS WITH A DESTINATION
    OUTSIDE OF SINGAPORE IF THE ONWARD FLIGHT IS WITHIN 72
    HOURS.
  - CREW CLEARANCE THROUGH SPECIAL IMMIGRATION COUNTER.

 ▶TIPN
```

```
  CURRENCY ********

  IMPORT:
  - LOCAL CURRENCY (SINGAPORE DOLLAR-SGD) AND FOREIGN
    CURRENCIES: NO LIMIT. HOWEVER, AMOUNTS EXCEEDING SGD
    20,000.- (OR EQUIVALENT)(INCL. TRAVELER CHEQUE, BEARER
    CHEQUE, BILL OF EXCHANGE, PROMISSORY NOTE) SHOULD BE
    DECLARED ON ARRIVAL.

  EXPORT:
  - LOCAL CURRENCY (SINGAPORE DOLLAR-SGD) AND FOREIGN
    CURRENCIES: NO LIMIT. HOWEVER, AMOUNTS EXCEEDING SGD
    20,000.- (OR EQUIVALENT)(INCL. TRAVELER CHEQUE, BEARER
    CHEQUE, BILL OF EXCHANGE, PROMISSORY NOTE) SHOULD BE
    DECLARED ON DEPARTURE.

  USE TIFA, TIFV AND TIFH FOR SPECIFIC INFORMATION
  CHECK ▶TINEWS/N1◆ - VIRTUAL APEC BUSINESS TRAVEL CARD (ABTC)

  TEXT DISPLAY COMPLETE
  ▶
```

Appendix 6

Regulations on passenger service management of public air transport

《公共航空运输旅客服务管理规定》已于2021年2月24日经第4次部务会议通过,现予公布,自2021年9月1日起施行。

第一章 总 则

第一条 为了加强公共航空运输旅客服务管理,保护旅客合法权益,维护航空运输秩序,根据《中华人民共和国民用航空法》《中华人民共和国消费者权益保护法》《中华人民共和国电子商务法》等法律、行政法规,制定本规定。

第二条 依照中华人民共和国法律成立的承运人、机场管理机构、地面服务代理人、航空销售代理人、航空销售网络平台经营者、航空信息企业从事公共航空运输旅客服务活动的,适用本规定。

外国承运人、港澳台地区承运人从事前款规定的活动,其航班始发地点或者经停地点在中华人民共和国境内(不含港澳台,下同)的,适用本规定。

第三条 中国民用航空局(以下简称民航局)负责对公共航空运输旅客服务实施统一监督管理。

中国民用航空地区管理局(以下简称民航地区管理局)负责对本辖区内的公共航空运输旅客服务实施监督管理。

第四条 依照中华人民共和国法律成立的承运人、机场管理机构应当建立公共航空运输旅客服务质量管理体系,并确保管理体系持续有效运行。

第五条 鼓励、支持承运人、机场管理机构制定高于本规定标准的服务承诺。

承运人、机场管理机构应当公布关于购票、乘机、安检等涉及旅客权益的重要信息,并接受社会监督。

第二章 一般规定

第六条 承运人应当根据本规定制定并公布运输总条件,细化相关旅客服务内容。

承运人的运输总条件不得与国家法律法规以及涉及民航管理的规章相关要求相抵触。

第七条 承运人修改运输总条件的,应当标明生效日期。

修改后的运输总条件不得将限制旅客权利或者增加旅客义务的修改内容适用于修改前已购票的旅客,但是国家另有规定的除外。

第八条 运输总条件至少应当包括下列内容:

(一)客票销售和退票、变更实施细则;

(二)旅客乘机相关规定,包括婴儿、孕妇、无成人陪伴儿童、重病患者等特殊旅客的承运标准;

(三)行李运输具体要求;
(四)超售处置规定;
(五)受理投诉的电子邮件地址和电话。

前款所列事项变化较频繁的,可以单独制定相关规定,但应当视为运输总条件的一部分,并与运输总条件在同一位置以显著方式予以公布。

第九条　承运人应当与航空销售代理人签订销售代理协议,明确公共航空运输旅客服务标准,并采取有效措施督促其航空销售代理人符合本规定相关要求。

承运人应当将客票销售、客票变更与退票、行李运输等相关服务规定准确提供给航空销售代理人;航空销售代理人不得擅自更改承运人的相关服务规定。

第十条　航空销售网络平台经营者应当对平台内航空销售代理人进行核验,不得允许未签订协议的航空销售代理人在平台上从事客票销售活动。

航空销售网络平台经营者应当处理旅客与平台内航空销售代理人的投诉纠纷,并采取有效措施督促平台内的航空销售代理人符合本规定相关要求。

第十一条　承运人应当与地面服务代理人签订地面服务代理协议,明确公共航空运输旅客服务标准,并采取有效措施督促其地面服务代理人符合本规定相关要求。

第十二条　机场管理机构应当建立地面服务代理人和航站楼商户管理制度,并采取有效措施督促其符合本规定相关要求。

第十三条　航空信息企业应当完善旅客定座、乘机登记等相关信息系统功能,确保承运人、机场管理机构、地面服务代理人、航空销售代理人、航空销售网络平台经营者等能够有效实施本规定要求的服务内容。

第十四条　承运人、机场管理机构、地面服务代理人、航空销售代理人、航空销售网络平台经营者、航空信息企业应当遵守国家关于个人信息保护的规定,不得泄露、出售、非法使用或者向他人提供旅客个人信息。

第三章　客票销售

第十五条　承运人或者其航空销售代理人通过网络途径销售客票的,应当以显著方式告知购票人所选航班的主要服务信息,至少应当包括:
(一)承运人名称,包括缔约承运人和实际承运人;
(二)航班始发地、经停地、目的地的机场及其航站楼;
(三)航班号、航班日期、舱位等级、计划出港和到港时间;
(四)同时预订两个及以上航班时,应当明确是否为联程航班;
(五)该航班适用的票价以及客票使用条件,包括客票变更规则和退票规则等;
(六)该航班是否提供餐食;
(七)按照国家规定收取的税、费;
(八)该航班适用的行李运输规定,包括行李尺寸、重量、免费行李额等。

承运人或者其航空销售代理人通过售票处或者电话等其他方式销售客票的,应当告知购票人前款信息或者获取前款信息的途径。

第十六条　承运人或者其航空销售代理人通过网络途径销售客票的,应当将运输总条件的全部内容纳入旅客购票时的必读内容,以必选项的形式确保购票人在购票环节阅知。

承运人或者其航空销售代理人通过售票处或者电话等其他方式销售客票的,应当提示购票人阅读运输总条件并告知阅读运输总条件的途径。

第十七条　承运人或者其航空销售代理人在销售国际客票时,应当提示旅客自行查阅航班始发地、经停地或者目的地国的出入境相关规定。

第十八条　购票人应当向承运人或者其航空销售代理人提供国家规定的必要个人信息以及旅客真实有效的联系方式。

第十九条　承运人或者其航空销售代理人在销售客票时,应当将购票人提供的旅客联系方式等必要个人信息准确录入旅客定座系统。

第二十条　承运人或者其航空销售代理人出票后,应当以电子或者纸质等书面方式告知旅客涉及行程的重要内容,至少应当包括:

(一)本规定第十五条第一款所列信息;

(二)旅客姓名;

(三)票号或者合同号以及客票有效期;

(四)出行提示信息,包括航班始发地停止办理乘机登记手续的时间要求、禁止或者限制携带的物品等;

(五)免费获取所适用运输总条件的方式。

第二十一条　承运人、航空销售代理人、航空销售网络平台经营者、航空信息企业应当保存客票销售相关信息,并确保信息的完整性、保密性、可用性。

前款规定的信息保存时间自交易完成之日起不少于3年。法律、行政法规另有规定的,依照其规定。

第四章　客票变更与退票

第二十二条　客票变更,包括旅客自愿变更客票和旅客非自愿变更客票。

退票,包括旅客自愿退票和旅客非自愿退票。

第二十三条　旅客自愿变更客票或者自愿退票的,承运人或者其航空销售代理人应当按照所适用的运输总条件、客票使用条件办理。

第二十四条　由于承运人原因导致旅客非自愿变更客票的,承运人或者其航空销售代理人应当在有可利用座位或者被签转承运人同意的情况下,为旅客办理改期或者签转,不得向旅客收取客票变更费。

由于非承运人原因导致旅客非自愿变更客票的,承运人或者其航空销售代理人应当按照所适用的运输总条件、客票使用条件办理。

第二十五条　旅客非自愿退票的,承运人或者其航空销售代理人不得收取退票费。

第二十六条　承运人或者其航空销售代理人应当在收到旅客有效退款申请之日起7个工作日内办理完成退款手续,上述时间不含金融机构处理时间。

第二十七条　在联程航班中,因其中一个或者几个航段变更,导致旅客无法按照约定时间完成整个行程的,缔约承运人或者其航空销售代理人应当协助旅客到达最终目的地或者中途分程地。

在联程航班中,旅客非自愿变更客票的,按照本规定第二十四条办理;旅客非自愿退票的,按照本规定第二十五条办理。

第五章 乘　　机

第二十八条　机场管理机构应当在办理乘机登记手续、行李托运、安检、海关、边检、登机口、中转通道等旅客乘机流程的关键区域设置标志标识指引,确保标志标识清晰、准确。

第二十九条　旅客在承运人或者其地面服务代理人停止办理乘机登记手续前,凭与购票时一致的有效身份证件办理客票查验、托运行李、获取纸质或者电子登机凭证。

第三十条　旅客在办理乘机登记手续时,承运人或者其地面服务代理人应当将旅客姓名、航班号、乘机日期、登机时间、登机口、航程等已确定信息准确、清晰地显示在纸质或者电子登机凭证上。

登机口、登机时间等发生变更的,承运人、地面服务代理人、机场管理机构应当及时告知旅客。

第三十一条　有下列情况之一的,承运人应当拒绝运输:

(一)依据国家有关规定禁止运输的旅客或者物品;

(二)拒绝接受安全检查的旅客;

(三)未经安全检查的行李;

(四)办理乘机登记手续时出具的身份证件与购票时身份证件不一致的旅客;

(五)国家规定的其他情况。

除前款规定外,旅客的行为有可能危及飞行安全或者公共秩序的,承运人有权拒绝运输。

第三十二条　旅客因本规定第三十一条被拒绝运输而要求出具书面说明的,除国家另有规定外,承运人应当及时出具;旅客要求变更客票或者退票的,承运人可以按照所适用的运输总条件、客票使用条件办理。

第三十三条　承运人、机场管理机构应当针对旅客突发疾病、意外伤害等对旅客健康情况产生重大影响的情形,制定应急处置预案。

第三十四条　因承运人原因导致旅客误机、错乘、漏乘的,承运人或者其航空销售代理人应当按照本规定第二十四条第一款、第二十五条办理客票变更或者退票。

因非承运人原因导致前款规定情形的,承运人或者其航空销售代理人可以按照本规定第二十三条办理客票变更或者退票。

第六章　行　李　运　输

第三十五条　承运人、地面服务代理人、机场管理机构应当建立托运行李监控制度,防止行李在运送过程中延误、破损、丢失等情况发生。

承运人、机场管理机构应当积极探索行李跟踪等新技术应用,建立旅客托运行李全流程跟踪机制。

第三十六条　旅客的托运行李、非托运行李不得违反国家禁止运输或者限制运输的相关规定。

在收运行李时或者运输过程中,发现行李中装有不得作为行李运输的任何物品,承运人应当拒绝收运或者终止运输,并通知旅客。

第三十七条　承运人应当在运输总条件中明确行李运输相关规定,至少包括下列内容:

(一)托运行李和非托运行李的尺寸、重量以及数量要求;
(二)免费行李额;
(三)超限行李费计算方式;
(四)是否提供行李声明价值服务,或者为旅客办理行李声明价值的相关要求;
(五)是否承运小动物,或者运输小动物的种类及相关要求;
(六)特殊行李的相关规定;
(七)行李损坏、丢失、延误的赔偿标准或者所适用的国家有关规定、国际公约。

第三十八条 承运人或者其地面服务代理人应当在收运行李后向旅客出具纸质或者电子行李凭证。

第三十九条 承运人应当将旅客的托运行李与旅客同机运送。

除国家另有规定外,不能同机运送的,承运人应当优先安排该行李在后续的航班上运送,并及时通知旅客。

第四十条 旅客的托运行李延误到达的,承运人应当及时通知旅客领取。

除国家另有规定外,由于非旅客原因导致托运行李延误到达,旅客要求直接送达的,承运人应当免费将托运行李直接送达旅客或者与旅客协商解决方案。

第四十一条 在行李运输过程中,托运行李发生延误、丢失或者损坏,旅客要求出具行李运输事故凭证的,承运人或者其地面服务代理人应当及时提供。

第七章 航班超售

第四十二条 承运人超售客票的,应当在超售前充分考虑航线、航班班次、时间、机型以及衔接航班等情况,最大程度避免旅客因超售被拒绝登机。

第四十三条 承运人应当在运输总条件中明确超售处置相关规定,至少包括下列内容:
(一)超售信息告知规定;
(二)征集自愿者程序;
(三)优先登机规则;
(四)被拒绝登机旅客赔偿标准、方式和相关服务标准。

第四十四条 因承运人超售导致实际乘机旅客人数超过座位数时,承运人或者其地面服务代理人应当根据征集自愿者程序,寻找自愿放弃行程的旅客。

未经征集自愿者程序,不得使用优先登机规则确定被拒绝登机的旅客。

第四十五条 在征集自愿者时,承运人或者其地面服务代理人应当与旅客协商自愿放弃行程的条件。

第四十六条 承运人的优先登机规则应当符合公序良俗原则,考虑的因素至少应当包括老幼病残孕等特殊旅客的需求、后续航班衔接等。

承运人或者其地面服务代理人应当在经征集自愿者程序未能寻找到足够的自愿者后,方可根据优先登机规则确定被拒绝登机的旅客。

第四十七条 承运人或者其地面服务代理人应当按照超售处置规定向被拒绝登机旅客给予赔偿,并提供相关服务。

第四十八条 旅客因超售自愿放弃行程或者被拒绝登机时,承运人或者其地面服务代理人应当根据旅客的要求,出具因超售而放弃行程或者被拒绝登机的证明。

第四十九条　因超售导致旅客自愿放弃行程或者被拒绝登机的,承运人应当按照本规定第二十四条第一款、第二十五条办理客票变更或者退票。

第八章　旅　客　投　诉

第五十条　因公共航空运输旅客服务发生争议的,旅客可以向承运人、机场管理机构、地面服务代理人、航空销售代理人、航空销售网络平台经营者投诉,也可以向民航行政机关投诉。

第五十一条　承运人、机场管理机构、地面服务代理人、航空销售代理人、航空销售网络平台经营者应当设置电子邮件地址、中华人民共和国境内的投诉受理电话等投诉渠道,并向社会公布。

承运人、机场管理机构、地面服务代理人、航空销售代理人、航空销售网络平台经营者应当设立专门机构或者指定专人负责受理投诉工作。

港澳台地区承运人和外国承运人应当具备以中文受理和处理投诉的能力。

第五十二条　承运人、机场管理机构、地面服务代理人、航空销售代理人、航空销售网络平台经营者收到旅客投诉后,应当及时受理;不予受理的,应当说明理由。

承运人、机场管理机构、地面服务代理人、航空销售代理人、航空销售网络平台经营者应当在收到旅客投诉之日起10个工作日内做出包含解决方案的处理结果。

承运人、机场管理机构、地面服务代理人、航空销售代理人、航空销售网络平台经营者应当书面记录旅客的投诉情况及处理结果,投诉记录至少保存3年。

第五十三条　民航局消费者事务中心受民航局委托统一受理旅客向民航行政机关的投诉。

民航局消费者事务中心应当建立、畅通民航服务质量监督平台和民航服务质量监督电话等投诉渠道,实现全国投诉信息一体化。

旅客向民航行政机关投诉的,民航局消费者事务中心、承运人、机场管理机构、地面服务代理人、航空销售代理人、航空销售网络平台经营者应当在民航服务质量监督平台上进行投诉处理工作。

第九章　信　息　报　告

第五十四条　承运人应当将运输总条件通过民航服务质量监督平台进行备案。

运输总条件发生变更的,应当自变更之日起5个工作日内在民航服务质量监督平台上更新备案。

备案的运输总条件应当与对外公布的运输总条件保持一致。

第五十五条　承运人应当将其地面服务代理人、航空销售代理人的相关信息通过民航服务质量监督平台进行备案。

前款所述信息发生变更的,应当自变更之日起5个工作日内在民航服务质量监督平台上更新备案。

第五十六条　承运人、机场管理机构、地面服务代理人、航空销售代理人、航空销售网络平台经营者应当将投诉受理电话、电子邮件地址、投诉受理机构等信息通过民航服务质量监督平台进行备案。

前款所述信息发生变更的,应当自变更之日起5个工作日内在民航服务质量监督平台上更新备案。

第五十七条　承运人、机场管理机构、地面服务代理人、航空销售代理人、航空销售网络平台经营者、航空信息企业等相关单位,应当按照民航行政机关要求报送旅客运输服务有关数据和信息,并对真实性负责。

第十章　监督管理及法律责任

第五十八条　有下列行为之一的,由民航行政机关责令限期改正;逾期未改正的,依法记入民航行业严重失信行为信用记录:

(一)承运人违反本规定第六条、第七条、第八条,未按照要求制定、修改、适用或者公布运输总条件的;

(二)承运人或者其地面服务代理人违反本规定第四十四条、第四十五条、第四十六条第二款、第四十七条,未按照要求为旅客提供超售后的服务的;

(三)承运人、机场管理机构、地面服务代理人、航空销售代理人、航空销售网络平台经营者违反本规定第五十一条第一款、第二款,第五十二条第一款、第二款,未按照要求开展投诉受理或者处理工作的。

第五十九条　有下列行为之一的,由民航行政机关责令限期改正;逾期未改正的,处1万元以下的罚款;情节严重的,处2万元以上3万元以下的罚款:

(一)承运人、航空销售网络平台经营者、机场管理机构违反本规定第九条第一款、第十条第二款、第十一条、第十二条,未采取有效督促措施的;

(二)承运人、航空销售代理人违反本规定第九条第二款,未按照要求准确提供相关服务规定或者擅自更改承运人相关服务规定的;

(三)航空信息企业违反本规定第十三条,未按照要求完善信息系统功能的;

(四)承运人或者其航空销售代理人违反本规定第十九条,未按照要求录入旅客信息的;

(五)承运人、航空销售代理人、航空信息企业违反本规定第二十一条,未按照要求保存相关信息的;

(六)承运人违反本规定第三十二条,未按照要求出具被拒绝运输书面说明的;

(七)承运人、机场管理机构违反本规定第三十三条,未按照要求制定应急处置预案的;

(八)承运人、地面服务代理人、机场管理机构违反本规定第三十五条第一款,未按照要求建立托运行李监控制度的;

(九)承运人或者其地面服务代理人违反本规定第四十一条,未按照要求提供行李运输事故凭证的;

(十)承运人或者其地面服务代理人违反本规定第四十八条,未按照要求出具相关证明的;

(十一)港澳台地区承运人和外国承运人违反本规定第五十一条第三款,未按照要求具备以中文受理和处理投诉能力的;

(十二)承运人、机场管理机构、地面服务代理人、航空销售代理人、航空销售网络平台经营者违反本规定第五十二条第三款,未按照要求保存投诉记录的;

(十三)承运人、机场管理机构、地面服务代理人、航空销售代理人、航空销售网络平台经

营者违反本规定第五十三条第三款,未按照要求在民航服务质量监督平台上处理投诉的;

(十四)承运人违反本规定第五十四条、第五十五条,未按照要求将运输总条件、地面服务代理人、航空销售代理人的相关信息备案的;

(十五)承运人、机场管理机构、地面服务代理人、航空销售代理人、航空销售网络平台经营者违反本规定第五十六条,未按照要求将投诉相关信息备案的;

(十六)承运人、机场管理机构、地面服务代理人、航空销售代理人、航空销售网络平台经营者违反本规定第五十七条,未按照要求报送相关数据和信息的。

第六十条　航空销售网络平台经营者有本规定第十条第一款规定的行为,构成《中华人民共和国电子商务法》规定的不履行核验义务的,依照《中华人民共和国电子商务法》的规定执行。

第六十一条　承运人、机场管理机构、地面服务代理人、航空销售代理人、航空销售网络平台经营者、航空信息企业违反本规定第十四条,侵害旅客个人信息,构成《中华人民共和国消费者权益保护法》规定的侵害消费者个人信息依法得到保护的权利的,依照《中华人民共和国消费者权益保护法》的规定执行。

承运人或者其航空销售代理人违反本规定第二十三条、第二十四条、第二十五条、第二十六条、第二十七条,未按照要求办理客票变更、退票或者未履行协助义务,构成《中华人民共和国消费者权益保护法》规定的故意拖延或者无理拒绝消费者提出的更换、退还服务费用要求的,依照《中华人民共和国消费者权益保护法》的规定执行。

第六十二条　机场管理机构违反本规定第二十八条,未按照要求设置标志标识,构成《民用机场管理条例》规定的未按照国家规定的标准配备相应设施设备的,依照《民用机场管理条例》的规定执行。

<h3 style="text-align:center">第十一章　附　　则</h3>

第六十三条　本规定中下列用语的含义是:

(一)承运人,是指以营利为目的,使用民用航空器运送旅客、行李的公共航空运输企业;

(二)缔约承运人,是指使用本企业票证和票号,与旅客签订航空运输合同的承运人;

(三)实际承运人,是指根据缔约承运人的授权,履行相关运输的承运人;

(四)机场管理机构,是指依法组建的或者受委托的负责机场安全和运营管理的具有法人资格的机构;

(五)地面服务代理人,是指依照中华人民共和国法律成立的,与承运人签订地面代理协议,在中华人民共和国境内机场从事公共航空运输地面服务代理业务的企业;

(六)航空销售代理人,是指依照中华人民共和国法律成立的,与承运人签订销售代理协议,从事公共航空运输旅客服务销售业务的企业;

(七)航空销售网络平台经营者,是指依照中华人民共和国法律成立的,在电子商务中为承运人或者航空销售代理人提供网络经营场所、交易撮合、信息发布等服务,供其独立开展公共航空运输旅客服务销售活动的企业;

(八)航空信息企业,是指为公共航空运输提供旅客定座、乘机登记等相关系统的企业;

(九)民航行政机关,是指民航局和民航地区管理局;

(十)公共航空运输旅客服务,是指承运人使用民用航空器将旅客由出发地机场运送至目的地机场的服务；

（十一）客票，是运输凭证的一种，包括纸质客票和电子客票；

（十二）已购票，是指根据法律规定或者双方当事人约定，航空运输合同成立的状态；

（十三）客票变更，是指对客票改期、变更舱位等级、签转等情形；

（十四）自愿退票，是指旅客因其自身原因要求退票；

（十五）非自愿退票，是指因航班取消、延误、提前、航程改变、舱位等级变更或者承运人无法运行原航班等情形，导致旅客退票的情形；

（十六）自愿变更客票，是指旅客因其自身原因要求变更客票；

（十七）非自愿变更客票，指因航班取消、延误、提前、航程改变、舱位等级变更或者承运人无法运行原航班等情形，导致旅客变更客票的情形；

（十八）承运人原因，是指承运人内部管理原因，包括机务维护、航班调配、机组调配等；

（十九）非承运人原因，是指与承运人内部管理无关的其他原因，包括天气、突发事件、空中交通管制、安检、旅客等因素；

（二十）行李，是指承运人同意运输的、旅客在旅行中携带的物品，包括托运行李和非托运行李；

（二十一）托运行李，是指旅客交由承运人负责照管和运输并出具行李运输凭证的行李；

（二十二）非托运行李，是指旅客自行负责照管的行李；

（二十三）票价，是指承运人使用民用航空器将旅客由出发地机场运送至目的地机场的航空运输服务的价格，不包含按照国家规定收取的税费；

（二十四）计划出港时间，是指航班时刻管理部门批准的离港时间；

（二十五）计划到港时间，是指航班时刻管理部门批准的到港时间；

（二十六）客票使用条件，是指定座舱位代码或者票价种类所适用的票价规则；

（二十七）客票改期，是指客票列明同一承运人的航班时刻、航班日期的变更；

（二十八）签转，是指客票列明承运人的变更；

（二十九）联程航班，是指被列明在单一运输合同中的两个（含）以上的航班；

（三十）误机，是指旅客未按规定时间办妥乘机手续或者因身份证件不符合规定而未能乘机；

（三十一）错乘，是指旅客搭乘了不是其客票列明的航班；

（三十二）漏乘，是指旅客办妥乘机手续后或者在经停站过站时未能搭乘其客票列明的航班；

（三十三）小动物，是指旅客托运的小型动物，包括家庭饲养的猫、狗或者其他类别的小动物；

（三十四）超售，是指承运人为避免座位虚耗，在某一航班上销售座位数超过实际可利用座位数的行为；

（三十五）经停地点，是指除出发地点和目的地点以外，作为旅客旅行路线上预定经停的地点；

（三十六）中途分程地，是指经承运人事先同意，旅客在出发地和目的地间旅行时有意安排在某个地点的旅程间断。

第六十四条　本规定以工作日计算的时限均不包括当日,从次日起计算。

第六十五条　本规定自2021年9月1日起施行。原民航总局于1996年2月28日公布的《中国民用航空旅客、行李国内运输规则》(民航总局令第49号)、2004年7月12日公布的《中国民用航空总局关于修订〈中国民用航空旅客、行李国内运输规则〉的决定》(民航总局令第124号)和1997年12月8日公布的《中国民用航空旅客、行李国际运输规则》(民航总局令第70号)同时废止。

本规定施行前公布的涉及民航管理的规章中关于客票变更、退票以及旅客投诉管理的内容与本规定不一致的,按照本规定执行。

References

[1] 刘得一,张兆宁,杨新涅.民航概论[M].北京:中国民航出版社,2011.
[2] 万青,张辉.飞机载重平衡[M].北京:中国民航出版社,2020.
[3] IATA. Dangerous goods regulations[M]. Geneva:IATA,2020.
[4] IATA. The air cargo tariff manual rules[M]. Geneva:IATA,2020
[5] MORRELL P S,KLEIN T. Moving boxes by air[M]. London:Routledge,2019.
[6] 陆东.民航旅客运输[M].2版.北京:人民交通出版社股份有限公司,2021.